Johannes H. Egbers was born in The Netherlands to a Dutch father and a German mother. He lived under German occupation, the debacle of Operation Market Gerden, and one of the fiercest battles of WW2, Operation Veritable.

After his engineering studies, he lived and worked as an engineer and managing director in five European countries and five States of the USA. He was ten years on the faculty of Lehigh University as a professor of engineering management after retirement. King Baudouin of Belgium knighted him in the Royal Order of the Belgium Crown for promoting transatlantic understanding. He is a US citizen and lives in Delaware.

This memorial is dedicated to the brave men of Operation Market Garden and Operation Veritable, especially those who gave their life, their health and their future, in victory and defeat, so that many generations could be free and pursue happiness.

Johannes H. Egbers

WORLD WAR 2: THE WAR THAT CHANGED HUMANITY

From local interacting communities to global technology-enabled individualism.

AUSTIN MACAULEY PUBLISHERS™

LONDON • CAMBRIDGE • NEW YORK • SHARJAH

Ordering Information
Quantity sales: Special discounts are available on quantity purchases by corporations, associations, and others. For details, contact the publisher at the address below.

Publisher's Cataloging-in-Publication data
Egbers, Johannes H.
World War 2: The War That Changed Humanity

ISBN 9798891553095 (Paperback)
ISBN 9798891553101 (ePub e-book)

Library of Congress Control Number: 2023923220

www.austinmacauley.com/us

First Published 2024
Austin Macauley Publishers LLC
40 Wall Street, 33rd Floor, Suite 3302
New York, NY 10005
USA

mail-usa@austinmacauley.com
+1 (646) 5125767

WW2, as an epic global war, is still a source of multiple reviews, historical analyses, and often controversial opinions and conclusions.

This expository semi-autobiographic reflection, in addition to personal experiences, includes information from multiple sources that are so readily available and accessible in the present time, such as Google, Bing, and Wikipedia, which are gratefully acknowledged.

Special mention, however, deserves the pictures and information from the 1945 Red Cross Booklet: 'De Gemeente Ubbergen in de Frontlinie'. (The County of Ubbergen in the frontline). Several pictures are of poor quality. Photography was not developed as in modern times, and the quality of photographic material was substandard during and immediately after WW2.

Table of Contents

Preface

Since *Homo sapiens* emerged some 300,000 years ago, humanity has lived mainly in communal and tribal groups establishing social norms and rituals in all parts of the globe.

Throughout history, humanity has been endowed with the unalienable instincts of good and evil. As far as we know, humanity is the only species with an awareness of moral values. Compassion, mercy, forgiveness, romance, and love make human life rich and livable. On the negative side, evil, hate, discrimination, greed, and power addiction led to war, suffering, and violence. In recent history, the global war of WW2 is an apt example.

Scientific and technological advances that emerged during and after WW2 changed how humanity lives and interacts.

Global knowledge advanced, far beyond pre-war awareness, through multiple technological developments such as television, computers, wireless communications, and comfortable jet-engine propelled travel.

WW2 changed traditional perspectives and the way humans interact.

***

Wars impact civilian life.

The primary focus during times of war is on those involved in the conflict, the battles, and military operations on land, sea, and air, by those who serviced voluntarily or were conscripted combatants.

Powerless and defenseless civilians are drawn into the ravages of war. Devastating surroundings, torn-apart families, death, injury, lack of food and shelter, physical and mental suffering, and a lifetime of trauma are often the fate of civilians who were mere victims of those who decided the destiny of millions.

While estimates about the number of war casualties vary significantly in times of chaos and destruction, there is ample evidence that more civilians die during wars compared to members of military organizations. One estimate, later, discussed concludes that during WW2, over 15 million combatants died, and more than 30 million civilians. In Russia alone, over 15 million civilians lost their lives.

This writing intends to highlight the lasting impact of this global war from a civilian perspective.

WW2 differed from ancient battles when thousands lined up for man-to-man combat. Different also from decades of violence such as the Thirty-Year War (1618-1648) or the Eighty-Year Independence War of the Netherlands (1568-1648) to free itself from Spanish rule, during which, by mutual agreement, a twelve-year cease-fire halted the fighting to resume the conflict then again, a state of affairs difficult to imagine in the progressing events of modern times.

Also, different from the more recent WW1 global war when soldiers were still forced to attack each other with bayonets on their rifles in the muddy hellish fields and trenches of Belgium and France.

While some person-to-person confrontations still existed during WW2, for most combatants, the enemy became more distant and unseen with the development of modern war technology, especially with the development of aerial warfare and rocket technology. With the development of drones and similar remotely operated weapons, future wars will probably be even more remote from opponents and far more destructive.

One phase of WW2, Operation Market Garden, is highlighted because of personal experiences and as one of the few Allied debacles on the European continent in its all-out effort to conquer evil and blind addiction to power.

While the intent is to present a broad overview of conditions experienced by all citizens, personal experiences could not be avoided in the hope that it may be seen to explain and clarify and not to enhance personal emphasis.

Many detailed and excellent military reviews and analyses have been written about WW2, some objective, some biased views seen through nationalistic eyes.

Military strategies or controversies between generals are not intended but could not be totally avoided. The emphasis is on how common citizens experienced war due to the decisions made by some sincere but also some power-addicted and evil rulers. Throughout history, the fate of citizens depended on the strategies and decisions of powerful leaders.

The initial superior Nazi war technology spurred a response by Allied Forces that erupted technology developments into an all-out revolution in many scientific fields such as aviation, communication, atomic energy, space research, and probably most influentially, computer technology and artificial intelligence.

WW2 thus became more than a devastating multi-nation war, and also as a war that irreversibly changed humanity's social interaction and mode of life triggered by a war-instigated technological evolution, mainly in the nations of Western civilization, but also globally.

"There is no other history as the history of the people," wrote historian Lucien Febvre (1878-1956) who, together with Henri Hauser and Marc Bloch, formed the Annals School of History in France, concentrating on the social effects of war, looking beyond the political realities to the social and economic background and, probably most importantly, the mentality of the time, which is so often lacking in historical reviews where contemporary moral and societal standards evaluate history.

Since many evaluations have been written, some excellent and factual, such as Cornelius Ryan's book: *A Bridge Too Far*, others are rather biased, so why add more? Because by sharing information and experiences the effects of this global war on lifestyle and society at large can hopefully be better understood and, where necessary, corrected.

Can memory still be trusted after more than sixty years? The influence of time, social and cultural progression, and change cannot be denied.

Priorities and perceptions change such as environmental awareness that did not exist in those past years.

Perhaps, a clearer perspective is possible from a distance when emotions have faded, and truth and reality have become more evident.

Even the Christian and Islamic Religions are based on what was written decades after the actual founding events.

Humanity can learn from history and try not to repeat the same mistakes.

Evil exists and must be recognized and prevented, wherever possible, without violence and bloodshed, but not all conflicts can be solved peacefully.

We must never fail to remember those who made post-WW2 peace, freedom, and prosperity possible by sacrificing their lives or by life-long invalidity, mentally or physically, those who sacrificed so much so that others may be free and prosper.

Lest we forget.

Every gun that is made, every warship launched, and every rocket fired signifies, in the final sense, a theft from those who hunger and are not fed, those who are cold and not clothed.

President Dwight D Eisenhower
WW2 Forum

…but man, proud man!
Dress'd in a little brief authority,
Most ignorant of what he's most assur'd.
His glassy essence,
Like an angry ape. plays such fantastic tricks before high heaven,
As make the angels weep…

William Shakespeare
Measure for Measure II

A tyrant will always first appear as a protector
Plato 375 BC

Section 1: Pre-War Conditions and Way-of-Life

A Pre-War Community

To better understand the social impact of WW2, it is necessary to have a perception of the pre-war conditions, the rhythm of life, and the social/economic/political mentality from where the changes emerged.

As a paradigm of life before the global war erupted, please picture a sleepy, quiet village called Ubbergen in a hilly landscape of the Lowlands, as the Netherlands was called in ages past, between the town of Nijmegen on the river Waal and the German border just a few miles away.

Immense geographic forces of the Ice Age had curved the landscape. Glaciers from the north formed a ridge or moraine in the low marshlands, a small forested hilly wonderland in the delta formed by the river Rhine flowing from Switzerland and Germany through the Netherlands into the North Sea, and the River Maas or Meuse entering from France and Belgium. These rivers formed a delta that historically divided the Netherlands into different north and south cultures since the Dark Ages. On the north of the rivers, Nordic tribes dominated, while the 'below the rivers' south was Celtic territory.

The ancient Batavian tribe preferred the higher lands. Romans settled there and called the city Noviomagum in our time, known as Nijmegen, a town that played a major role in WW2, as discussed later. Chestnut trees were favored by the Romans, who preserved chestnuts as a winter provision. Those magnificent trees are still in the area.

Life progressed slowly during the 1930s after the economic chaos of the Roaring Twenties, the 1929 Stock Market Crash, and the subsequent Depression, the time where this story begins, the period of only some twenty years between WW1 and WW2, sometimes referred to in Latin as *Interbellum*.

The village's main road was a sort of dead-end road ending at the German border, the forbidden land only accessible by a few who had to submit several permits and documents for the privilege to cross the border.

Gentle, strong, Belgian horses pulled coal-loaded carts from the Nijmegen railroad station to the village, ignoring the occasional encouraging soft whips by the yawning carter. They knew where to go. Horses had, just like people, names, and characters. They belonged. The hilly country was a real test of the strength of a horse.

At the foot of the hill, all speed that could be mustered was applied which slowly declined going uphill. We had to keep the head of the horse up running along but never knew why. At times, a horse would collapse from a heart attack, which caused a problem removing their massive bodies. Occasionally a horse would bolt out of control for no apparent reason. It took courage and skill to calm a strong horse down.

Since people were not very mobile, merchants tried to press a meager existence bringing their products and services to the customers through hard physical work.

The milkman used all his strength, pushing his heavy cart up the hills, aided by a loyal German shepherd under his cart.

The '*visboer*' would praise his freshly caught fish which he would clean and prepare after a client agreed to buy. A rather gruesome operation disposing of the waste through a hole in his cart.

The '*scharenslijper*' (scissor sharpener) would sharpen knives and tools, turning the heavy stone wheel with his foot.

A common sound was the cry of the '*lompen en oud papier*' collector who would ask for rags and paper. Or anything else one would want to get rid of.

The coal and potato deliverers would carry their heavy sacks on their backs wherever needed, even three or four levels high.

The electric street car's frequent tingle operated by the upstanding driver dissolved gently in the mild daily routine.

Most articles in the small grocery store came in bags or sacks, sugar, flour, beans, and whatever, weighed on a scale the grocer and the customer could see and watch. No problems with the burden of choice here as in modern superstores, sugar was sugar and beans were just beans without the varieties offered in modern supermarkets.

Most commoners rented a small piece of land to supplement their meager income on which vegetables and potatoes were grown and harvested. Seeds were developed under old windows installed horizontally to the ground. Long beans were sliced in a hand-operated rotational slicer after they were kept heavily salted in terracotta vessels for the winter supply. Brown beans were collected as full plants, dried, put in sacks, and separated by hitting the sacks with a flail. Potatoes were dried and stored in homemade containers.

At the end of the winter, potatoes became spongy and hard to peel. Coffey was bought as beans and ground also in hand-operated rotating grinders. Food was not bought in cans but harvested from the earth and processed at home. Common people's daily food was simple and varied very little, based on bread and potatoes mixed with a variety of vegetables or beans, while on Sundays, a small piece of meat was added.

Occasionally an automobile entered the scene, so few that children would register every plate number and proudly show them around when an automobile had been spotted from other provinces.

The village of Ubbergen was quiet and peaceful, sometimes close to boring. The border with Germany, only a few miles away, was a foreboding area, an eerie place from where you stayed away, and as common citizens seldom entered!

Constable Gerbrands, a slightly overweight quiet neighbor, maintained order where there was very little to maintain. His most serious case would be finding the careless young culprit who caused damage to some stored roof tiles. Or guiding an overly happy tavern visitor home. He was actually not needed.

He just was. Riding around on his old bicycle, people greeted him jovially, as someone who needed to be there to play his minor role on the village stage but was not necessary. No fear he induced. He just belonged as paddles on a sailboat, only needed during emergencies that never happened.

A serious duty of the constable was to see to it that all bicycles had a small metal plate indicating that the unpopular bicycle tax was paid for the population's main mode of transportation.

Dominating the village were some gracious manors occupied by aristocrats with impressive long names. Prince-consort Bernard of Queen Juliana had ten first names, which, it must be assumed, is adequate. Some ultra-rich Nouveau Riche businessmen settled down with their families who tried to earn acceptance in the restricted circles of the aristocratic elite.

Most villagers were serving in some capacity at those manors except for a small number of tiny shops as the one owned by two aging sisters where a pack of North State cigarettes used to cost 25 cents.

Important was the center village tavern where the male population would gather on Saturday evenings and on Sundays after Mass.

Except for two families from elsewhere, the villagers had been faithful conservative Roman Catholics for many generations, making the priest and the appointed mayor the local notables. They in turn did their best to satisfy the wishes of the manor occupants. It was all very much accepted as the way things should be.

In the Netherlands, religion was practiced by region. In 'Below the Rivers', most of the population was Roman Catholic, lively, fun-loving, and brown-eyed Celtic people with a southern and darker complexion. Large and impressive monasteries dominated the landscape, and the intellectual center was, and still is, at the Radboud University in Nijmegen.

'Above the Rivers', people were mainly Nordic and Calvinistic with several denominations, more severe, blue-eyed, and more stoic.

For ages, river crossings were possible only by ferry until the late 1930s when bridges were constructed, with the inevitable consequence of gradually diminishing the religious and cultural divide.

In the southern region, priests assured villagers that if they regularly went to Mass and confession, their place in Heaven was guaranteed. The message instilled peace in the hearts of the believers, who lived a more joyful life than their Nordic compatriots, who were more subdued and sterner under the influence of Calvinistic pastors, who often preached predestination and in general, a more morose religion.

For centuries, the rivers divided cultures that gradually became less separated by bridges, modern transportation, and technology.

Located in the center of the village of Ubbergen was the stately manor called Waalheuvel, (Hill on the river Waal), with its own forest, greenhouses, ponds, and rose gardens mentioned only because of the role the impressive structure played during the war. The master of the manor was a very successful industrialist and national Senator but also an accomplished violinist and art collector.

Artists from Italy, laying on their backs on scaffolds had painted wonderful lofty scenes on ceilings depicting scarcely clothed babies and angels. Any form of nakedness was an absolute taboo because it would lead to sinful thoughts, except when it was displayed in art because artistic nudity was art and beyond suspicion of naughtiness.

The mansion was adorned with beautiful antique furniture, murals, and tapestry, in contrast with the average abode. When entering the manor house, common people would whisper when permitted to be there for repairs or delivery.

The Waalheuvel Manor depicted above as it is in recent times, was occupied during the war by the German military and later an emergency hospital during war operations from October 4, 1944, till June 30, 1945.

In the village, the edifice known as 'The Villa' is still impressive but not as grand as it was in its pre-war glory days.

A serious discussion developed about the emblem on the manor family's main transportation, a 1936 Cadillac with a stylistic angel on its hood with exposed breasts. Should she be covered? Was a mini-bra necessary? A serious question it was requiring the consult of the local priest. The idea was dropped after thoughtful consideration. It was art after all. And art, as said before, does not induce naughty ideas.

As a devout Roman Catholic, the lord of the manor and his pleasant, elegant wife had twelve children, four girls and eight boys, who were, also as was expected, reared by governesses.

Three gardeners, two cooks, and four other domestic servants inside the manor ensured a smooth and elegant atmosphere. The chauffeur also served as a part-time butler and handyman.

The lord of the manor called his estate a 'good-running hotel' because of the legion of family, business, and political visitors. The formal dinners were high-class events after the English model. Participants were expected to adhere to the unwritten but very important rules of behavior and dress. No deviations were tolerated!

The village had no doctor, so when needed, villagers had to go to the nearby village of Beek where Doctor van Hasselt had a practice and who was also a loyal Roman Catholic. He and his wife had fourteen healthy children. While waiting to see the doctor, people sat silently and whispered only occasionally. Nobody knew why. It was the way things were done.

On the wall of the waiting room was written in Old Dutch, '*Houd goede moed ende wilt volherden, wat niet is het kan noch werden*' (Have courage, what has not happened, still can be). Doctor visits were seldom made. Most sicknesses were treated with traditional remedies. People did not have annual physical check-ups and did not know what blood pressure or cholesterol was. Nobody had ever heard about allergies.

When a patient had to be transferred to a hospital, which happened rather seldom, transportation was by car or streetcar. It was not unusual for a patient to be transported in a hammock. Hospital visiting hours in the nearby city of Nijmegen were limited to one hour and a maximum of two people. The head nurse strictly maintained discipline. A strong anti-septic scent dominated the hospital.

One of the most feared and frequent illnesses was tuberculosis leading to a slow suffocating death. The main cure was an open-air treatment in Switzerland for those who could afford it. Local possibilities were in hospitals such as the Sanatorium in nearby Beek which played a major role during the 1944 liberation battles.

The manor's carriage house was converted to a garage for the owner's 1936 Cadillac and 1938 Chrysler Royal. American cars were prestigious. Even the Queen changed her Rolls Royce for a Cadillac with a glass separation between the front and back seats and two folding seats called strapondins.

Back-seat occupants could communicate via a microphone with the chauffeur, but the driver could not respond, only nodding understanding or failing to understand. There were class restrictions for those allowed to drive a Chevrolet, an Oldsmobile, a Nash or Cadillac/LaSalle. Unwritten but strict rules dominated a class-divided society.

On the ground floor of Waalheuvel's carriage house were its former stables with elegant colorful tiles and copper railing as witnesses to past taste and glory, in modern times converted into a garage. My family lived upstairs where there was a kitchen, a living room, and a bedroom for my parents on the first floor and two small rooms for my sister and me, and an attic on the second floor under the roof. Only the living room was heated. My mother cooked on a coal-heated stove. She would spread kerosene over peat to start the fire and then add the anthracite coal.

The carriage house was and still is an excellently designed structure with high-quality time-related architecture. The interior and exterior were designed and built when money was apparently no issue. No car was ever permitted in the garage without first being washed and cleaned outside. The structure is now nationally protected property for its architectural value.

Babies born in the village came into the world at home assisted by midwife Roman Catholic Sister Aloncia, a nun who very progressively moved quickly to her many patients on a small motorbike with her habit waving in the wind while riding with a stunning speed of some thirty miles per hour.

Everything done had its traditional rules and expectations. Acceptable first names were those of grandparents or Saints.

The Waalheuvel carriage house as it is in recent times, outwardly the same, but its interior has been renovated.

Within the mansions and manors, the ambiance was typical upstairs/downstairs. A bell board was installed in the kitchen where the domestics could gather around a table. A light on the board would show where calls came from and thus where the service was expected. When the bell rang, the reaction of the servants was nervously immediate.

The elite families felt responsible not only for supervising servants during working hours but assumed responsibility also for their mental health in their private lives. When the female domestic servants were reading a book called '*De klop op de deur*' (The knock on the door), it was taken from them because its content was deemed unsuitable because of its socialistic tendencies.

Ten-year-old Pietje Heinen (Pietje as the usual abbreviation of Pieter) son of the postman and his wife who lived on the Holleweg was popular because of his life-loving carefree ways. There were about ten children who all looked very different. When talking about Mrs. Heinen, people would shake their heads in silence. As children, we were too ignorant to understand.

Young Pietje had a wonderful boy soprano voice, and he liked to sing. On quiet summer evenings when the village was silent except for the chirping of the birds, he would stand before the open window and let his clear boy's soprano echo over the village and make people smile. Everyone's favorite was the popular Italian song Mama since about 1938 (*Mama con tanto Felice*). Everyone liked Pietje who was a twin with a brother who was totally different in appearance and character.

Riding his bike enthusiastically and excitedly during the early days of liberation, Pietje collided with a tank and was instantly killed. Tanks are very unforgiving. He was my first death experience. With many to follow. A nun opened the door of the temporary morgue in Waalheuvel where we looked, confused and stunned at the ash-pale silent face of what had been only hours ago my life-loving joyful best friend. His short life left a lasting imprint on my heart.

Another important appearance in the village was the septic tank service operator, an important but not very well-smelling part of village life. The steel cart was pulled by a restless black Olderburger steed called Frits. After a restricted day pulling the heavy steel cart with its usual repugnant but common aroma.

Frits was known as being 'on the muscle', meaning that he was a frisky and energetic horse keen to race and be freed of the restricting load he had to slowly pull all day and allowed to go to a nearby meadow for the night followed by another village ritual when another Pietje, a little red-haired boy would ride Frits across the village to the meadow's freedom.

Villagers could hear him coming from afar with the undeniable sounds of a horse in full gallop and on it little red-haired Pietje Peters running as fast as a happy Frits could. No saddles, of course. And no other traffic. Another event that belonged to the everyday routine and made people smile.

Children walked to school in nearby Nijmegen, about 45 minutes away, and brought their own lunch. My mother would pack a lunch for me in a metal former soap container. We walked regardless of the weather and often had wet feet since our only pair of shoes was frequently resoled or repaired. In wintertime, we often suffered consequently from 'winter toes' that would swell and itch terribly.

The school had seven classes, seven teachers, and no one else except a custodian. The first two-year teachers were female, thereafter they were all male. In every class were fast and slow learners and handicapped pupils, I sat one year next to a boy who had what was called a 'water head' (hydrocephalus), a grotesque large head.

It was not yet possible to drain the fluids of babies with this illness as it is in contemporary times. Handicapped classmates were accepted as if it was supposed to be that way. Monday, Tuesday, Thursday, and Friday were full school days on Wednesday and Saturday only in the morning.

A nerve-wracking day came at the end of every school year when the headmaster, the teacher of the highest class, would come into the class to let us know who was allowed to progress to the next year and who had to do the year over again.

Headmaster Drost was a very dignified man respected by parents and pupils. When I once used a rather vulgar expression, not unusual among common folk, especially in dialects, he took me aside and told me very seriously that such words were not acceptable. Lesson learned! When *Mijnheer* (mister) Drost would lecture about the saintly Father of the Fatherland, Prince William of Orange, he would have tears in his eyes, and we were in awe.

Modern historians dug up some information about a much less perfect *Willem van Oranje* according to the tendencies of our era where we are more factual but also much more downgrading and cynical. In the pre-WW2 days, the effort was to place role models on a pedestal they may not have deserved, but nevertheless encouraged people to aim for higher standards.

The school had a small library with all books carefully wrapped in paper to avoid any trace of malignant use. Most books were about the South African Boer Wars from 1899 till 1902 which were still fresh in my memory.

A popular song was '*Mijn vrouw en kinderen ze sturen naar moordenaars kampen henen. Oh, wat een schande, schande voor Engeland*' (my wife and children were sent to murder concentration camps, oh what a disgrace for England). Deeply touched, I despised the wrong done to our kinsmen and women who had settled in South Africa the same time the first settlers came to North America.

Image and reputation are fragile and change with time. And so it happened with the Boers, the heroes of my youth are now called Apartheid racists.

Popular songs were South African such as *Bolandse Nooientjie* and *Sari Marais* and the beautiful rather melancholic Indonesian *Krontjong* (from a ukulele-like instrument) songs such as *Terang Bulan* (bright moon) and *Ajoen* (swinging in the high coconut tree) from a 16th Century Indonesian and Portuguese background.

Two Jewish radio performers were very popular, actress Heintje Davids and tenor Joseph Schmidt.

Most teachings were to 'learn by heart', filling the brain's data bank with numbers of dates and general information. Pupils had to recite the required information so repeatedly that it could be recalled when half asleep. In modern days, information is obtained externally from Google and other sources replacing the old brain data bank. Past generations had to rely more on what was stored internally. Filling a person's data bank has the advantage of parallel processing which allows consideration of information outside what computers and other technological stunning developments tell us.

One classmate was Heinz Balbierer, a tall gentle somewhat awkward boy who during the occupation had to wear the hated yellow badge that identified him as a Jew. His family had fled Germany, only to face the same prosecution in the Netherlands during the German occupation.

My efforts to find his name among those who died in the concentration camps did not reveal information. He and his family just disappeared as so many have during times of war and disaster. Known only to God.

In school, pupils learned discipline. When the whistle signal came from the school headmaster, pupils would line up outside, walk silently to class, stand next to their seats, and sit down when the teacher nodded. And yes, there was some physical punishment, especially the pulling of ears. But it was the norm and accepted.

A bad offender was shut up in the coal storage room. Nevertheless, through strict discipline and high standards students received excellent education thanks to dedicated teachers. Parents always supported the teachers, even when they had been wrong.

I fell in love with the girl in front of my seat, as boys do at that age without understanding why. Her name was Jopie Ruwers and she had beautiful thick long hair. I became her hero when I prevented my friend Wimpie van Buren who sat next to me on the two-seat bench, from putting the ends of her long hair in the inkwell located in the middle of the benches.

She gave me a pencil and I swooned over it for weeks. Writing had to be perfect with the new 'crown' pens we would get new ones once a month.

Two major school events were the birth of Princess Beatrix in 1938 and we were given traditional '*Bischuit met muisjes*' on the occasion, a traditional biscuit with sugar caraway seeds, and the opening of the bridge across the river Waal, the bridge that would later play such a crucial role during the war. We all sang that the ferry could start a trip around the world now and go in retirement. Since the bridge was built with riveted connections, we celebrated with chocolate rivets filled with s sweet cream.

Continued education after grade school was determined by the social class one belonged to. Boys of 'blue collar' parents went to work or continued craft training at the *Ambachtschool,* and the girls went to work or enter the *Vrouwenarbeitschool,* the 'women's work' school.

Lower middle-class children went to the MULO, a continued education school; the middle-class pupils went to the *Hogere Burger School*, the 'higher citizen school' and the offspring of the elite, if at all possible, to the *Gymnasium.* Dutch, German, English, and French were mandatory for the MULO and HBS pupils while Greek and Latin were added for the *Gymnasium* students. There were exceptions, of course, but in general, education was determined by social class. Less than five percent of the students attended universities.

When children had time to play, they were expected to entertain themselves. Boys made catapults from tree branches and old bicycle inner tubes to shoot small stones, a dangerous weapon. Bows and arrows also were self-made. Arrows were taken from the reed mats used in the gardens. Football (soccer) was played either with old tennis balls from the elite courts or ones made of paper with rubber bands around it. Imagination was given free rein. Girls played with balls thrown against walls while singing songs, developing amazing skills and also used skipping ropes.

Communal entertainment came from the local soccer games manned by local unpaid players, the Annual Fair and Circus in Nijmegen where the main desired food was French fries wrapped conically in old news journals, listening to the radio such as the *Bontedinsdagavondtrein,* (the Tuesday night joy train), local gymnastic, music band, theater, dance and art clubs.

Formality was strictly maintained during dance classes. Boys and girls would line up across from each other. When the gramophone music started, boys would move forward, bow, and ask the girl opposite to his position for the dance. She would make a courtesy and the dance began.

Close bodily contact was not allowed. The trick for the boys was to line up across from the girl you wanted to dance with, which caused at times some undignified but anxious competition. Yet the ambiance remained within strict rules of etiquette.

Entertainment was locally produced and often of questionable quality. Only the radio programs from the town of Hilversum would provide some limited external influences. Performance standards were maintained according to communal standards and not very high compared to recent times with easy access to the best in every form of art is readily available.

There was a tendency to over-sentimentalize and the available training was not very progressive. Yet the local performances, often on a small scale and in private houses, were appreciated and enjoyed.

People knew each other well, at times too well. Even from the laundry drying on the line exposed an unwelcome intimacy and thus had its rules and traditions such as the way socks should be hung or shirts and how 'unmentionables' could be prevented from exposure. Electric dryers were unknown.

The elite had a device called a '*mangel*' where sheets and similar linen were pressed and flattened between two cylinders driven of course by human energy. For some reason, female knickers were called a '*directoire*' which I did not understand. A board of directors? Only in later years did I find that the name came from a French decorative art period between 1892 and 1899.

There was no refrigeration, but a 'fly box' was in the cellar in which meats and milk were stored with a front door with a metal mesh to prevent insects entering. Once a week a horse-drawn enclosed carriage entered the village bringing square ice bars to the pub, and some elite mansions for refrigeration. The heavy square bars were handled with steel hooks. When a bar was hacked into shorter lengths, children would eagerly pick up the ice splinters to suck on them.

Shoes were several times resoled and repaired. Women and girls demonstrated amazing skills in repairing holes in stockings and socks using a wooden hand tool with a smooth round top held in their left hand inside of the sock, repairing the damage with their right hand. Nylon was still unknown.

The elite ate white bread, unaware that it was less healthy and caused many to suffer from constipation. Common people ate healthier and cheaper dark bread. Before antibiotics were developed, it was a common occurrence that people had infections. The only remedy to avoid infections was to apply iodine which hurt terribly!!

Religious education depended on the school attended and private lessons at home or church. On a small plateau under majestic chestnut trees and surrounded by the mesmerizing scent of jasmine on the fence, stood and still stands a small chapel since the 14th Century where the few Protestant families of the region would gather to listen to the pastor of a nearby village. So small was the chapel that one could shake hands from the pews with the minister in the pulpit.

As children, we also received our religious education there. The young minister Ds. van der Linde was a very pleasant young pastor who served several churches and befriended the monks in the huge monasteries around Nijmegen with as center the Roman Catholic University. He later became a Catholic priest and a professor at the university.

The above seven-hundred-year-old chapel, which was once alive, now stands somewhat forlorn and forgotten, a symbol of a time long gone when one could inhale the scent of the jasmine with eyes feasted on the majestic chestnut trees above and around. Its simple beauty elicits scenes of this long-lost era, of melancholic memories of imperfect yet gentler days, in which right and wrong were more clearly defined and behavior more valued.

Even though we lived only a few miles from Germany, crossing the border was not done. It was as if entering a strange forbidden land. I only remember going once with my father when he was sent there on a special mission, and I was allowed to go with him. Standing with my father at the back of a cheering crowd enthusiastically waving at something or someone with their right arms stretched out shouting '*Sieg Heil*'. We did not participate of course. Several people turned to us questioning why we did not follow their example. After my father's explanation that we were not German, they concluded that we were 'Ausländer' foreigners, as if we were an inferior species.

The other occasion was the only visit with my mother and sister to my maternal grandparents in Northern Germany. Traveling about 150 miles by train would take a day. At the border, the train halted, and all adults had to leave the train to clear customs and passport control which took hours. Boisterous, happy giggling young girls of the BDM (Bund Deutscher Mädel), the league of German girls and the female side of the Hitler Youth, entered on an apparent outing.

They all were in high spirits wearing white blouses with black skirts and ties, obviously happy and elated while my sister and I felt lost and lonely. My mother returned and we continued to Oldenburg where we switched to a slow-moving train with balconies and where people sat around a coal stove in the middle of the cabin. The steam locomotive constantly rang a bell to keep cattle off the tracks.

My German relatives maintained a very neutral stand on the political turmoil of the time. When the oldest part of town was demolished to be replaced by pleasant small but comfortable new housing by the National Socialistic Regime, the change was noted with subdued approval.

The people in the rural small town of Brake along the Weser River in Germany wanted to be left alone. Uncle Dirk, who spent his entire life on the river but never learned to swim, transported cargo on his small barge driven by a one-cylinder glow-head diesel producing a sleep-inducing rhythmic sound with its 80 rpm. This diesel engine will run even if you put cod oil in it my father assured me.

But there were exceptions. Uncle Carl Maier was an impressive artistic-looking philosophical man who emotionally criticized the upcoming Nazi regime while his wife, my mother's sister Hanna, tried in vain to keep his tone down.

Totally on the opposite side was Uncle Gustav Renken, a local contractor and a fanatic member of the SA '*Sturmabteilung*', (Storm detachment, the pseudo-military arm of the Nazi Party). He and his three sons had round heads with short hair. Gustav was wearing his brown uniform continuously with the swastika on his arm. In the US he probably would have been called a redneck.

During family gatherings, the family tried to keep relations cordial, especially in the presence of my grandparents, and with the help of Gustav's pleasant wife, my mother's sister Insa, the discussions were kept trivial and neutral.

Once every two or three years we would visit Uncle (*Oom*) Willem and Aunt (*Tante*) Bertha in Olst, a village on the River IJsel about ten kilometers north of the town of our ancestry, Deventer, one of the oldest cities in the Netherlands and was once known as a tree trade town (*Hanzestad*) in medieval times when it had a Latin School, the university of that time, and a Bishop Seat which was of great importance.

Tante (Aunt) Bertha was my father's younger sister, a very kind slightly buxom woman who liked to giggle in her own specific way. Uncle Willem was a stoic quiet man who had been over 40 years the station master at the village railway station, in its community a very responsible and respected job.

He had to open and close the road crossing gates for the tracks near the station when the daily train would pass and would hold a round signal on a stick, red showing that the train could not move and green that it was ready to move again after he had blown his whistle. Slowly, the magnificent hissing locomotive would advance, and the machinist would wave farewell leaning with one elbow outside the locomotive contours. *Tot morgen Willem* (See you tomorrow Willem) he would shout addressing each other by their first name.

Railway stations were extremely impressive places for a young boy with their mighty locomotives letting steam off from time to time reminding of a fire-spitting dragon in the fantasy mind of youth. A man carrying a huge oilcan would oil connections and a second railroad worker would go along the train hitting wheels with a hammer to ensure that there were no brake pads stuck on the wheels.

There were second and third-class apartments in the carriages, with wooden banks in the third class for the common citizens and cloth upholstery in the second class for the elite.

Why was there no first class? No one knew. For the queen, it was assumed. Windows would be opened via a leather strip with holes in it that could be fastened to protruding pins. But it was risky to open windows because there was a real chance you would be covered with black soot from the locomotive.

As a convinced Socialist Uncle Willem studied Esperanto, the language designed to be the common language for the new socialistic world. He grew up as an orphan in a harsh environment.

After the war, I took him across the border into Germany where I was living at that time. It was his first journey outside the Netherlands and basically the first time away from his village and surroundings. When we passed customs, he looked around sitting next to me on the front seat of my car in a contemplating mood and said after a while, "People here look about the same as they do at home." One can only wonder what he had expected!

Many events were basic and primitive. When a pig was slaughtered, the throat was cut. Men would hold the animal down while women collected the blood in a pan stirring blood to prevent clogging and make sausage with it. The pig would be hoisted on a ladder and fastened to complete the slaughter, as it had been done so for countless generations.

Many roads were still rural and unpaved. Some major roads had round square stones called '*Kinderkoppen*' (children's heads) or stones made of river clay. To install the road deck first the ground was leveled, then a layer of sand was added.

One man would bring the stones in a wheelbarrow to his colleague who was kneeling on the ground while placing every single stone by hand followed by several strikes with a special hammer. Their skill was fascinating. After a stretch of road was finished, a thin layer of sand was added. It was back-breaking work.

Yet the idyllic impression of life in the village had, as all coins have, an opposite side.

Ultra-rich the Netherlands with its wealth obtained from three hundred years of colonization of what was called at that time the Netherlands East Indies, now independent Indonesia, failed to protect its vulnerable citizens and kept the accumulated wealth within the upper classes.

It was the era before social support systems would develop, which made the programs of the Nazi Party very attractive to the lower, mostly abandoned class of citizens.

Beggars rang the bell often to ask for a small gift, at times accompanied by skinny slovenly dressed, and bad-smelling children. My mother would make a sandwich for them but never money.

A very tragic figure was a homeless man I only knew as 'White sand' because he earned a few pennies to sell white sand used to clean kitchen floors. As a desperate alcohol-addicted wretch, he drank even the most dangerous alcohol and died of delirium,

Nicknames were the common way to identify each other. Neighbor Jansen had developed a special way to enter his bicycle. The common way for a male to enter a bicycle was to stand on the pedal and swing a leg over the bicycle to sit on the saddle, Jansen had an extension installed on the rear wheel axel which he entered with his left foot to then swing his right leg across to the saddle.

Thus, he was known as '*Jansen de Springer*' (Jansen the jumper). Nicknames were a necessity since centuries of inbreeding and traditional customs to name children for their grandparents resulted in several villagers with the same name. The Code Napoleon of 1811 demanded that every citizen select a family name that could not be changed anymore. Some people did not take it too seriously and used their nicknames such as *Naaktgeboren* (born naked), *Vroegindewei* (early in the meadow), *Nooitgedacht* (never expected) and many more.

Time has taken its toll by filling every free space in the village with houses where I spent my wonderful youth among good people who, despite all trivial problems and tensions, lived peacefully in the village.

Before WW2, the village smelled differently, with scents of kerosene, peat, cooking, and stove inside, the scent of horses, manure, and trees outside, and the smell of incense in the houses of my Catholic neighbors.

Inside the manors, a rich undefinable perfume dominated. But most of all was the wonderful smell of jasmine growing along the fences under the grand chestnut trees, a smell I never encountered again and, at least for me, enriched the memories of the wonderful years of my youth.

Across our house was an old majestic brown beech that stood as a proud protecting center as only old trees can. We used to carve our initials in its bark. Now the tree is gone, and a modern house is in its place.

Life was traditional with a strong sense of proper behavior, its often-boring customs, social standards of unwritten but strongly abided traditions, normal communal interaction without the distractions of television and computer technology, and thus more time to interact, discuss, argue, debate, sing and joke.

The not-so-very-good local band named the Harmony marched proudly during special events, some dressed in uniform, some in some with parts of a uniform, and some without a uniform. It was all supposed to be this way.

There was very little trash before the throwaway and plastic era. Package materials were used and reused. On a meadow behind our house, old wooden objects were gathered during the year and burned in a communal festal activity to 'burn the winter away' on the evening before Easter.

To the best of my memory, we survived without a lawyer in our village or even in the County. For testaments and other legal matters, one had to travel to a notary in nearby Beek or Nijmegen. Notaries were highly respected in society, a position that could only be achieved after many years of university education.

Business agreements or sales were concluded with a handshake instead of the endless legal terms and documents required in modern times. Breaking a handshake agreement would cause a scandal. And scandals were still taken very seriously.

It is difficult to capture a time with words, its feeling and mindset differ so much from contemporary reality, as will our time probably to future generations. Old films seem overdramatic, yet it was the norm of the time.

The pre-WW2 was a locally focused world with its own communal standards and traditions and a clear understanding of acceptable behavior, of rights and wrongs, at times too strong and fierce in its condemnation. Any departure from those standards would not be accepted.

No ZIP codes were required when addressing a person via the mail. Just a personal name and the name of the village sufficed. Postman Heinen knew where everybody lived. House numbers or street names were not needed. The main door of a house had a mail slot through which the mail was put to either fall on the ground, or into a receiving box behind the slot. There was of course only sporadic mail and no advertising as far as I remember.

Marriage was taken very seriously. Divorce was just not allowed. A couple who intended to live their lives together would first get engaged, a very serious commitment already that took several years during which money was saved for the basic needs a marriage would require. When the date of the wedding was established and announced, the couple had to register at the Town Hall.

An announcement was posted so that anyone who would oppose the wedding could register their objections. A wedding was first for the law at the Town Hall and thereafter in the church. Brides were expected to wear a white dress as a token of their virginity. Pre-marital sex was strictly prohibited.

Women who were pregnant before the wedding or had a baby or within the usual nine months after the wedding would lose respect in society, a matter that was taken seriously at a time when a scandal was still seen as a breach of good standing and behavior.

A remarkable difference with post-war society was that the domains of men and women were strictly maintained. Women were expected to take care of the household and children, while men were expected to be the providers.

The family patriarch often ruled as a small potentate, yet in many families, women were the absolute authority. The only educational opportunities for women were in health care, education, and administration, but even in these professions, women were mostly assigned to lesser tasks and paid less.

It was still common to refer to females as '*het zwakke geslacht*', the 'weak gender', by contemporary standards, a rather demeaning and unrealistic reference when the woman in many families was holding the family together while showing amazing strength and tenacity during difficult and dangerous times.

Gender relations were based on Christian principles and traditions in a time that the Christian religion still had a major influence on society from Calvinistic Denominations in the North of the Country and as well from the Roman Catholic Church 'south of the rivers'. Women were expected to support and assist their husbands and were subservient legally as well in society at large.

When a village citizen died, a man dressed in formal black attire with a high hat would go from house to house, pull the bell, open the door, and stand inside the door to recite in a monotone voice the name, address, and date of the passing and when the funeral would be. Neighbors were expected to be pallbearers. The ride from the homes where most villagers died to the church and from there to the cemetery would be with a black funeral carriage pulled by two black horses with black plumes on their heads.

The ornate funeral carriage, all in black of course, with glass sides so one could see the flower-draped coffin had an inscription that read '*Hodie mihi, cras tibi*'; My turn today, yours tomorrow. Without ever having had a Latin education, everyone knew its translation and meaning. Relatives would wear a black band around their arms for thirty days as a sign that they were still within a period of mourning. That's the way it was and expected to be followed as a communal ritual.

Not a perfect world it was, but a rather peaceful and reliable way of life founded on a solid base of communal interaction and affairs, on how one was expected to behave and what was proper behavior in accordance with centuries of tradition and what was permitted both within and outside of the law.

An interesting ritual that lasted even in a few post-war years was to put your shoes outside your room in a hotel before going to sleep. The next morning the clean and shiny shoes were back where you put it the night before. 'Reputable' hotels would allow a couple a room only after proof of marriage.

Scandals were taken seriously; they could lower your standing in society and, although not written on paper, influence your career and income.

A difficult decision was to determine how to address people in a respectful or familiar way as it is in German and French languages. Another puzzle was to address someone in a letter which required a choice between a dozen different ways depending on the person's education and position, a decision that would be problematic if you did not know the person's background and chose the highest standard only to find out later that it was totally and embarrassing wrong!

Homosexuality was barely whispered about and for most people totally unknown. It was heard at times that there had to be something out of the ordinary in a mystic 'sinful' way, but not many knew what it was and those who suspected something did not dare to talk about it.

Life was slower and communal, steady by its own standards, and reliable. For most, it was easier to become happy because when you have very little, even a small gift such as an orange at Christmas can be a source of awe and gratefulness.

Humor targeted mostly the everyday smallness of people without the biting more cynical style of modern times where laughing comes from artificial technology instead of the heart.

Right and wrong behavior was clearly established.

Till a war erased its ignorance and innocence.

Mobilization and the 'Phoney War'

The Netherlands had avoided involvement in the stygian death fields of WW1 and was proud and confident of its neutrality. It was a very rich nation obtained from the wealth of what was called the Netherlands East Indies, independent Indonesia in modern times.

Dutch diplomats in Berlin sent warnings after 1933 that times had changed with the rise of the National Socialism (Nazi) in Germany, emphasizing that the threat from an expansion-driven Nazi regime for an invasion into the Netherlands should be taken seriously.

But it was not. After more than a century without war, a mindset dominated that it should be this way. There was initially no great concern about what happened in neighboring Germany. It was their business. Friendly relations were maintained with all neighbors. The Netherlands was known as a peaceful nation and had no resources such as oil to be of great interest to the new German regime.

The Netherlands certainly did not have an aggressive and competent military force to be a threat to anyone. Moreover, good relations with important trade partners were imperative.

Did the Netherlands not provide a refuge for the German Emperor in 1918 and treated him with respect and gave him a mansion to retire? And did not the nation pursue a foreign policy of neutrality?

Yet there were some signals and observations of what happened in Germany for the past seven to eight years that were not well received and with an uneasy feeling of a mixture of concern and unbelief, especially the German demonstrations of military power and the boasting attitude of fanatic leaders and a seemingly tranced submissive population.

Films and pictures of magnificently organized parades, of thousands of marching soldiers welcomed by almost hysterical shouting masses were seen with admiration and a great sense of mistrust.

Uneasy feelings returned when only six months later when German troops invaded Czechoslovakia. The German expansion drive had apparently not changed. Chamberlain stated openly that Hitler could not be trusted.

It was well known that Germany needed oil for their military operations and that it did not possess regions that could produce the required energy sources. But the Netherlands could not be of any assistance in this respect except perhaps for the modern port of Rotterdam and its refineries.

The mood declined even more when Poland was targeted, and Russia and Germany agreed in August 1939 to a non-aggression pact which left Poland in a vulnerable position.

To offset this threat, a more optimistic mood returned when England and France sided with Poland guaranteeing their support to the beleaguered nation and promising to declare war if Germany dared to attack Poland. They were, after all, the powerful and victorious combatants of the previous war! Hitler would not dare to attack Poland now it was argued.

Ignoring and defying the joint French/English support for Poland, the European political situation turned negative again when German military power invaded Poland only a little later on September 2, 1939, which forced England and France to declare war on Germany according to their promise.

The first step toward another multi-nation war was taken. But hope remained that it would stop there. It was reasoned that there were indeed many Germans living in a region of Czechoslovakia and there had been great differences of opinion over centuries whether East Prussia was Polish or German, a mood reflected by the Canadian Prime Minister Mackenzie King when he blamed the German invasion of Poland for not giving the city of Danzig back to Germany.

The Netherlands had no such German enclaves, so why worry?

It became nevertheless clear to common citizens that their fear of a repeat of the horror of WWI was increasingly realistic. In September 1939, Russia and Germany agreed to divide Poland among themselves. The suffering nation was absorbed by its aggressive neighbors. Fanatic dictatorial Communist and National Socialistic ideologies had eliminated, for the moment at least, a proud and peaceful nation called Poland.

After declaring war on Germany to curtain the ongoing aggression, France and the British Empire hesitated to confront Hitler's superior military strength directly with the hellish conditions and stalemates of the previous war in mind.

A period started that Churchill called the 'twilight war' and the 'bore war', but the term 'phoney war' in the end was accepted for the period from September 1939 till May 1940 when Germany attacked France, Luxembourg, Belgium, and the Netherlands and thus a direct confrontation could no longer be avoided.

The reaction in the Netherlands after the war declaration by France and the British Empire was one of concern and sympathy. Something needed to be done to stop German aggression. The war declaration by two powerful nations should be the right response. It was considered serious and upsetting but should not affect us because we were a neutral nation and no threat to anyone. Life in the Netherlands went on its normal routine.

As young citizens, we went to school, did our duties, played, and observed the work of clever craftsmen. My favorite was the village carpenter. The scent of the different woods and the hot glue smelled like perfume to us when we would just sit quietly and observe craftsmen at work.

Power tools were not yet invented. The curling slivers of the plane were fascinating. So differently in modern times, the pace was slow and steady in an era where quality dominated over time and profit. Only hand-operated tools were used, which required skill and craftsmanship.

Political opinions in the village differed. We are human and, as a nation, value free speech and opinion. The Netherlands had maintained over centuries, a commitment to freedom of opinion and tolerance.

A few supported former Prime Minister Colijn in a belief that resistance was useless against superior and powerful enemies. So why spend all the money on defense? A realistic point of view that was later put into practice by Denmark. Resistance would only cause death and destruction, it was argued, and had no chance of success.

Not very well appreciated was the minority of *Het Gebroken Geweertje,* the 'broken rifle' of the War Resisters International formed with the idealistic but unrealistic intent to forever prevent another war. People who belonged to this political movement were wearing a pin showing a broken rifle and conscientiously objected to any type of military service.

Several women's organizations supported the movement. It was very well intended but considered by the majority rather unpatriotic. Idealism will not prevent evil intent. It was argued that these people want the police to protect against local lawlessness and crime but not have an army on a national level to protect the nation.

Another few village experts were convinced that the strength of a superior national defense, the so-called Water Line Defense Line, a wide inundated corridor, would make it impossible to progress to the main cities of Rotterdam, The Hague, and Amsterdam. The military strategists still had the territorial land-war mindset of past wars.

Fokker, of WW1 fame, had designed a superior two-engine double-tailed plane named the G-1. The nation had about 23, so the same experts argued that Germany would not dare to attack. Had not Major-General Alting von Gensau, proudly declared '*Wij zijn paraat*!' We are ready! ('Double names' assured one belonged to the elite!)

Was it realistic? German artillery developments had advanced its range so that the major cities could have been under fire without crossing the Water Defense Line! That the major threat could come from the air in modern warfare was not seriously considered.

There also was general confidence that the League of Nations would be able to defuse serious confrontations with the horrors of the First World War still in mind. Did not all nations agree that such a human catastrophe should never happen again?

The Netherlands military was underfunded and obsolete. It was known and accepted, despite the nice parades with beautiful horses, but was somehow not taken too seriously. It did not mean that every soldier would not do his utmost to defend the nation, but only when it was necessary.

Social class dominated in the military as it was in society at large, where the division between officers, NCOs, and soldiers was maintained rigorously. Name and university education guaranteed an officer's status whether qualified or not. Once an officer, you remained an officer. It was the class one belonged to. In the worst case, an officer could be dismissed, booted out of the military dishonorably, but could not be degraded below an officer's status. It also was not possible to enter the officer's rank from a non-officer military rank.

Compulsory service by a lottery system was accepted by most more as an unavoidable necessity and should be over and done with as soon as possible. For most young men, military service was something one had to do but without the national, military pride and pleasure of Germany.

Most village citizens did not know how to interpret the European political scene. Decisions would be made regardless of what they would think. How to survive and what could be done to protect family and belongings was the dominating concern.

The German invasion of Poland in September 1939, however, made even the Dutch Government nervous, On August 28, 1939, a Mobilization declaration was issued. Some 200.000 men were ordered to report for military duty arriving at their destination via extra trains. The measure tripled the existing military to about 280.000 men of a total population of slightly over 8 million.

Many recruits lost their jobs with the inevitable result that families lost their income. The government military allowances were insufficient for many families to survive, which led to locally organized food distribution and eating facilities.

Military leave was canceled. But the new actions were not effective enough to cause a sincere turnaround in technology or preparedness. Compulsory service had been reduced early in the 1930s from 24 to 6 months to save money, a period that proved insufficient to train recruits.

At the time of the mobilization, the training period was about 8 months. Budgets to bring the obsolete military up to modern standards had been cut. Germany and France required training periods of about two years.

The Netherlands spent 4 % of GNP on the military and defense. Germany spent over 25%.

That the nation was also wide open for espionage was another weakness. German intelligence could freely enter and see what was going on, observe what and where military defenses were built, and the strengths and kinds of exercises that were being held.

The Netherlands had a long tradition of being welcome to foreigners, strangers, and refugees. Germany took advantage of its liberal idealism with the eager help of some Dutch Nazis.

When Mobilization was declared, our village was suddenly overwhelmed with Dutch soldiers. Officers found, as was expected in a class-oriented society, housing in the lush elegance of the manors. NCOs and soldiers where available space could be found, such as the next-door youth hostel and in the garage of our house. For the village youth, it was all very interesting and adventurous.

Along the road to Germany, explosives were placed around trees lining the main access roads. On main roads, openings were excavated in which steel beams could be placed under an angle toward a possible aggressor to halt advancing tanks, called by the common folks somewhat derogatory 'asparagus'.

While all the actions taken made some impression, the reality was that the Dutch military remained obsolete. The Dutch Army had no tanks, only a few light armored vehicles. Clothing was about the same as it had been in the 1914-1918 war uncomfortable and ineffective such as the lower leg windings named poeties.

Bicycles were still used for transportation and horses to pull artillery guns; they were nice to look at, however, out of date in modern motorized warfare. The rifles were mainly the P14, a model designed in 1914. Some 300 artillery units were from 1904, some even from 1878.

When Mobilization was declared, the military mindset it was clearly demonstrated when 12.000 horses were ordered to be confiscated, along with bicycles and cars, keeping memories of WW1 and previous 19th Century battles in mind. While the German military was modern and motorized, the Dutch generals still expected WW1 conditions.

The military had no modern communications systems and used only cable systems and dispatch by motorbike riders. There were many shortages such as maps and binoculars. The Dutch military was not taken very seriously by its neighboring nations.

A typical pre-war soldier with a rifle-mounted bayonet and unpractical leggings (putties). The bayonet played still a major role as it had during WW1 during man-to-man combat. Memories were only twenty years old. Similar conditions were anticipated.

The Dutch Commander in Chief General Winkelman shifted the main defense line from t inundated Water Defense Line to a hilly area in the center of the nation west of Arnhem called the Grebbeberg for several reasons among which was a defense further away from the main cities such as Amsterdam.

The general atmosphere was somewhat chaotic, especially in finding adequate quarters for the troops in farm barns and schools to sleep and eat.

The average Dutch soldier took it all in stride, kept its great Amsterdam streetcar sense of humor, and most of all, put its trust in the national commitment to neutrality.

In the village, young soldiers flirted and whistled when a young woman passed. It all was a rather pleasant and interesting event. Even somewhat boring at times. There was very little military display, no parades or shows of strength and it all appeared somewhat low-key. The Dutch people, other than the German citizens at that time, were not intrigued by military grandeur and are still not in modern times.

In 1938, the *Luchtbeschermingsdienst* had been introduced, the Air Protection Service consisting of volunteers who had as its primary purpose to warn civilians of the potential dangers coming from the air. The organization remained active during the war years but lost its effectiveness when Jews were forbidden to participate and the desire to serve away from home sharply declined during war activities and when later starvation became a reality.

Air Protection Service volunteers had an identification batch on their arms and were equipped with a helmet, first-aid kid, and gas masks. The horrible experiences of WW1 chorine attacks by the German army were still fresh in everyone's memory. My father's duty included a night watch in a tower high on the ridge looking for possible war-related events which did of course not happen before the invasion. He did not like being away from home and spending unpleasant long nights in a dark tower.

Shelters were constructed and anti-aircraft stations installed. Even though the Dutch Government greatly underestimated the possible impact and strength of the German air attacks, it was realized after WW1 that some threats would come from the air. But not massive hundreds or even thousands of planes nor paratrooper battalions falling from the sky. One volunteer per 200 and 300 families was the goal of the Air Protection Service.

Among the developments was the installation and testing of alarm sirens. Whoever invented the device did a very effective job. Not only could the sound penetrate deeply but it's howling up and down dynamic sound created a dark strident, and doomsday impression. I deplored its sound which would make an already nerve-wracking situation worse.

Blackouts were ordered. Black roll-up curtains had to be installed on all windows. Car lights had to be covered with black paint or covers except for a small slit and even bicycle lights had to be dimmed in a similar way, a rather futile demand since it was questionable if enemy aircraft could even see the very weak bicycle lights.

Streetlights were also shut down or dimmed to uselessness. It all made the nights hauntingly eerie and very difficult to find your way. Later curfews during the occupation made it impossible to be outside at night anyhow, not even during health emergencies.

The use of biological warfare was taken seriously. To test gas masks Dutch soldiers were locked up in the heater room of our house under the garage and exposed to benign but most unpleasant tear gas. How well I remember the frantic bouncing on the closed door when a soldier's gas mask failed to provide the needed protection. Not a pleasant experience.

Being member of the partially uniformed voluntary civil protection force gave some middle-aged, often overweigh family fathers an unrealistic sense of importance, leading to with subsequent amusement and joking as it was later so well portrayed on English TV series with their outstanding talent to see the humorous side of well-intended but somewhat over-dignified commitment.

Mobilization did not change the most routine ways of life and usual operations but did cause some concerns.

My father, a sensitive, gentle man, had been the chauffeur for wealthy families during the days when automobiles were still unreliable and uncomfortable when the driver would sit in the open air as had been the tradition when the horse-pulled carriages were the main transportation.

Aristocratic families would spend, as was the common tradition, the summer in their rural castles and manors and moved to their stately houses in

The Hague for the winter to participate in diplomatic, aristocratic and the very rich circles visiting operas, parties, receptions, concerts and other festivities.

To be a chauffeur in those days required a lot more than just driving a car. It took maintenance and mechanical skills to crank the engines into action and repairing the frequently flat tires which required putting a patch on the inner tube, a back-breaking job and very unpleasant during inclement weather.

My maternal grandfather owned and operated a windmill in Friesland along the North Sea coast of Germany. When the terms of the Versailles Treaty completely devastated the German economy, he went bankrupt and, as it is well known, inflation became totally out of control making the German currency worthless. To help the family, two of his daughters, Grete and Maria (Mia) my mother found domestic work in the Netherlands. The little they earned was worth a fortune in support of their German family.

When employed in The Hague, my parents met, fell in love, and married. My aunt Grete returned to German Friesland, but my mother remained in the Netherlands. My father spoke fluent German, and my mother good Dutch even though they never had any language education.

It has been stated that the two languages, Dutch and German, must be 'about the same', which is not true. Most Dutch people learn English easier and faster than German.

My family had throughout the ages and since the emergence of the Netherlands as a free independent nation in 1648, a staunch 'Orange' supporter, loyal to the Dutch Royal Family. The 'Father of the Fatherland', William the Silent, who led the rebellion against the Spanish occupation was, in addition to other titles, a Prince d'Orange in France and thus the reason for the royal family to be called the House of Orange.

In the US, having multiple cultural or national heritage as a nation of immigrants is normal and accepted. But in Europe difficult border crossings prevented a multi-national and diverse society. When in marriage the two spouses are from nations that became enemies, tensions can be expected.

In front of our house, the red, white and blue national flag was proudly displayed equipped also with the orange pennant. My mother had become a Dutch citizen, but she dearly loved her German family and her Frisian heritage. Native loyalty differences may have existed between our parents but we, children, were not aware of it. We never heard our parents argue.

It was known in the village that my mother was German. She was well respected by her high standards, yet German and thus looked at with a certain suspicion. Differences in culture and religion were avoided. Marriages between Protestant and Roman Catholic couples just did only seldom happen and were fiercely objected to, even between the different Protestant denominations.

Aware of the increasing political turmoil in Europe and despite its trust in the neutrality of the nation, the government introduced a distribution system for sugar in October 1939 to test the system more than a true need, which proved to be a very worthwhile experience in later years. Sugar could hence only be bought with food stamps and with a limited amount per person and family.

When Germany invaded Denmark and Norway in March 1940, the mood in the nation declined significantly. Soldiers became more concerned, especially in a village only a few miles from the German border.

They knew that they would be the first to encounter the assumed enemy but also were aware that they would have no chance nor capability to defend themselves in case of a German attack and that their obsolete weapons would have no chance against modern German armory. Resistance in Denmark lasted only six hours and only sixty-two days in the difficult terrain of Norway.

In April 1940, a full-strength mobilization was ordered, and we knew that things looked very serious.

But the local ambiance nevertheless remained cautiously optimistic.

The lord of Waalheuvel Manor purchased a small Opel Kadett anticipating that gasoline supplies would be limited. The small Opel was much more efficient compared to the gas-guzzling Cadillac. It was well known that the Axis, Germany, Italy, and Japan lacked oil supplies. Several drums filled with gasoline were stored in an empty chicken cup behind our house and caused some excitement when there was a small grass fire nearby. But nothing serious happened.

People also began to hoard supplies in anticipation of possible shortages.

Tension mounted, but hope remained that just as in previously in WW1. The Netherlands would remain neutral and be spared the ravages and suffering of war.

Section 2: War, Occupation, and Liberation

Events Leading to a Global War

"The cause is hidden, the effect is visible to all!"
-    Ovid

The First World War, WW1, from 1914 to 1918, caused immense human suffering from German aggression and arrogance.

When the time came to meet for a treaty between the former combatants, the victorious side was determined to ensure that Germany would never be able again to cause a similar catastrophe.

France and England's mood during the Versailles Treaty 'negotiations' was understandably bitter for the many lives lost in the muddy hell of endless and senseless battles. So many of their citizens returned from the battlefields as life-long physical and mental invalids. If they had returned at all. Retaliation and punishment were on the negotiator's mind, an understandable mindset. Never again should Germany be allowed to rise and become Europe's Nemesis again.

Consequently, the outcome of the Versailles Treaty devastated Germany and its economy. US President Wilson warned in vain that desperate people act desperately and could become radical, as happened during the Russian Revolution in 1917. Its impact was well known.

The Versailles Treaty and an initial blockade of imports and export by the Royal Navy of the German ports had the intended effect. The German economy collapsed with inflation, unemployment, and the monetary value out of control.

Statistics of those who died from malnutrition vary between 400,000 and over 900,000. The once proud German nation became despondent, and its self-esteem declined to an all-time low.

Bound to the terms of the Treaty, the German government tried to regain control but failed.

Historians and political scientists agree that the ultimate cause of WW2 must be traced back to the Treaty of Versailles.

For six months from June 1918 till January 1919, Prime Minister David Lloyd George for the United Kingdom, George Clemenceau for France, Vittorio Orlando for Italy, and President Woodrow Wilson for the US argued, quarreled, and bickered about the terms. France and England wanted to be sure that Germany would never be able to cause the horrific suffering of WWI again. Germany was barely allowed a voice in the discussions.

An intense difference of opinion emerged on what the terms should be. To bring German colonies under the protection of the League of Nations was unopposed. Nor was the redrawing of the German borders with France and Poland. That would reduce German territory by 13%.

France would obtain the Elsass Loraine region even though it was a German-speaking area and Poland would obtain East Prussia which had been German for many generations.

Reparations for the damage however became a point of contention. France and England demanded very high payments while President Wilson warned again of the possible consequences of destroying the German economy which could have a serious consequences politically and economically when desperate people would turn to radical extremism.

There was agreement to allow only a limited German military to assure that Germany would at best become a mediocre military power.

The Rhineland region remained under French authority, where people experienced the hardship of occupation by a foreign power just as Germans had controlled many European nations.

The naval blockade had devastated the German economy. The powerful British navy started the blockade in 1915. Despite German efforts to maintain an autarkic economy, the blockade had its intended effect. Unemployment rose to over 30 percent.

In addition to losing millions of their men in the hell of the war, now, the common German soldier who survived, many of them disabled, now were close to starving to death upon their return from war. The German people no longer saw any hope for a positive future. A vivid picture emerged of a desponded and desperate population. As so intensely described in the books of Erich Maria Remarque.

Doubt about the effectiveness of the Versailles Treaty was also expressed by General Ferdinand Koch, one of the WW1 Supreme Allied commanders who rightly predicted:

"This is not a peace treaty, but an armistice of about twenty years."

Along came a former WW1 corporal on the political German scene named Adolf Hitler who promised:

1. To no longer comply with the terms of the Treaty of Versailles.
2. Full employment, free education, and free health care.
3. To restore national dignity by introducing the concept of a superior human race.

When the naval blockade ended, the misery continued because the economy was in such disarray that it was unable to recover. An attempt by the government to stimulate the economy by printing more money failed and turned into uncontrollable inflation.

Add to this the collapse of Wall Street in 1929 and the subsequent global economic malaise. Germany was a nation in despair and without hope.

Desperate people act irrationally, clinging to any irrational promise from the extreme left or right demagogues.

Germany was in a state of chaos and hopelessness. Every war has many casualties. Most are obvious. Lives are lost by both soldiers and civilians. Young people are maimed. But when the violence ended the misery did not end for the conquered nation, especially not for powerless women and children. The population lost motivation and hope, the essential elements for a healthy nation to prosper.

The outcome is known. A former Australian army corporal and talented demagogue named Adolf Hitler entered the German stage and tried to convince depressed people that they were superior human beings by hiding behind Nietzsche's the anti-Christian *Übermensch* concept about a higher level of the human species, an idea that was not new and known in the Greek and Roman eras. It also fitted the concept of 'aristocracy'.

Many German aristocrats were sympathetic to the superhuman idea because it fitted well in their 'blue blood' convictions. An amazing number of aristocrats joined the Nazis and became high-ranking leaders in the German military. The support of many societies' elites influenced the population at large.

It did not take long for Hitler's National Socialist German Workers' Party (*Nationalsozialitische Deutsche Arbeiterpartei, NSDAP*) to gain support from desperate people. The skinny, bloated, undernourished children of 1919 were the voting young adults in 1930. They remembered.

Hitler ruled dictatorially, but it cannot be denied that his regime achieved stunning technological and economic advances in the short time between 1933 and 1940. The devastated, forlorn nation of 1919 became one of the most advanced global nations by 1939.

While every detail and part of the Nazi regime is condemned, and rightly so, this was not always the case before WW2. Hitler had many admirers for the radical and successful changes that had been achieved, among them former English King Edward and, for instance, US Government officials traveled to Germany to study the *Autobahn* system.

A defeated nation found renewed motivation and self-confidence. A resurgence of national pride, greatly improved living conditions, a fast-growing economy, and increasing international respect. And fear.

The fast rebirth and success of the conquered nation made their leaders overconfident, and power addicted. To stem Germany's increasing demands, successes, and expansion drives, an agreement was signed in Munich in September 1938 between Germany, England, Italy, and France that accepted Germany's occupation of part of Czechoslovakia called Sudetenland but also stated that it would be Hitler's last territorial claim in Europe.

The occupations of Sudetenland could be reluctantly accepted because the region had been for centuries, part of German-speaking nations. When British Chancellor Neville Chamberlain happily waved the signed document, there was a sigh of relief. The catastrophe of WW1, with its immense suffering, still fresh on many minds, was apparently avoided.

The outcome is known. Chamberlain soon had to admit that Hitler could not be trusted after the Nazi regime expanded its grip over Continental Europe. He resigned and was replaced by Winston Churchill.

Germany and Japan's arrogant confidence in their advanced military capabilities caused widespread concern and global tensions.

New military technology advanced rapidly, especially in aviation and long distant warfare. Just as a new technology abruptly ended the World War with the dropping of the A-bombs on Japan.

Initial success and the easy conquests of several nations by the German military led to the inevitable truth that power corrupts.

And absolute power, Lord Acton wrote, corrupts absolutely.

The negative outcome of the Treaty of Versailles was fortunately not repeated after WW2 when the Marshall Plan was introduced in Europe to aid a devastated nation in rebuilding its economy. It also helped the US industry transfer its amazing war-related production to a peacetime international economy.

Japan's recovery was stimulated by General McArthur's decision not to allow Emperor Hirohito to be persecuted and declared a general amnesty for all war crimes in 1948. He was convinced that the emperor's support was needed for Japan's recovery.

The lessons learned from the post-WW1 mistakes were successfully implemented by the post-WW2 leadership, allowing the former advisories, Germany and Japan, to become peaceful nations and economically and politically strong international contributors.

Common German citizens, who after WW1 suffered greatly from the understandable but devastating terms of the Treaty of Versailles, benefited from the experience and the wisdom of the post-WW2 leadership who did not make the same mistake again by allowing the defeated nation to re-cooperate and become economically strong again.

Unprovoked Aggression

May 10, 1940, promised to be a glorious spring day, a quiet Sunday to relax and disperse all the mounting concerns and tensions, inhale the fresh air and enjoy all the new life that so wonderfully emerged after a harsh winter. It was a very quiet, sunny morning during which only the chirping of the birds could be heard.

It turned out to be a day when life changed irreversibly for millions, a day to be remembered and impossible to erase from many minds.

A promising morning it should have been, the common quiet day of rest, often of long, somewhat boring, tedium hours when children had to stay in our Sunday clothing with strict orders not to soil them and certainly not cause any damage that needed repair. The Sabbath was also a day of many heated disputes among Protestants about what was allowed and what was not, while Roman Catholics were more tolerant and enjoyed the day of rest.

An unusual noise woke me up at early dawn, a disturbing ominous unwelcoming, and threatening noise. With my knees on a chair before the small window in my tower bedroom in which barely a bed could fit, I looked at the early morning spring skies searching for the source of the noise coming obviously from above in the first glimmers of a new day.

What I saw was startling and frightening. Seeing one airplane in the sky was already a unique event in those days; seeing hundreds of planes in tight formations slowly filling the skies was overwhelming. Never had any of the planes seen before. There were even a few double-wing planes reminding of WW1 aerial battles, probably used for reconnaissance only.

It did not take long for the harsh reality to sink in, a nightmarish feeling from which you wanted to awake from as from a bad dream but knew that you would not. A dark cloud entered the brain that throws a shadow over the routine expectations and considerations to be replaced by uncertainty and fear.

An unsettling awareness entered minds that were relying on the normal occurrences of daily life, of the mailman passing on his bicycle and the sounds of children playing somewhere, of what was constant, accepted as the way it should be, to be replaced by an indescribable feeling that all that should be, had lost its foundation and caused one to wander in a dark uncertainty into nowhere.

News and stories about wars had been frequent and frightening, and at times, one had to admit, even interesting, but disconnected from personal life as if it did not and should exist only somewhere else. Wars happened in foreign worlds, not ours. Suddenly what had been remote became a harsh naked reality.

The undeniable truth entered our consciousness; our nation was attacked by Nazi Germany, just as other nations, such as Poland, Austria, Denmark, and Norway. And who knew what other nations? German expansion mania was in full swing. The impact of the Germanic superior-human obsession, the ideology of belonging to a dominant race, was pursued with vicious and unrelenting power.

Gone was all rhetoric about justified or unjustified restrictions of the Treaty of Versailles. The Munich Agreement was reduced to a worthless piece of paper. An ugly beast was out of its cage, seemingly unconquerable, using its devastating power wherever it wanted to go like a medieval mystic fire-spitting dragon, ending one hundred years of peace and neutrality in the Netherlands.

My parents also were awake. We dressed quickly and nervously and walked outside. Fear and uncertainty make you shiver as one does when cold. Neighbors were gathering in confusion, dumbfounded, exchanging useless comments about a truth that slowly sank in. The Netherlands, our beloved nation, once wallowing in its precious neutrality, was being invaded,

People have different ways of reacting to danger. My Roman Catholic friends and neighbors would kneel and recite Hail Marys and the Rosaries, which disturbed me when I wanted to hear what was going on outside, especially when we were hiding in shelters with fighting was all around us.

Others remained silent, stunned, internalizing the disaster while hearts bounced in their chests. One of the neighbor's teenage girls started to laugh hysterically. Here and there, I heard men curse in frustration and anger.

The lone Dutch soldier left in the next-door youth hostel fired at the planes with his obsolete rifle, an ineffective and irrational act. All the other soldiers had left, aware that any resistance in and around our village was useless. The lone soldier who had stayed behind later changed his uniform to borrowed civilian clothing.

My father loved German music. Mostly the operettas from Franz Lehar and Emmerich Kalman. The stars of those days were the Jewish tenors Richard Tauber and Joseph Schmidt. Later that morning, in anger and frustration, my father took his once loved 78 rpm gramophone records, his precious possessions that had been sounding in our house repeatedly from the manually operated gramophone and smashed them to pieces.

Records were expensive and took months to save money for them. My mother was in the kitchen and cried; the only time I ever saw her cry.

The two reasons for invading the Netherlands we later understood, were that Hitler considered the Dutch population part of his Aryan master race illusion and his plan was to integrate Dutch territory into his grand Germanic concept.

The second reason was that Hitler considered the Netherlands the preferred location from where to invade England. That the country was rich and still on the gold standard would help Hitler's precarious financial status because of his excessive military expenses, which was an extra bonus.

Rows of trees along the road to Germany came down with heavy thumps after the explosives had been ignited, unnecessary destruction of beautiful old trees that did not restrain the German advance at all. They were ready. They knew. The 'asparagus' obstacles in the roads were quickly burned down with torches. German intelligence had done its job, and they came prepared.

The only people who welcomed the German invasion were the few Dutch Nazi sympathizers. They anticipated a new era in which they would rule our nation under the protection of their mighty German masters. Instead of being outcasts, their future of glory had arrived in which they would take over all positions of authority. Some tried in vain to convince their neighbors that a better future would be ahead.

As far as we could tell, there were two families in our village who sympathized with the German National Socialistic idea, called *NSBers* from (*Nationaal Socialistische Beweging*) the Dutch Nazi political party. Before the war, it had not been seen as very unusual and somewhat reluctantly accepted. Tolerance was a Dutch tradition.

Nazi propaganda under Joseph Goebbels, Minister of Propaganda and Public Enlightenment, had been convincing and effective, as were the truly impressive parades and demonstrations.

The ideas of work for everyone, a car designed by Porsche for every family, government care for the elderly, no unemployment, sports and entertainment for the young people and health care for everyone, and free university studies for everyone seemed very appealing in Germany after the devastating post-WW1 years and had, as a result, also had its admirers in the Netherlands, especially among those who were condemned to remain at the lowest levels of society and at the mercy of often indifferent masters. Slavery comes in a variety of forms and practices.

Effective German propaganda also promised freedom from the Treaty of Versailles restrictions, which was welcomed in Germany after the economy collapsed and unemployment reached records never known before. What the Nazis promised, and implemented, was well accepted. German national pride which had been at an all-time low was boosted. The adder in the grass, his dictatorial power addiction, was carefully hidden.

Why would millions of rational people enthusiastically follow what is now seen as perverse and cruel? It is a rational question to ask.

When Anton Drexel wrote the 25 principles of the National Socialistic Party, which were edited by Adolph Hitler in 1920, Germany was in a state of the utmost despair and chaos.

On the stage came an Austrian painter who claimed that his party would no longer abide by the demeaning terms of the Versailles Treaty. His ideas of a super Germanic race and his hate of Communism and Jews were taken by many with a shrug of the shoulders. Jewish perception in society was anyhow that one had to be careful dealing with them. The average German was mainly interested in survival.

When Hitler succeeded in gaining power in 1933, remarkable things did indeed happen. In just a few years, German technologies dominated globally. An intoxicated nation began to believe in a former screaming corporal as the Italians did in a shouting former blacksmith/stonemason/journalist Benito Mussolini. Effective use was made of the human herd instinct.

Political and societal movements do often not stop when objectives have been achieved, their inertia propels the movement beyond the initial objectives.

Thus Hitler forced the German people to tumble into another catastrophe when a small, power-obsessed man, corrupted and blinded with success and ambition, believed just as Roman emperors had, that his ideas and decisions were perfect and divine, an illusion that caused millions to suffer immensely and die while he, in the end, must have realized the magnitude of his crime, hidden in a bunker with no way out but destroying himself and family including children.

That is if the information we have represents the true facts since there have been numerous claims that Hitler escaped elsewhere. It really does not matter anymore. Wherever he may or may not have survived, he could not have avoided feeling responsible for the immense suffering he had caused if he had a conscience.

Self-righteous people may be blind enough even to justify the most horrible crimes they committed, as Stalin had when millions of his people were starved to death.

There were some 22 political parties in the Netherlands in 1937, of which ten had accumulated enough votes to earn seats in parliament. The National Socialist Movement under Anton Mussert, an academically educated engineer, had just over four percent of the votes and thus four seats out of one hundred in parliament.

***

Toward seven in the morning, the first German soldiers appeared. There was no local resistance, only some delaying obstacles that needed to be removed.

The Dutch military strategy was to stall the attack and defend against a German advance along the many rivers and canals that crossed the nation, such as the nearby Maas en Waal Canal, a connection between the rivers Maas (Meuse) and Waal where concrete bunkers, also named pillboxes or, *Kazematten,* casemates, were constructed from where the rivers were covered within the reach of guns and artillery, making any advance across the waters very dangerous.

All defenses were made with the expectation that, if there would be a threat at all, it could only come from the east, from Germany. No threats were ever expected from our good neighbors and friends in Belgium. The Netherlands has borders only with Germany and Belgium.

From behind curtains, we saw the first enemy troops marching in single lines on both sides of the street. They were young, looking around with suspicious and worried eyes, certainly not with any trace of the often praised, glorious, and joyful warriors idealized in previous German, particularly in Prussian culture. They must have known that they were vulnerable to sudden resistance from unknown hiding enemies.

Looking back, one can only wonder why these foot soldiers were sent in first instead of their superior and mobilized armored equipment. Were these young foot soldiers just baits to entice the enemy to shoot at them so they could be located? Why would Hitler's generals not send their feared Panzer Units in first, knowing that the Dutch Army was obsolete?

Soon thereafter, however, the superior strength of Hitler's army was displayed with a sheer unending procession of tanks and armored vehicles guided by black-uniformed stern-faced commanders, artillery units, motorbikes with side seats, and MAN and Mercedes supply trucks, moving all steadily as if in a pre-planned military parade.

An officer, with the apparent order to ensure that no sudden attacks could be expected from hiding Dutch soldiers, walked beside our house emptying his pistol to see if there was any response. There were none. All soldiers were gone, and the only weapons some civilians may have had were old hunting guns.

The enormous capacity and advanced technology weaponry of Hitler's military might passed by heading west. Unlike the obsolete Dutch military, their army was modern, disciplined, and advanced beyond what we had ever seen before. This invasion was carefully and expertly planned.

Hesitantly we slowly emerged from the houses after we had quickly gone inside when the first soldiers had appeared, depressed and uncertain of what future would be ahead.

A half-track stopped in front of our house. We were ready to quickly disperse when a soldier called us back and asked if he could please have some water to drink. How could it be possible that this superiorly organized army would not have enough water for their soldiers to drink? But we did not dare to question, intimidated as we were about the overwhelming military power.

Hesitantly and cautiously, my mother opened the garage door, took the hose used for washing cars, and turned the sprocket slowly.

But the soldier refused to drink and told my mother first to drink a little, which she did reluctantly. What caused this German soldier to fear being poisoned by water coming obviously from a residential source? What had he been told or instructed? He drank, looked very tired, and said thank you. Can you refuse an enemy a drink of water?

After he drank, the soldier said to our surprise, '*Sind wir denn wirklich in die Niederlanden?*' (Are we then really in the Netherlands?) Did they not know? Were these common soldiers not informed about the planned invasion and just followed orders and were not told where they were going? '*Befehl ist Befehl*'. (An order is an order) was their motto. You do; you don't question or hesitate. German absolute discipline was their strength.

As cruel, fanatic, and obsessed organizations of the Nazi regime, the SS, Gestapo, and '*Grüne Polizei*' (Green Police) were feared and despised for their unrestricted and unpredictable violations of human rights, the average German soldier's behavior was kept within the limits of its strict discipline. While Nazi fanatics suffered from arrogant blindness, the common soldier did what he was told to do, not more and not less.

It was rumored that in 1939 in Poland young Hitler Youth members had caught and raped a young Polish woman. A court-martial convicted them, and they were executed. No deviations from the strict limits of their orders were accepted.

A deranged mind like that of Hitler, who ordered Polish people to be shot at random to 'make more room', was certainly able to act as cruelly and dementedly toward his own.

The rumor may well be true. The US military also executed 147 soldiers for rape, murder, and robbery during WW2, most by hanging. Only one was executed for desertion, Private Eddie Slovik of Detroit.

A German soldier knew what he was allowed and not allowed to do and followed it with his instinct of order and organization and would not adventure outside its given boundaries, whatever the circumstances. Discipline was deeply ingrained in the way they behaved and performed. Women did not have to fear being molested during the occupation.

This was not always the case when Allied Forces arrived when my father and I barricaded our entrance door to protect my older sister.

Most of the German soldiers we observed seemed initially to enjoy the invasions as an interesting expedition, overconfident that nobody or nothing could stop them. Most of the higher officers expressed the arrogant assurance of belonging to a superior race.

As pieces in a complex puzzle, the average German fitted neatly in its assigned spot and made it possible to maintain thousands of miles of the front line from Russia to North Africa and Western Europe. Military experts may disagree, but this was the impression we had of our enemies.

Via the radio immediately after the invasion before it became a tool in the German propaganda machine, we listened eagerly against hope for some uplifting news but learned that the Queen and Royal Family had fled to England and that fierce fighting was reported at the Grebbeberg Defense Line.

On the fourth day, we heard the tragic and devastating news that the heart of Rotterdam was bombed into ruin with an unknown number, mainly civilian casualties, a cruel and immoral act that forced the Dutch Government to surrender after four days of fighting when the German Command let it be known that Utrecht and other cities would be bombed next if the Dutch military would not surrender. There was no choice. Only three of the famous Fokker G-1 planes were ready; the Luftwaffe had total control of the air. The four-day war was over.

Courageous escapes were made by naval vessels and even more by merchant marine ships that went to England and later played an important role in the transatlantic convoys.

Hitler assigned Arthur Seyss-Inquart, an Austrian layer and one of his admirers, as the *Reichskommissar*, the absolute authority in the Netherlands. Born in Moravia in former Czechoslovakia, Seyss-Inquart studied law in Vienna. In his early years, he was a political independent and did not join the German Nationalistic Socialistic Party till 1938.

Ruthless as his leader, he was the total authority. What can be said about him positively to remain objective, was that he four years later ordered to limit the scorched earth policy for the retreating German military.

Four years later, when the isolated northern half of the Netherlands was reaching a critical stage, American General Bedell Smith (nicknamed Beetle), a staff officer of General Eisenhower, negotiated the dropping of food by American and British bombers for the starving population on Operation Manna.

It would mean, however, that the bombers that came day after day to destroy wherever German targets were found, would be allowed to fly at vulnerable low altitudes, even as low as 100 feet, an obviously difficult decision for Seyss-Inquart to make.

During their discussion, the American general is said to have addressed Seyss-Inquart as follows:

"Well, you are going to be shot anyhow."

To which Seyss-Inquart responded, "That leaves me cold."

"It will," was the general's curt reply.

Seyss-Inquart was tried in Nürnberg in 1946 and the last of the Nazis hanged.

His last words were, "May this execution be the last act of the tragedy of WW2 and may peace and understanding exist between people."

For justice to be fair, it must be fast, so it was after WW2.

It can be questioned, however, if the emotional atmosphere of true, deep-felt, and justified anger about the atrocities committed created a mindset of revenge in which true justice was questionable.

The Netherlands' population nicknamed him 'Six and a quart', a satiric reference to being mediocre in the Dutch educational rating system of that time, rating from 1 to 10, although he apparently was an intelligent man with a high IQ of 141.

Thus, the military war ended. A foreign power ruled the Netherlands.

But with its military surrender, internal resistance grew, as it had been before when the Low Countries were under Spanish and French occupation. There is a deep commitment to freedom and independence in their culture.

And even in desperate conditions of powerlessness and being puppets in the hands of a powerful enemy, the first seeds were growing to regain the precious state of independence.

When danger, fear, and uncertainty dominate, when the future seems dark without a glimmer of hope, people cry out to higher and spiritual powers for guidance and hope, as they had during horrible medieval epidemics, such as the plague that would kill at random.

After the surrender of May 14, 1940, and when the occupation began, church attendance increased dramatically among many who had not been inside a church before. Preachers and priests tried to stimulate a more positive outlook with careful but well-understood condemnations of brutal regimes.

Some dared even to condemn the Nazi regime openly, such as the courageous Pastor Paul Schneider in Germany who paid for it with his life after being tortured to death even before the 1939 war began.

The messages from the pulpits had to be subdued because even Nazi members were attending Mass and listening to sermons in Protestant Churches. Israel's long fight to be free from Egypt's tightening grip was a perfect subject to hint at the present situation.

On the belt buckets of every Nazi army soldier, '*Gott mit uns*' (God with us) was ironically inscribed, intending to ascertain the absurd idea that God would bless a brutal dictatorial and merciless regime.

Societies change when freedom and independence are lost when free speech is no longer possible. When one always had to be alert and careful of what to say and do, leading inevitably to a humbler mindset questioning the basic meaning and values of life.

When faced with imminent life-threatening danger, people cry out, "Oh my God" which seems to rise without thought from bewildered souls, as it was heard during the horrible September 11 NY attacks.

People seek support from spiritual and religious sources when faced with trauma and imminent danger. Prosperity tends to suppress spiritual needs, while people cling to the hope spiritual faith can provide during adverse conditions of poverty, hunger, and war.

After the May 1940 surrender, the depressing realization entered conquered nations that there seemed to be no signs, not even the slightest indications, that there were any powers or nations in the world that could control, eliminate and conquer an apparently superior enemy that had taken our freedom and future.

The German technical and organizational skills had transferred a nation at the economic bottom of all Western nations to a superior member in many aspects, most importantly military technology in seven years.

Belgium and even France also had to surrender. The European continent was completely under the control of Hitler and his cronies. Only England was still free, blessed with its island geography. But from what we knew and observed, England could also not stand against the overwhelming might of Germany's modern and well-trained military power.

England would be the next victim, it was just a matter of time, as it had been for all other European nations that had been overthrown.

A bleak, dark future appeared on the horizon despite the courage and determination of the growing underground resistance.

As common people could see, the future no longer embraced the intensely needed glimmer of independence and freedom. And most depressingly, a future without hope.

Occupation, the First Two Years

The four years of German occupation are divided into two sections for a reason:

During the first two years, living conditions were poor but tolerable, but the outlook was one of hopelessness and despair.

During the second two years, living conditions became desperate, but the involvement of the USA and the German defeat at Stalingrad returned the hope that even the Nazi monster had met its limits and could be defeated.

After the forced capitulation of the Dutch military, we wondered what our future would or could be. Uncertainty and anger dominated. And depression.

It did not take long for the Dutch Nazi sympathizers to be appointed to all positions of authority whether competent or not mainly as city and village majors. Thus, 4% percent of the population tried to control and manage an angry 96 percent, which is not a very effective political system by any honest evaluation.

Despite the danger of being accused of sabotage, it was amazing how incompetent and slow many employees were as long as their contribution did not affect the support and need of the citizens. Many Dutch Nazis dressed in pretentious displayed uniforms, wallowing in their sudden position of power.

Most feared, and possible, was, that the Netherlands would become a sort of added hinterland of the German *Reich*, just like poor Luxembourg. It would mean becoming part of Germany according to Hitler's illusion of a great Germanic nation making it possible for men to be drafted against their will into the military.

Who could stop them? England? Not likely. The Empire barely escaped disaster thanks to courageous young men mainly from Britain but also from foreign nations such as Poland, Czechoslovakia, Canada, and others, in the Battle of Britain.

Over a thousand young men and planes were lost while the Germans lost twice that many. England nevertheless could encounter the same fate other European nations experienced. Strong nations such as France and Poland had not able to stop the Nazi onslaught. Nobody could. So far.

The mood during the first two years of occupation can best be summarized as a time without hope, too convincing were the Nazi's military successes, too superior their technology, and too arrogant their confidence.

The impact of hopelessness is immense on the daily experience of life as if a gloomy veil is spread over all that happens and is expected to happen. Hope is the essential ingredient to ensure future appeal. Without hope, nothing matters.

Only a few strong minds gathered enough courage to still believe in a better world despite the obvious depressing reality. The majority carried on a dark daily drag of existence and survival. All that was seen and heard squashed the last glimmers of brighter days and daring dreams.

All day a catchy song would blare from everywhere. 'Wenn *wir fahren gegen Engeland*', (when we go to England) as if it was a pleasant journey on a cruise ship. A happy song it was. "So long my love, let's sing a little song and drink a glass because we are 'traveling' (*fahren*) to England." Who could stop them? We could not imagine anyone could.

The Dutch Indies, (Indonesia) however were still free. But another dream was soon scattered when Japan rolled over it despite courageous resistance during the battle of the Java Sea and at many other locations.

All Dutch and other European citizens were put in horrible concentration camps; men and women were separated, families were torn apart, and property and personal belongings were confiscated. Japan never acknowledged its cruel crimes after the war nor compensated for the losses and damage they caused.

All we could see and hear was that two advanced military technological giants, Germany and Japan aided by a minor loudmouth dictator Benito Mussolini in Italy ruled the world.

Initially, the occupying authorities tried to ensure that there was nothing to fear and that all was well for a reason. Subdued and peaceful nations require less military control and could assist in producing the supplies needed for their expansion plans now that the German industrial output was stretched to its limits by a shortage of labor when all capable men were in the military.

Only two weeks after the Dutch surrendered the *Reichskommissar* Arthur Seyss-Inquart, Hitler's appointed absolute ruler of the nation, said in the *Ridderzaal,* the Knight's Hall of the Dutch Parliament in The Hague:

"We did not come to suppress a culture or take a nation's freedom away. We did not want to come with the force of weapons. We want to be protectors and remain friends to obtain a higher task that we as Europeans have."

And later on, July 26, he added:

"The political choice of this nation is a matter for the Netherlands people to decide. We do not seek changes in the form of government or influence the relations of the people with the House of Orange; these are things for the Netherlands people to determine freely."

It sounded good! But the national mood remained skeptical. Was it sincere or just a smoke screen to hide its true purpose?

While everything related to National Socialism had earned a reputation of being self-serving and associated with oppression, there were still some even among the well-educated and aristocracy, who sincerely believed in its benefits as a political system.

The soft approach did not work.

Too strong was the anger of the Dutch population over the loss of self-determination, the hatred for the senseless killing of innocent citizens, and the needless death of so many soldiers.

Nazi propaganda films in Germany gave the impression that the Dutch people had greeted the German invasion enthusiastically with open arms by cleverly mixing Dutch festivity films into their politically motivated news journals. These films were not shown in the Netherlands where it would be immediately recognized that they did not represent the truth.

Members of the small NSB Party who had hailed the German aggression, a very small percentage of the population, acted initially somewhat subdued when they were not certain how much support they could expect from the invaders. But soon they acted authoritatively and arrogantly.

The German approach was a pre-planned 'velvet glove' strategy to stimulate a sense of calmness and normality in which people would cooperate, cause less trouble, and provide the much-needed industrial output. The economy did well for a short while from exports to Germany where the military needed more supplies than could be satisfied nationally.

Working for exports to Germany was actually assisting the enemy. Yet people needed work to support their families.

For some three hundred years tea, coffee, spices, and many other products had been imported from what at that time was called the Netherlands East Indies. The invasion immediately made these imports impossible.

It soon became clear that all food supplies were scarce. With the approval of *Reichskommissar* Seyss-Inquart, the government had no choice but to introduce and manage a distribution system that would try to ensure a fair chance for every citizen to receive a fair minimum from the gradually shrinking food supplies. Shortages had already caused sharp price increases for certain food products. A free-market system would have made it impossible for lower-income citizens to survive.

Some seven hundred distribution centers were opened employing about 12,000 people. Shops received products from regulated government supplies in accordance with the number of stamps they had issued.

The distribution system tested during the Mobilization for sugar was expanded gradually for all foods and later also to clothing, fuel, and even kitchen hardware. In later years, even potable water could only be obtained with distribution stamps.

To obtain the needed stamps (*bonnen*) one needed a permit *(stamkaart)* and to obtain the permit a personal identification card (*Persoonsbewijs*) was required, with the inevitable outcome that those who were hiding from German terror, Jews, and resistance members, former soldiers who had been ordered into prisoner-of-war camps but refused to go, had no access to the food stamps and were without minimum supplies.

Exchange or selling stamps was strictly forbidden but proved to be difficult to enforce.

The distribution system remained active for a while after the war but gradually declined. Coffee was only available with stamps till 1952.

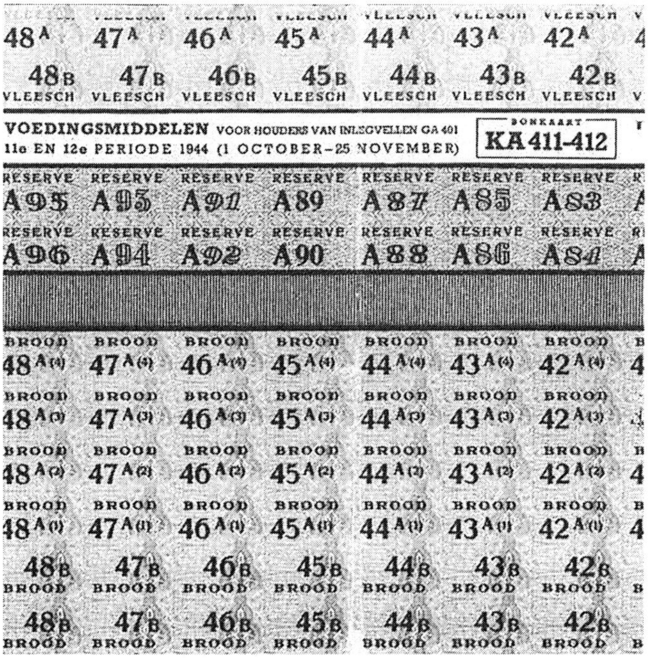

VOEDINGSMIDDELEN VOOR HOUDERS VAN INLEGVELLEN GA 401
11e EN 12e PERIODE 1944 (1 OCTOBER–25 NOVEMBER) | BONKAART KA 411-412

The picture shows typical stamps for meat, bread and general use. Specific numbers were declared eligible during certain weeks.

Adding to the food supply misery was that the national currency devaluated. Silver and copper coins disappeared and were replaced with zinc. In the period between 1940 and 1944, prices tripled.

The quality of most available products rapidly declined. White bread disappeared and was replaced with dark bread that included pulse, peas, rye, and potato flour. The inside was sticky, acidly mixture, and at times almost fluid. Ersatz tea made of cherry blossoms and other ingredients was horrible, and so were many replacements.

Even sawdust was occasionally added to bread. Tobacco replacements never were successful nor any of the 'ersatz' products. Shoes made of carton materials were uncomfortable and useless in inclement weather. The traditional Dutch wooded shoes increased in use. Fuel, such as coal from the national Limburg mines was also restricted by stamps, if available. Gasoline was only available for the military.

The lack of food also made people take great risks such as a family in nearby Berg en Dal who all died from food poisoning after eating deteriorating fish.

There always are people who take advantage of misery and suffering. Greed is always present. During the occupation, two dominating societal groups emerged, a small percentage of farmers and black-market traders.

Most farmers tried to be fair and responsible but had the difficult task of deciding whom to assist and who not. Since they were unable to help the large number of people begging for food, any food, there were far too many citizens begging for some food compared to the number of farmers who were able to help.

There can be a certain understanding for the farmers who took advantage of their new dominant position since they had been barely able before the war, to scrap enough to survive from their crops at minimal prices at minimal prices. The occupation had reversed positions; no longer did the farmers have to sell their produce. Now their former customers were the ones pleading for their produce, at any price.

But for the farmers and traders who turned to the black market no words of understanding can be found. These good citizens became rich from catastrophe and hunger by serving the rich at the cost of the poor and common people.

To put things in perspective a few examples of the outrageous profits that were made in relation to the average income of some 25 Guilders (Florins) per week. The Dutch silver coin, the guilder, was identified by the abbreviation Fl. used as the figure $ for the US dollar. The abbreviation comes from the word florin, the name of a coin formerly used in several nations and has its origin in medieval Florence.

Black Market				
Article	Pre-war price		Medium	Maximum
A pound of sugar	Fl.	0.30	7, 50	75.00
Pound of butter	Fl.	0, 80	38, 0	140.00
Pound of coffee	Fl.	0, 25	100, 00	300.00
Pound of tea	Fl.	1, 50	200, 00	1000, 00
A bread	Fl.	0, 16	3, 00	30, 00
A candle	Fl.	0, 03	1, 50	10, 00
Cigarettes	Fl.	0, 25	10.00	80, 00

This limited overview clearly shows that the common Dutch citizen with an income of Fl. 25 per week, from which also the rent had to be paid, had no chance to meet the black-market demands. Only the rich upper ten of society were able to pay the extreme prices.

In an effort for farmers to produce more needed food products, special compensations were given to farmers who plowed meadows into arable acreage for potatoes and produce.

Buying directly from farmers was prohibited since it would undermine the distribution system, but it could not be prevented. Many took long walks, as we did, or went by bicycle to farms hoping to buy any food. Begging is demeaning. The large number of people looking for any food made it also very difficult for the farmers to be fair. '*De boer op*' (to the farmer) it was called.

For some farmers, it was, however, highly profitable. My courageous mother never gave up, and we went from farm to farm in the later-flooded Ooi Polder. Though she spoke Dutch very well, her German accent did help our quest for food.

Returning with some cabbage, beets or potatoes was risky because the cleverly positioned Dutch Nazis supported by German soldiers, knew the few roads from where we had to come back and would not only confiscate the precious collected food at will, but also bicycles, the ever more needed and only way of transportation, and whatever else they could steal.

Slowly, the cord around the necks tightened and the mood deteriorated as the Nazis intended cooperation failed because of stubborn silent resistance.

When Jews were not allowed to be employed in public offices and came under increased pressure, a spontaneous strike erupted in February 1941 in solidarity with the plight of the Jews on the initiative of members of the Amsterdam Communist Party who existed mainly among the dockworkers.

The strike quickly spread, and some 300,000 people participated. But the reprisal of the German authorities was ruthless. After two days, the strike was ended by military force.

When the usual hydrocarbon fuels were no longer available, local transportation such as the frequently used buses, and most communal transportation turned to the limited numbers of electric-driven streetcars. It soon became clear that this was totally inadequate.

People were packed into the streetcars as sardines and even hanging dangerously outside. For longer distances, the same became true with railway transportation.

Electricity made from coal from the Dutch Limburg mines could provide energy for electric streetcars and coal for the locomotives that were the only, albeit totally inadequate, means of transportation. But the German war machine also needed the coal and had the absolute priority leaving insufficient supplies needed for civilian use.

Pony-driven taxis appeared and man-operated tricycles after Asian tradition. But bicycle and tricycle tires wear quickly with excessive use, and there was no new supply after the existing tires were all used.

Bicycles were and still are the typical Dutch way of moving around, a healthy and good exercise, while the mostly flat but nevertheless windy land made the bicycle possible and practical for human transportation and goods.

As of April 1942, Jews had to wear the yellow Star of David identification on their clothing.

Jews were taken from their houses and streets and transported to elimination murder camps such as Auschwitz-Birkenau as it is known from the Diary of Anne Frank and many other books and documents. Amsterdam used to have a very large and active Jewish community, but in September 1943 the German authority boasted that Amsterdam was "free of Jews."

The courageous longshoremen's strike had failed and yet showed that the Dutch population would not be swayed by the Goebbels propaganda machine nor by harsh measures. The strike gave some self-confidence again.

An order was issued that all privately owned radios had to be taken to local town halls and there stored to prevent listening to the hope-giving radio news from the BBC in London and the Dutch *Herrijzend Nederland* Broadcast also from London. Both stations were heavily disturbed making it exceedingly difficult and more often impossible to hear what was said through the cracking interference.

Eliminating all radio information turned out to be ineffective because it was not known how many radios there were among the population. Not all radios were turned in. Many radios were not turned in and were carefully and cleverly hidden.

Trusted neighbors would cautiously gather trying to exchange with each other what was understood despite the irritating sounds and make some sense of what was heard sharing it with friends and neighbors. Only fractions of the announcements could be understood. The high-frequency oscillating and penetrating noise was made to prevent us hearing the news from London.

After listening intensely, everyone present exchanged what they heard or believed that they had heard in a subdued manner. Thereafter the radios were again expertly hidden. An underground verbal communication system emerged that became surprisingly fast and effective in the still communal style of living.

Next came an order to turn in all gold and silver, coins, jewelry, and anything containing silver or gold.

My parents owned two tiny gold coins, called Gouden Tientje, Little Gold Ten Guilders. What is today a minor possession was at that time carefully saved for some unforeseen disaster or emergency. After careful consideration, the coins were hidden behind the lining of a box.

Gold and silver coins later proved to be of great importance for ultimate survival. The black-market preferred coins because coins cannot be traced by authorities and can be easily hidden to evade taxes.

When shortages develop, black markets thrive! Before the war, our butcher would come by the house once a week to ask what my mother would like to buy. Much to my mother's chagrin, he always brought more than she had ordered. But as soon as the war started, she could not get anything anymore from the same butcher. The black market was a lot more profitable.

Some farmers also would gladly give you what you wanted if you paid in coins, silver, or gold. With the inevitable result that the rich suffered less and the poor the most.

When the war ended, the Dutch finance minister allowed every adult ten guilders. All bank accounts were blocked and not released until citizens could verify their account's validity, a remarkably effective way to detect and prosecute black market merchants and traders for their excessive profits. Yet gold and silver coins remained unaccounted for when stashed away often buried in the ground as it had been practiced for centuries.

People are clever and find ways to survive. The preservation of life is deeply engraved on human instincts. If you cannot buy food anymore, then grow it yourself. Thus started an intense agricultural phase of life.

As soon as school was out, to the fields we went growing and harvesting potatoes, cabbage, beans, carrots, and much more. It was not uncommon, because many people in the lower income levels of society had to grow food to survive. Some of it was truly enjoyed, nature's miracles were frequently observed during Sunday afternoon walks.

We even ventured to grow tobacco on the wet Dutch soil. Quite successfully actually. With pride and anticipation, my father and I saw with anticipation the ripening brown bottom leaves and discussed taking them home or leaving them for another day. When we returned the next day, all the ripe tobacco leaves were stolen.

Another serious blow to my father's already depressed soul. It was another sign that people's moral behavior and commitments are vulnerable during desperate situations and the struggle for survival. We would cut brown tobacco leaves with old shaving knives and roll them in any paper we could find.

The result was better than cherry blossoms but still dismal. Clever little mechanical hand-operated machines appeared on the market to 'roll' a cigarette after inserting tobacco and paper. The gadget would produce the cigarette after wetting the paper with your tong in the hope it would stick together after closing the gadget and the cigarette would roll out.

To provide access to some meat we build cages for rabbits. Rabbits are gentle and nice because they convert grass into meat, and they procreate rapidly. Our first duty coming out of school was cutting grass for the rabbits. But it had to be dry because their bellies would swell if the grass was wet and then die. I did not understand because rabbits had to eat also after a rainy period in the wild.

I liked rabbit, especially the little ones that are very cute. There were two problems; who would slaughter them and whether there was enough fat in the animals for cooking the meat. We had no oil or butter. My father could not kill them. But we did have some meat about once in four weeks.

Everything German was hated which caused family problems because it was well-known in the village that my mother was German by birth.

What made things worse were visits from Uncle Otto.

Otto Hinrichs was my mother's only brother. After successfully finishing the highest level of secondary education (*Gymnasium*) in Germany, he applied for the Merchant Marine Academy hoping to become an officer on a merchant's vessel but was refused because he was supposed to be colorblind (Farbenblind).

A year after being rejected he was called back and told that he could enter because he was not colorblind but was previously refused because he was not considered of a high enough social class. But under Hitler's regime, such social class restrictions were eliminated. Result? A supporter of the new regime!

When the war started, he was the first mate on a freighter docked in Curacao but escaped back to Germany where he was immediately enrolled in a training class for submarine commanders. But only after submitting a family tree (*Ahnenpass*) to show that there were no Jews in his ancestry. He was one of the two who survived out of a class of 32.

During the first years of the occupation, he would visit us when stationed in Lorient in France expressing regret that he, as a marine merchant officer, had to torpedo defenseless freighters in the Atlantic Ocean. But he was nevertheless convinced of the ultimate Nazi victory.

During the post-war Nuremberg trials, the prosecution considered the sinking of defenseless merchant ships as a war crime but dropped the idea when it became clear that the Allies had done the same thing. So, when the prosecuting party did a certain act, it was no longer considered a crime or violation. A rather questionable attitude regarding law and justice!

My mother asked her brother not to come to our house anymore because having a German officer come to our house was increasing our neighbor's suspicion.

When the tide of the war changed, so did my uncle. My mother would meet him in a nearby Arnhem where he told her that he was now stationed in Bergen, Norway, and that it was most likely the last time they would see each other because his submarine, the U1061, was unable to do anything anymore but lay silently in deep water as much as batteries would allow, being continually attacked by overpowering Allied Forces with deep-sea explosives.

In addition, he said, even if I survive, I will be killed by the Norwegians when I must surrender because they hate us intensely.

Post-war records show that the U1061 made its last patrol in February 1945. What happened is somewhat of a mystery. But I remember how the radio after May 5, 1945, repeatedly urged German warships still at sea to return to their home port because the war was over.

Two of his fellow U-boat commanders defied the order. *Oberleutnant* Heinz Schaeffer directed his submarine, the U-977, also stationed at Bergen in

Norway, to Argentina after he allowed married men to be dropped off at one of the islands. He later became a guest of the US navy.

Another colleague *Oberleutmant* Otto Wermuth of the U-530 also headed for Argentina where he arrived in July. There have been unrealistic suggestions claiming that Hitler and Eva Braun had been on one of these escaping submarines to Argentina which must be disregarded as unrealistic.

When the war ended, 156 U-boats surrendered, their own crews scuttled 221, and two escaped to Argentina. It was rumored that my uncle steered his submarine on the rocks to save his crew and was in jail waiting for Court Martial when the war ended. He apparently was cleared by the Norwegian resistance and was back in Germany a fortnight after the war ended and became a captain again of a German freighter. Yet he remained a somewhat bitter disillusioned man.

Many years later I gained a better understanding of his mindset and attitude. Nazi Germany had manufactured and operated some 1156 U-boats and lost 785 of which 632 sunk at sea, destroyed about evenly by ships and aircrafts. These losses were among the highest percentage of any WW2 war operation.

Submarines could at that time remain only a relatively short time underwater, mainly during attacks because of the limited battery energy available when submerged. Most times had to be spent at sea level when they were using diesel power. At sea level, they were more exposed and vulnerable. Post-WW2 submarines used atomic energy and could remain constantly submerged.

WW2 submarines were called 'Iron Coffins'. For a reason.

Over 2603 merchant ships were sunk. Of the 40.900 men recruited for the German submarine service, 28000 lost their lives (68 %!!) and 5000 were taken, prisoner. About 30.000 men on Allied merchant ships lost their lives (Information from the naval historical Society of Australia). The chance of survival in the German submarine navy was the lowest of all military operations, about 10% and must have impacted morale.

Stories emerged from the very young crews sobbing and crying entering what they knew had to be their deadly fate. Dying in the claustrophobic environment and slowly suffocating when all oxygen was spent must have been desperate and awful. Conditions were horrible in foul-smelling air, with poor food and one toilet for the entire crew.

More and more citizens were arrested and sent to concentration camps, including Jews, but also suspected communists, members of the resistance, Romani, those suspected of homosexuality, and many others, unpredictably. Fear and a sense of hopelessness reigned without any form of fair justice. My parents prepared a small suitcase so that my father would be ready with the minimum necessities if arrested or deported.

Things were going from bad to worse. The devastating attack on the US navy on Pearl Harbor on December 7, 1941, seemed to make a recovery of the US military impossible from what we could hear on the biased news.

Surprisingly, my father slowly shook his head in disagreement.

"America's capability is unlimited," he said softly but convincingly. "The Axes will regret that this ever happened."

His prediction was right. The first weak glimmer of hope appeared on the horizon when the mighty United States was forced to enter the World War.

Small things also went initially embarrassingly wrong such as the fate of the magnificent French Blue Riband carrier and largest passenger liner of that time, the *Normandie*, launched in 1935.

The luxurious liner was docked at Pier 88 in New York, taken over by the Coast Guard five days after the attack on Pearl Harbor, renamed Lafayette, and in great haste transferred into a troop carrier in accordance with the international law of angary which allows a nation to seize property belonging to a neutral nation 'under circumstances of necessity'. But haste led to inadequate safety and caused a fire that burned the ship down.

Salvage was out of the question. The incident became immediately part of the Nazi propaganda and much *'schadenfreude'* by the Axis enemies, a typical German word for the pleasure derived from someone else's misfortune. It was supposed to show US inability to be ready for an all-out war, which proved to be a fatal misconception.

With the gradual tightening of living conditions, resistance increased according to the law that every action leads to a reaction. A Viking proverb proclaimed, "It is better to fight and fall than to live without hope."

Resistance against the hated occupation gradually became more cunning and effective when the occupation progressed despite fierce counteractivities of the most fanatic Dutch as well as German Nazis. Resistance can be divided into courageous and effective operations and foolish even negative acts.

Effective resistance operations were:

1. Intelligence gathering:

Information about the German military location, strength, and armory was of great value in analyzing the enemy's movements and strategy and most importantly, saved lives. The invasion on D-Day in Normandy was at least partly determined by the French Resistance's information which suggested that the German defense was not as strong there compared to the shorter crossing of the Channel further north on the flat French and Belgian coast.

It must be taken in consideration that the information from these sources, including from those who were parachuted into German-controlled territory, was limited and incomplete. The German counterintelligence was aware of ongoing spy activities. They infiltrated false information and closed large areas from any civilian permission to enter making objective observations impossible from a ground level.

One local and successful example of intelligence transfer was when Canadian forces were closing in on the town of Deventer. A member of the resistance had carefully gathered information about mining fields, obstructions, and the strengths and defenses, smuggled this information at the risk of his life through the fighting lines, and handed it to the grateful commander of the Canadian forces, General Gibson.

The information saved the town from the fierce fighting and subsequent loss of life and destruction as it happened in the neighboring town of Zutphen. The resistance member never received adequate recognition for his brave act. General Gibson kept the resistance information in his personal archive.

2. Hiding Fugitives:

The fanatic Nazi leadership was neurotic about anything and anyone that did not fit their narrow concepts. To develop a superior race, homosexuals, Romani, people of color, resistance members, and of course their most hated enemies, Jews and Communists had to be eradicated. Those who had the courage to hide those fugitives did not only put themselves at risk but also their families and everything they owned.

Those arrested, often by the betrayal of fellow citizens, lost their lives or suffered hell in horrible concentration camps. Heroes were those who were hiding Jews such as my wife's highly admired and respected family doctor

Cohen who was hiding with his family at a secret place where my wife's father would bring food and milk whenever possible.

Every move had to be very carefully studied and planned to appear as a routine occurrence. In the Dutch language, a word surfaced for those who were hiding: *'onderduikers'*, a word that can be best translated as 'submerged people'.

3. Hiding and Returning Airplane Crews:

The initial losses of bomber crews were immense by the British during day raids and at night by American formations. Before fighter planes such as the P-51 were capable of longer flights to protect the bomber armadas, the losses were very high by anti-aircraft flak or shot down by German fighters. Helping downed and often wounded crews was an act of aiding the enemy in the Nazi mindset punishable with immediate execution.

Yet courageous men, as well as women, guided many surviving crews of Allied planes that were shot down, back to England via France and Spain, which needed close cooperation with the resistance in Belgium and France. Despite the danger, they often succeeded. These resistance members were not always the prominent of society and were mostly common burghers.

4. Stealing Food Stamps:

Stealing food stamps by raiding food stamp distribution offices to provide basic needs for those who were in hiding was also a very hazardous but effective resistance operation. German and cooperating Dutch authorities understood that every stamp distribution center was vulnerable and subsequently kept the stamps in safes and vaults.

With the help of loyal Dutch people who were employed at the distribution centers, detailed and secret information was obtained that made several operations successful, most notably the January 1944 raid on a Tilburg food stamp distribution center when 105.000 stamps were captured.

5. Providing information:

Garman's propaganda was clever and deceiving. But the average citizens had enough common sense to just ignore the outbursts of false and biased information. Propaganda's impact should never be underestimated, especially when it is done by clever experts claiming that Germany was winning every battle. Its hatred for all that was not 'pure' Germanic was spread everywhere, on the radio, in pamphlets, and in literature.

News from London was always so disturbed that it was impossible to understand much with its annoying penetrating up-and-down interference. Our radio was in a closet where it was carefully hidden. Friends and neighbors would crowd around the closet. The sound level had also to be kept low out of fear that Nazi sympathizers would hear it.

Resistance organizations had the connections and capability to provide accurate accounts, at times not up to date but taken as true and objective. Facts that contoured the barrage of propaganda were of immense importance to maintaining people's morale and motivation of a population in distress. The resistance organization provided what was desperately needed.

Negative Resistance Operations:

1.   Killing German soldiers and Dutch Nazis

Shooting or murdering a member of the German military or Dutch traitors was always followed by brutal retaliation that cost many innocent citizens their lives. As hated as the Germans were, such actions did not help the Dutch population.

German retaliation was inhuman and excessive. But what would any military organization do when one of its members was shot at random by unknown citizens? A failure to retaliate would encourage similar violent acts.

Reckless and destructive members of the resistance shot down the Dutch traitor General Seyffert and just by accident injured the German Military 'Security' Commander in the Netherlands, SS *Gruppenfuerer* Hanns Alwin Rauter aware that their acts would result in fierce retaliation that would cost the lives of innocent people taken at random from the streets and execute, such as the 117 innocent citizens who were rounded up randomly and executed in a remote place called the *Woeste Hoeve* including my wife's uncle.

Those were useless and destructive initiatives from callous people knowing that their foolish acts would not in any way reduce the German military strength and would probably not hurt them, but instead cause the loss of life of innocent fellow citizens.

Much admired were two young sisters and a friend who would coax Dutch traitors and German soldiers into a park or forest where they shot them. The sisters Oversteegen survived and died at age 92; their friend was caught and executed.

Such actions certainly required courage but were far from effective in that one or more soldiers or traitors would have no impact on the strength. German retaliation was too severe and inexcusable. Any military organization however would take drastic action to prevent the shooting at random by citizens.

2.   Late Joiners

There are always clever people who have a talent to take the most advantageous action at minimum risk such as those who joined the resistance during the last weeks of the war when the German forces were in chaos and too occupied with survival, which lowered the risk of being arrested to practically nil. Dutch Nazis knew that their cause was lost at that time and were no longer a threat.

Several Nazis did all they could to regain a more positive reputation. Some of those late joiners were marching in the front of the liberty parades while many of those who risked their lives faded away without recognition, some disappointed and bitter. I witnessed a similar late joining resistance member in our village who was also prominent during commemoration ceremonies after the war. A Dutch proverb says that the horses that deserve the oats seldom get it.

***

Courageous resistance members emerged from often unexpected levels of society, people who risked their lives of themselves and of their families to save or help those in need.

There were unfortunately also tensions within resistance groups who disagreed on strategy and organization. The French resistance was divided into three separate sections: The followers of General Henry Geraud, the Geraudist were backed by the USA. The followers of General de Gaul, the Gaulists were backed by Great Britain, The Communists who were at least in principle backed by Soviet Union.

The rivalry between these groups was cleverly exploited by the German counterintelligence.

***

Germany needed all their national manpower for the war efforts in Russia, Africa, along the Atlantic Coast and were very short of manpower to run their factories.

Forced labor was introduced. All together some 500.000 men were forced to provide services of which about 250.000 were deported to Germany. For many, it was a death sentence since the manufacturing facilities were targeted by Allied bombing raids that converted many cities, and especially industrial areas, into infernos. A close friend of my parents came by to say goodbye in a total state of despair, almost apathetic, deeply depressed about being deported. He never returned.

Most devastating during the first two years of occupation, however, was the absence of hope. So superior, so overwhelming strong was the German military hegemony that all hope for a German defeat and a return to liberty was fading. No realistic possibility could be seen that it would ever change, and it took the last feeble ray of hope out of life.

Despite my parent's orders to never leave a door open to the garage where now not three but eight cars were hiding, a most unpleasant member of the Dutch Nazi organization forced me to open the door. I do not recall all the type of cars that had been stored to escape the ever-present greedy eyes of the Dutch Nazi members. One was a REO Speedwagon I remembered because I liked the name. The next day all eight were taken including the 1936 Cadillac.

What could the German or its Axis partners do with such a fuel-inefficient automobile as the gas-guzzling Cadillac, I heard my father argue in vain knowing that Germany and its Allies were short of fuel.

The Cadillac would be sent to befriend Turkey as a gift we were told but doubted if it was true. Yet we later heard that Germany and Turkey had signed a Friendship Treaty on June 18, 1941, which made the statement more plausible.

Only after the war, we learned that Turkey had allied itself with Nazi Germany to regain the territories lost after the collapse of the Ottoman Empire to England, France, and Greece.

In addition to all the other miseries to survive, a new problem had to be faced by my desponded parents.

Hitler had decreed that the children of German women were German, no matter who the father was. Not a new concept really because in many cultures and religions such as Judaism, children adopt the culture or religion of the mother based on the reality that it always can be determined who the mother is, but not the father before DNA testing existed.

According to Hitler's edict I was supposed to be German and was obligated to join the hated Hitler Youth, the visiting Hitler Youth leaders told us. I had to appear before them, and they judged that I was an acceptable species being blue eyed and blond which fitted in Hitler's perception of what a superior Germanic race should be.

My mother deserves a medal for diplomacy. She did not resist, which would have been interpreted as resisting the interest of the *Reich*, a major crime in their eyes, nor did she give in, but calmly listened and confirmed that she would seriously consider giving her approval. It was the right strategy.

She tried to postpone and delay, hoping that the pressures of war and time would put the order on the back burner. As it turned out to be she was right. Having Hitler Youth leaders coming to our house was another event that enhanced villager's suspicions and my father's outrage. It is a bitter sense of desperation when you are forced to submit to people you despise but cannot see a way out nor change fate.

So many were in a similar situation as for instance in Luxembourg where Hitler had made the nation part of the German Reich and therefore all young men were conscripted and forced to become part of a military they despised. Many of these young men became Russian prisoners of war.

They were however repatriated at the instigation of French delegates who convinced the Russian authorities that these Luxembourg young men were victims of the Nazi's irrational policies. A pro-French and subsequent anti-German sentiment evolved in Luxembourg. Luxembourgers can be identified since than by their mostly Germanic family names but French first names.

Fear and the struggle for the basic needs of life caused an inevitable change in the state of mind also of teenagers.

From the normal carefree somewhat unstable but joyful young people, we matured quickly without faraway dreams for a bright future and instead concentrating on surviving tomorrow, far too mature for our age in a daily struggle for food and safety! As so many have and still do in regions were hunger and violence is a brutal reality.

But most devastating realization during the first two years of occupation was the absence of hope.

Occupation, the Second Two Years

Rationing and privations gradually turned to a battle for survival in the harsh winter of 1943.

During the first two years, the living conditions were poor but bearable. The general mood expressed hopelessness for not seeing any signs that freedom and more normal standards of living could be regained.

During the second two years conditions became desperate and fearful, but on a far horizon a renewed and desperately needed hope emerged that the thus far unconquerable Nazi assault would encounter a similar or even greater force that could and would defeat them.

In 1943 and 1944, people became increasingly weaker from undernourishment and increasingly fearful because of tightening suppression. Most of the people also suffered from insomnia because of nights filled with the sonorous sounds of thousands of bombers accompanied by the aggressive noise of the flak and the too often doomsday sound of wounded bombers flying low and out of formation.

Day and night eerie alarm signals prevented sleep at night and long hours of hiding during the day. When the bomber armadas were going east, the alarm sirens would send its loathed signals in the air. Never will the deep resonant sound of the in the thousands of internal combustion engines of propeller-drive planes be heard again.

Dangers came from shrapnel from the anti-air canons and even more from bombers in distress that had to release their terrifying death-loads at random to survive. Free-alarm would be given when the armadas returned to their bases, assuming they were empty, which was unfortunately not always the case.

The flight routes to reach the main Allied targets, the vital German industrial *Ruhrgebiet* and the North Sea harbors of Hamburg and Bremen, went via the Netherlands. What to do at night after the alarm was given became a dilemma for many families, either take the safe way and hide in shelters or stay in bed and try to get some rest for the next day's tasks.

Life had to go on. The last drop of old supplies was squeezed out and gone, and there was no indication of any possible replenishment in the foreseeable future.

Yet even when the situation was becoming a fight for survival, some signs appeared that the tide may be changing, despite the efforts of the Nazi propaganda to assure skeptic audiences that the Axes had every situation under control. Whispered 'underground' communications worked amazingly well considering its forbidden and restricted ways.

For the first time, rumors floated around that the mighty dragon's insatiable expansion drive had been slowed down or even halted by the Nazi defeat and surrender at Stalingrad and the entrance of the US into the global effort to eliminate the Axis' evil.

During times of distress and fear, thoughts about the future shrink to a very limited span of time. Gone are dreams and visions, only the immediate counts, only the survival from physical harm and fundamental needs of shelter and food.

Priorities are dominated by basic human instincts to protect the life of oneself and loved ones, the survival of the species, of life. Existence was compressed to the basic instincts and tenacity the sustain life so obvious in all forms of nature.

But even in distress people were holding on to a weak but desperate hope that the Nazi monster had encountered a nemesis in capable Allies determined to defeat and destroy their plans of world-domination.

Food became very scarce. Even with food stamps the permitted ingredients were often not available. Living in a non-agricultural region made things more difficult for my family. My father went on a very early Sunday morning in the curfew darkness and total absence of any form of artificial light to buy some clandestine wheat to avoid the hated checkpoints controlled by Dutch Nazi sympathizers supported by a few German soldiers who confiscated whatever they wanted.

The wheat bought at high prices was ground down in the coffee bean grinder, a common kitchen utensil in those days. Since the wheat was bought clandestinely outside the distribution system it could be confiscated at any time while being charged with fraud or worse. For breakfast, we had wheat boiled in water when milk was no longer available. Not recommended.

Bicycle tires were totally worn and no longer usable. My father substituted the pneumatic tires with garden hoses which made the ride very hard and required more energy. Wooden shoes, or '*klompen*' in Dutch, while still worn by many farmers, became increasingly popular in different styles and forms. The wooden shoes made sense in the usually clayish rural lands, but on paved roads, they were inflexible and uncomfortable.

Before the war, my mother would buy what was called white flour 'tiger bread' on Saturdays as a special treat. The bread was so called because of the stripes cut with a knife on the dough. She would cut the end, put a little butter on it and gave it to my sister and me when the bread was still warm. When hunger set in, I hallucinated about what once used to be so common.

How can the conditions we lived under be best described? It is almost impossible to find the words that fairly represent the mood of a depressed society in which hopelessness, defiance, anger and resistance turned in the minds of a population fighting for survival. For some, the conditions led to apathy and depression, for other to intense hate and defiance transformed into an emotional energy and into a frantic commitment to retaliate and resist.

A visit to a dentist was already very unpleasant before WW2 with slow drills and absence of anesthesia. During the occupation it was made worse when the dentist had to activate the drill with his or her foot when no electricity was available. A truly perfect way of torture.

The following translation of one order can give an impression of the demeaning lack of freedom and civility.

ORDER

By order of the German army all men between 16 till 40 must report to perform work.

The men of this age must after receipt of this order immediately stand outside in the streets with the articles mentioned below.

All other people including children must stay inside the houses till this action is completed. When men within this age group are found inside their houses, their belongings will be confiscated. Those who have permits to be exempted from this order must also be in the streets.

The following articles must be available: Warm clothing, good shoes, blankets, rain protection, a knife, fork, spoon, a cup, and sandwiches for one day.

The daily compensation will be good food, smoking articles, and wages according to the ongoing tariff.

The families left behind will be taken care of.

Nobody is allowed to leave their communities.

Those who resist or try to leave will be executed.

****

Freedom in even the smallest form no longer existed. Soldiers would go from house to house to search for men who were hiding, some doing an indifferent job as if they were not very happy with their assignment, Others performed their assignment wallowing in a fanatic and mistrusting moment of power.

People were, however, inventive finding all kinds of places to hide, under floors or even, as my brother-in-law, in sewage pipes. Escape ways were also developed in closely built houses that would fool the search parties by stealthily moving from houses to be searched to houses that had been already searched.

Promises of wages, food, and tobacco were often just words. Most feared were orders to be transported to German industrial regions that were daily transformed in infernos by the raids of Allied bombers.

After D-Day, men were forced to dig anti-tank trenches. Any form of refusal or sabotage was immediately punished with execution. The trenches never had any effect during the fighting. They were remnants of WW1 war strategies. On the beaches, the 'hedgehogs' were installed above ground, steel devices intended to immobilize a tank by being stuck into the tracks immobilizing the tank and making it an easy target.

People are however capable of doing amazing things for instance the father of a friend who was deported as forced labor to Vienna in Austria. When the war ended, it took him two months to walk and hitchhike back 700 miles back to his home in Dordrecht through a devastated Germany without train, car or bus transportation.

The forced laborers, which is just a form of slavery, came from several occupied nations and were assigned mainly in industry and mines, and in fact, compelled the men to aid their despised enemy.

The natural response was to do as little as possible and attempt sabotage through poor quality, which made it very difficult for the mostly older German supervisors to trust their workforce. Ruthless punishment was the only weapon they could use when discovering any attempt that proved an actual or intended sabotage.

There were numerous other restrictions on normal personal freedom. No boats were allowed on rivers and canals, which caused great trouble for a lowlands nation that depended on transportation over water for people and goods. Curfew lasted from eight at night till six am. No one was allowed to be near bridges. A sign in front of bridges would hold a simple warning that anyone who was not allowed to be on a bridge would be shot.

Most common were random groups of native Nazis and German soldiers who would confiscate whatever they would like to have from food, bicycles and even clothing. One of my acquaintances had a picture of his two little girls with him trying to appeal to the confiscators' sense of compassion, which sometimes was effective, sometimes not.

We learned to hate, a dangerous emotion that restricts logic and common sense.

But a glimpse of hope rose on the horizon.

Despite all efforts by the Nazi propaganda media to prevent us from knowing, the outcome of the Battle of Stalingrad and the surrender of the enclosed German army spread like wildfire. For the first time, Hitler's seemingly unconquerable military machine of the Third Reich had found its limits when General Friedrich Paul, against Hitler's order, surrendered in February 1943.

It was a turning point. Those courageous Russian armies that fought under extreme weather conditions must be credited with achieving the first dent in the Nazi's armor. At the cost of millions of people who lost their lives or were injured.

Together with neighbor Anton Smit, we studied a map of Russia trying to find the strange names mentioned on the radio propaganda noting with surprise and satisfaction that the front line did not penetrate deeper into Russia, but all the so-called tactical victories slowly moved westward indicating an obvious retreat.

The mighty German military machine had stalled and found its demise in the sheer endless steppe of Russia under extreme cold weather conditions just as Napoleon had experienced over a hundred years before. A cautious feeling emerged that this could be a turning point. Nazi arrogance had over-reached its capability.

When English, Italian, Australian, and New Zealand troops halted the German North African offense into Egypt at El Alamein late in 1942, the news had been received positively but did not have the same impact as the surrender at Stalingrad. General Edwin Rommel's reputation was different somehow from other Nazi Generals still seen as an enemy, but a respected enemy, who fought for his country without committing war crimes.

Despite terrible losses from flak, fighters, technical failure and inexperienced crews, the Allies achieved control of the air.

Only later in life did we become aware of the astonishing achievements that took place; to launch daily 1200 B-17, B-24 and Lancaster bombers together with over 600 accompanying fighters in the cloudy English skies with its often-inclement weather and without modern avionics.

Twelve hundred four-engine planes with a full load of fuel and bombs, manned with very young inexperienced crews would start every 30 seconds to a lineup of the US 8th Air Force and RAF from multiple airbases. It took over two, often frightening hours, to organize the formations up in changing winds and so close that the effect of the propeller forces could be felt of a nearby frequently unseen plane.

Just as complex as managing the return of equal numbers of often severely damaged planes and wounded crews. The emphasis has been on the damage this massive armada caused and less on the achievement of managing hundreds of planes without modern avionics during often inclement weather over a limited region.

Even with all modern aviation technology such a feat would be almost impossible in modern days. Yet it was done by dedicated and motivated young people and their commanders.

During the first year of the occupation, searchlights were used to locate the bombers in the dark nights, and one was placed behind our house. With helpless horror, we saw that when two search lights had a plane its cross light, it was lost. The barrage of anti-aircraft canons had a clear target.

In such a desperate situation, the targeted plane would drop its bomb loads at random. The heavy bombers would even try to escape the cross lights by going into a steep dive. But in vain. Once visible, the merciless anti-aircraft guns would finish the plane off and most of them burned.

Desperate crew members would try to bail out. Some parachutes were on fire. Helpless, stunned and desperate, all we could do was to whisper a silent pray for the young men who were falling to their death.

When fighters such as the P-51 later escorted the bombers, the searchlights disappeared because the agile fighters would locate and destroy them.

The graves of the crews who perished are reminders of the high price freedom demands. Young they were, very young, some not even eighteen years old. Many graves are slowly forgotten and no longer attended. The agony and anxiety of the bomber crews who desperately and mostly in vain tried to keep their damaged plane under control, cannot be described in words.

Only one of the four engines was howling its final song of doom when I saw in a flash and horror how a British Lancaster bomber disappeared after barely staying above the roof and tree to engulf in flames transferring healthy young life into small ugly black ghostlike mummies.

The sonorous deep penetrating, day and night, sounds of the thousands of bombers will never be heard again. Over six thousand mighty engines from bombers and fighters sang a song of hope but also of a frightening doom that turned cities and towns into infernos.

The hundreds of bombers often colored the skies with white contrails that changed the skies and slowly dissipated.

Night and day the air was filled with violence, fear, suffering agony, and death.

As one of thousands: Lancaster Mk. LL678, 'Lily Mars', 514 Squadron RAF, was shot down by a Me 110 night-fighter over Deventer, the Netherlands, on June 13th, 1944. The aircrew was British, Australian, and Canadian. Three of the eight-man crew survived as prisoners of war.

And so were so many other bomber crews:

USA bombers	38,418
British Bombers	11,695
Total	50,113

These are terrible numbers. Are they accurate? Probably not. It does not matter. The numbers express how thousands of young men were forced to make a split-second horrifying decision to go down with their malfunctioning and damaged plane or jump from dazzling cold heights into enemy territory. So many were forced to sacrifice their young lives.

During alarms school pupils had to crawl under desks or line up against the wall in a hall away from windows. The eerie sound of the alarm was activated when planes were coming from the west (England) because the bombers were carrying their heavy destructive loads. Most German fighter and anti-aircraft efforts concentrated on planes flying toward Germany.

When they returned from the east, the free alarm signal was given assuming that bombs had been dropped. Severely damaged bombers made all-out efforts to reach the English coast under emergency conditions at the special aerodrome provided for damaged planes so that the many normal operational airfields would not become inoperative by crashed planes.

In school, we had to learn German. Just as with all such forced and unwelcome orders, compliance was close to sabotage by doing the minimum possible without getting in trouble. Suddenly we were not very smart anymore and had faked difficulties with pronunciation and reading foreign words.

Vitamin blocks were given in school looking like a chocolate bonbon but tasted awful. Some classmates from wealthier or farm-related families refused to eat them, but I ate them all and became very ill. Once home I vomited, and all the vitamins were wasted.

There had been no doubt in the minds of everyone, friends and enemies alike, that Germany would attack England soon. Nearby on the river Waal, many common river barges were moored with a cut-off bow to make landing easier and faster. The song that blared daily from morning to night made it clear that the attack on England was still imminent.

According to the Nazi propaganda it was going to happen even when the first American troops had landed. It was the only way for the German military to stop the devastating bombing of their industrial regions vital for their military supplies.

Hitler Youth had taken over a beautiful old Hotel Spijker in nearby Beek and they marched frequently through our village. Despite our hate and disgust, one had to admit that they were impressive. The sound of their large deep drums was mesmerizing, their parade in black uniforms perfected to the smallest detail.

On the front, their leader would be riding on a white stallion. And they could sing. My later experiences in the Dutch and US military also included some singing which was, to be frank, joyful but mostly chaotic. Germans learn to sing, and they do it well as they do everything well-trained and well-organized.

The most famous Nazi military march that somehow survived even after the war was the German Panzerlied (tank song) written in 1935 by Lieutenant Kurt Wiehle. Dutch Nazi sympathizers had their own version:

Al vielen kameraden voor het heilig ideal tot schuld van de Joden and van het Kapitaal. (Jews and Capitalist are guilty that our comrades died for our sacred ideal)

The music of the march intrigued even Italian, French, Swedish, and Chilean military units to include the melody in their repertoire after the war. Even in the Dutch military, it was unofficially sung, but humorously and with a touch of sarcasm adapted with the words of a well-known Santa Claus song. In 2017, the German army banned it from songbooks.

Humanity has a fundamental urge to follow a leader, an instinct better described by the German word '*Urinstinkt*', an instinct that makes a band of horses follows a leading stallion blindly.

Hitler and his experts used this instinct to perfection, culminating in shows and parades that made millions follow as in a trance. A dangerous but effective mental tool used in dictatorial cultures, by Napoleon, Mussolini, Stalin, and Mao Tse-tung.

The Russian debacle at Stalingrad slowly influenced the attitude of the German occupying forces. The promised ultimate victory that still was boasted loudly every day and everywhere became hollow and meaningless.

'*Duitsland wint op alle fronten*' (Germany wins at all fronts) it said on the widely spread posters and placards and loudly declared via the Nazi-controlled radio. Even though there were few left after the forced radio ban.

Yet the sporadic news from the Russian front included more references of 'technical re-positioning' that sounded very different from the previous glorious announcement of conquered cities and regions.

Cautiously phrased announcements made it clear that the tide had changed. Most of the occupation forces looked more tired and insecure, while the fanatic minority of the SS and Green Police became more ruthless and unpredictable.

A new experience entered our village with the arrival of semi-military troops from the Caucasus. We thought that they were from Azerbaijan but from later information, we learned they may have been from Georgia. Communications with them were difficult. They were Soviet Russian prisoners of war who had been given the choice to go to prisoner-of-war camps or perform so-called non-military duties with their two-horse or mule spans enjoying more freedom and better pay and conditions.

These war victims had chosen the best way out, not realizing that it led to their doom. While they possessed no weapons, they were forced to wear German uniforms. For the Allies and certainly for the Russians, they were collaborators and probably executed when caught. The officers were German and lived the high life in Waalheuvel Manor riding their magnificent horses stalled in our carriage house for pleasure, while their compatriots were dying by the thousands in the Russian steppe.

I never saw these foreigners doing anything practical when these units went on their daily tours with the most impressive two-horse spans at the front followed at the end with mule spans. They must have brought their typical V-shaped carts all the way from Eastern Europe. Simple people they were, kind and gentle.

At night, they would put their arms around each other's shoulders and dance in a row to the tune of a small flute. They were very fond of the German military doctor who was living in a nearby mansion. When the doctor walked to their headquarters in Waalheuvel, they would rush toward him to carry his attaché case. A small but meaningful gesture.

What happened to them? We do not know. But they may well have been part of the uprising of similar Georgian troops on the Island of Texel in the North of the Netherlands where many were killed, Victims they were, like pawns in the war game of chess, to be sacrificed at will, strangers in totally foreign environments knowing that there was no hope of ever returning to their faraway homes.

After the East Europeans disappeared, German troops occupied our village and took over possession of our garage. They were not Hitler's best, older, and obviously of lesser quality compared to their SS fanatics.

One of the obviously less impressive members of the elite forces, called Hans, who, standing behind me in front of our house, put his hands around me in a strong grip of a quasi-playful gesture. I tried to wrestle free but failed. His comrade standing nearby urged him to let me go, but Hans kept me in his tight hold I became frustrated and urged him repeatedly to let me go, but he obviously enjoyed that even more and tightened his grip.

Increasingly frustrated and angry, I suddenly thrust my head forcefully backward and hit the back of my head hard on his nose which started bleeding. Hans let go, pulled his leather belt in anger, and hit me hard. Angry and frustrated I cried and threw at him all the dirty insulting Nazi words we knew, such as '*Vuile Rotmof*'. (Dirty rotten Hun).

Finding insulting words for the Germans had been popular and easy. Since the incident happened in the front of our house, my angry vulgarities could be heard in the neighborhood including other German troops. Alarmed my sister ran to my father who came hurriedly and pulled me away.

When the situation calmed, we were worried. Insulting members of the occupying forces was a serious offense. Public anti-Nazi or German statements were legally forbidden and severely punished. My insulting cries had been heard loudly within the village center.

When a midwife made some deriding remarks about the leader of the Dutch Nazi leader Mussert while delivering a baby at a Nazi friendly family, she was arrested. The prosecutor, an obviously patriotic landsman, referred to the right of free speech within closed circles.

The Nazi-friendly judge however sentenced her to six weeks in prison stating, "According to the history of the law, her statements are perhaps not punishable, but the people's opinion (*volk's gedachte*) demands a verdict. It is beyond my understanding how she could make iniquitous remarks of someone like our leader who stands way above her."

An obvious remark that in a dictatorial regime where not the law but political opinion rules. The prosecutor was fired.

We were worried. The next day my father asked Hans' comrade who had witnessed the event if there would be consequences, but the soldier laughed and said, "I watched what he did. He had warned Hans three times." '*Dass hat er fabelhaft gemacht*' (He did that magnificently).

A day later, I got a slice of bread with cheese from Hans, an attempted peace offer. I should have refused, but when you are hungry even food from an enemy taste wonderful. We were lucky that there were no further complaints or inquiries.

The winter of 1943 was harsh. Any winter is harsh when there are not enough ways to keep warm. Balls of paper were first drenched in water and then dried to last a little longer, but they did not give much heat.

When coal was no longer available to keep Waalheuvel at a minimum temperature, it was decided by the owners to cut down trees in the woods belonging to the mansion making it harder for my father to keep the mansion heated because wood burns much faster, and it was back-breaking work for a man who was undernourished and weak.

It was an all-out effort, and I learned a lot. For instance, when a hand saw is stuck in the resin well of an evergreen tree, there is no possible way to move it anymore. Chainsaws were not known.

Hard work it was to cut mature trees with handsaws and axes. In a coal cellar under the garage extension, my father and I cut the little wood we could find with a one-handgrip saw which he had modified with a makeshift handle at the end so that we could saw with two people, my father at the main handle and I on the makeshift one.

I also learned that you cannot span an energetic horse like Oldenburger Frits in tandem with a Belgian slow-moving steed. When the order was shouted to move a large, felled tree with a two-horse span, Frits would jump forward, at times even breaking chains while the Belgian horse would slowly set things into motion.

Horses have characters that differ just like humans and must be recognized and used accordingly. Horse teams must fit. The times in the woods however were peaceful and so in contrast with the outside world. We felt somehow safer in the forests among the large trees as guardians around us.

There was no wood for us to burn from the trees that belonged to the manor.

Things went from bad to worse in 1943 when my father's employer, the manor lord, died. For many weeks, he aided his boss as a part time-nurse. Waalheuvel Manor was taken over by the German army after Van der Lande's widow moved to a smaller but still very elegant lavish mansion on the *Oranjesingel* in Nijmegen.

Being out of work was a catastrophe, it meant being deported to Germany as forced labor. But my father, fortunately, found a job being responsible for the two cars of the gasworks in Nijmegen where coal was converted into gas. Gasworks director Tesser lived in our village and was a member of the NSB which heightened the already ongoing superstition in the neighborhood.

One of the two cars my father was responsible for was a 1934 Chevrolet which ran on low-pressure coal gas from a large gas balloon installed on the rooftop. When it was windy, the car could not be driven. The balloon had made the car so unstable that it would turn over its side. The other car was a 1938 Ford which had two high-pressure gas cylinders installed on the roof.

There was no gasoline available for any civilian use. The coal gas was so contaminated that the carburetor needed to be completely dismantled and cleaned every week. The few trucks still around ran on gas from burning wood chips, a very troublesome operation that also was dangerous. A truck driver collapsed in front of our school from inhaling carbon dioxide.

***

It would often rain silvery strips of paper dropped by bombers to confuse German detection systems. I was later to learn that they were called scaffs and especially used over targets to confuse German detecting systems when the planes were most vulnerable and when the bombardier had to steady the plane over the target.

Later in 1943, another frightening sound was added by the erratic V-1. German propaganda celebrated the V-1 as the weapon that would ensure their victory. Yet the V-1 was slow enough for fighters to catch up and destroy them. They were very loud and above all unreliable.

In a later chapter, more information about this new weapon is mentioned. We mostly ignored them except when we heard their engines stop because when they did, they would come down with their deadly load.

During school hours we almost daily spend time under alarm conditions. As it was during one of the most traumatic days of my life. The frightening sirens had sounded alarm when bomber armadas were crossing eastward toward Germany and to our great relief, the free alarm signal was given when the bomber formations were returning westward back to England and were supposed to be empty after releasing their deadly cargo.

German anti-aircraft would fire also less at returning bombers concentrating most of their ammunition on the approaching planes that bombed vital infrastructures and factories in Germany.

A squadron of American B-24 bombers had been targeting factories in the city of Gotha in Germany but returned with a full load searching for their secondary target because adverse weather conditions had made it impossible to drop their bombs on their primary target.

Since the squadron came from the east, it was assumed that they were without their deadly cargo. Their secondary target may have been Kleve, a German city not far from Nijmegen also on the river but across the border. The end of the alarm phase was announced by the sirens.

Schools came out and my sister and I hurried home. There still were planes in the air which were ignored because there always were planes everywhere. People came out of their shelters when suddenly the bombs rained down intended for the harbor on the river. The result was horrific.

It was a clear freezing day on February 22, 1943, and some of the bombs fell on the main water supply to the city of Nijmegen, built on a higher elevation of the ridge, making firefighting impossible. The old town was ablaze, and its center burned down. My sister and I just made it home when the first hysterical children that escaped entered our village. We were intensely happy to see our father arrive safely.

The catastrophe was devastating. Over 1000 died among them many children.

The situation became chaotic and desperate. People jumped to their death from burning buildings when fires started on lower levels. Mr. Heinen, a family friend came by in a state of shock in search of his older daughter Betsy, a very attractive sparkling young woman we knew well and liked very much. After searching for Betsy for days in one of the many temporary morgues, all he ever found of his daughter was a piece of her gown fixed to a tree by a piece of shrapnel.

No words can describe the effect this ill-planned catastrophe had on the already depressed population. The alarm sirens spread their foreboding sound again even when people had gathered for a mass funeral.

Forty percent of the inner town burned down. Some bombs had hit the town's main water supply and made it inoperative. The only water supply for the firefighting had to be pumped from the ice-covered river to the higher situated town.

The daily fear, the lack of food, and many families who had lost all they had, and above all the many deaths and wounded, brought morale to an all-time low.

In our family, the mood had also reached its absolute low. Only the quiet strength of my mother kept us from falling apart. My father received orders to report at the end of the month at the Berlin office of the NSKK, National *Socialistische Kraftfahrers Korps,* originally a civilian truck driver's organization, but since the war started its truck drivers were forced to drive supplies including ammunition to the front in Russia.

Large military operations and occupations caused a severe shortage of German manpower, and thus civilians had to be engaged in semi-military activities such as logistics.

NSKK drivers however were forced to wear German uniforms and were as far as the Russians were concerned the same as soldiers even though they were unarmed. It was a certain death conviction. In a state of deep depression, my father told me what I had to do when he was gone to support my mother and sister. He was convinced that he would never come back.

But not every Dutch citizen suffered. There was a small percentage that found the occupation to be their time of glory. Nazi propaganda remained fierce and clever. Some 20.000 young men out of a population of about nine million joined the feared and fanatic SS, *Schutzstaffel* (protection army) together with Nazis from other occupied nations such as Belgium, Denmark, and Norway.

Sent to the intense cold Russian front they paid dearly for their treason. Less than one-third survived. The others were killed, many froze to death, or became Russian prisoners of war. Captured German SS soldiers were treated harshly, and many succumbed. They could not count on any form of mercy from the immensely suffering Russian people.

Most SS soldiers had their blood group tattooed under their arm, which was given with the explanation to receive quicker help when wounded, but in fact, it identified them like branded cattle, so there were also no way SS members could hide among common soldiers.

Some of the volunteers became Nazi heroes such as 19-year-old Gerardus Mooyman who had put 13 Russian tanks out of service in one day and received the highest Nazi decoration, the Knight's Cross of the Iron Cross with Oak Leaves, Swords and Diamonds (*Ritterkreuz des Eisenen Kreuzes mit Eichenlaub, Schwerten und Brillianten*). It is not clear if the Knight's Cross included the oak leaves, swords, and diamonds. Who cares?

Mooyman was brought back to the Netherlands and used for propaganda. Many towns in the Netherlands were forced to name a street after Mooyman which was quickly corrected after liberation. After the war, he was put on trial and received an eight-year prison sentence but was released after three years and became a successful businessman.

He died after a car accident in 1987. His open and reflective interview was well received in which he stated that he did not know about all the atrocities that were going on. According to the interview he was a 'misled idealist'.

Yet he nevertheless joined the enemy that imprisoned and killed thousands of his innocent compatriots, prosecuted Jews, prevented free elections, and allowed a foreign power to dictatorially rule his native land.

'*Wir haben es nicht gewusst*' (we did not know it) was the general excuse by many former Nazis who put the blame on the misleading and clever propaganda. Having lived through that time, I cannot accept their plea of innocence. They knew.

We all knew, maybe not the details of what was happening in the horrible German murder concentration camps, but we knew how innocent people were brutally incarcerated in the local Vucht concentration camp and the inhuman way our Jewish friends and others were treated, and how innocent people without any form of a fair trial were executed. How many disappeared and never came back!

Another convinced supporter of Nazi Idealism entered the stage of our lives, Mr. Vanderius (not his real name), engineer, manager, adventurer, intellectual, was a proud somewhat arrogant good-looking man educated at the elite Delft University. He had been in the oil fields of Indonesia, worked for Fokker and even had his certificate to captain a sea-going vessel.

Vanderius was a dedicated national socialist and was in high regard by the German occupation authorities. He lived in a beautiful mansion on the high side of the ridge.

An amazing large percentage of the well-educated men and women in my native country including aristocrats, sympathized with the Nazi culture and joined the hated invaders,

Aristocracy had been introduced by the ancient Greeks to bring people forward who could motivate others to follow the high road. Role models thus to motivate people to reach higher. When aristocracy became an inherited right, a false image of a superior class in society was established. How well do we know that children may not at all be what their parents were or did.

Maybe, Hitler's idea of a higher level of humans, which Nietzsche called '*Übermensch*', attracted aristocrats in several nations. Belonging to a superior human race fitted the perceptions of aristocracy throughout centuries.

At the time of the Nijmegen bombing catastrophe, Mr. Vanderius was the mayor of the town, a city in despair after the bombing. Later he became the Governor of the Province of Gelderland. My father was ordered to drive for the mayor during and after the catastrophic bombing of February 22, 1943, using one of the few still running cars the compressed gas-propelled 1938 Ford through burning streets after the air attack.

When the fire was slowly burning out, my father who had companied the mayor almost every day around the clock told him that he was ordered to be deported to Berlin.

"You are needed here," was Vanderius's curt response.

We never heard about the order to report in Berlin again. Were the documents burned during or in the aftermath of the bombing catastrophe? Or did Vanderius order it removed? All we knew was that a horrible catastrophe saved my father's life. And my future.

When the end of the war became more obvious, my father hesitantly said to his boss Vanderius when they were observing how female Nazi Soldiers (*Blitz Mädel*) were tearing everything apart in the Waalheuvel mansion before leaving.

"Is this the idealism you believe in?" he dared to comment.

To which Vanderius retorted: "Never judge a political ideal or religion by those who try to practice it."

Vanderius was arrested immediately after the war and was prosecuted as a war criminal. He was released after multiple people came forward whose lives he had saved.

When a German commander had ordered the execution of a dozen people taken at random when one of their soldiers was shot in a Nijmegen Park, Vanderius had rushed to the place of execution and told the German commander that if they had to shoot anyone, they should shoot him because he was the responsible authority, which they did not do of course.

The people who were lined up for the execution were let go. And so was Vanderius after the trial. He became the successful director of an industrial equipment manufacturer after the war—an unusually talented man and a convinced national socialist till the end.

All media kept spouting their totally unrealistic bias and propaganda but did not mention D-Day, yet we knew it immediately. Good news travels fast from person to person over long distances. Our confidence in the strength of the Allied Forces was absolute.

How long would it take to liberate us? A week or two was the best guess. General Patton's name became famous and legendary. Nothing and no one could stop his aggressive tank offenses!

Changes came in several aspects. Most local German military troops were older soldiers or the very young of the Hayot as the Hitler Youth was called. The best and most capable men were either on the Russian front or in France to defend against the Allied invasion, we presumed.

The brainwashed young men of the *Hayot* sang that they would die for their *Führer*; "And will write to my mother that I did my duty." They were fully prepared to sacrifice their lives. But I do not doubt that behind all the bravura were scared kids.

Even more fanatic became the few members left of the *Ordnungspolizei* also named Orpo and '*Grüne Polizei*' the Green Police because of the color of their uniforms, a much-feared ruthless arm of the Nazi Party. They must have realized that they would be made accountable for their cruel ways was not far off. Desperate people tend to do desperate things.

Another clear sign was the complete control of the air by Allied planes. Like birds of prey, they swarmed everywhere. When my sister and I were sent to our family for a week further north where there was more food available in agricultural regions, we were packed in the overloaded train like sardines in a can. On the last wagon was an anti-air artillery unit. Not a confidence-producing feeling.

More and more German troops came by on their way back to Germany obviously disorganized and disorderly. Very un-German. The lack of fuel created all kinds of innovative solutions such as planks fasted on the back of a truck with its end on the road. The front part of another truck without tires was fastened on the planks.

Just as American-Indians transported ill of disabled people behind a horse. Two soldiers came by on a two-seater French bicycle. When they had a flat tire, they just threw the bicycle at the side and walked on to the border. Once inside Germany, they could hide their identity. Their accent would clearly identify them as Germans if they would stay in the Netherlands.

There is a simple way of identifying if a person is Dutch or German by pronouncing a word beginning with 'Sch' such as Scheveningen. German people use a softer hissing sound in front of their mouths while Dutch people pronounce the word deeper in the throat as in Arabic languages.

A truck overloaded with ammunition became stuck in front of our house when it did not have enough power to make it up the hill while dive bombers were circling above. The situation was critical. The driver, an assumed NSKK forced labor man, warned us that an ammunition truck explosion would completely destroy our village.

We quickly grabbed our most precious belongings and went as fast as possible to an emergency shelter in a valley of the Waalheuvel forest where villagers had made it before the war, and we stayed there a day till additional help came to pull the ammunition truck up the hill. The shelter was built in the tight valley assuming that it must be the safest place. Yet a grenade fell near the entrance but did not explode because of the deep layers of leaves that had accumulated.

There was even less opportunity to sleep with increasingly heavier traffic taking place during the night to avoid being spotted from the air. When a heavily guarded convoy of large rockets came by, I called for my parents to have a look. They were V-2 the ultimate weapon of the Nazi's desperate hope for a reversal of the imminent defeat ahead.

Development of the V-2 rocket technology was transferred to the US where it was used for the Space Program and Earth circling satellites, from which amazing technologies emerged.

Life changed in many ways after D-day on June 6, 1943. It became obvious that more ravages of war were just around the corner. It was doubtful that the fanatic German Nazi leadership would give up easily knowing that they would be held accountable for the many crimes they had committed.

Discouraged and disorganized German columns continued to retreat to their native land. But small contingents of the fanatics of the SS became more frantic. Dutch citizens who cooperated with the Nazi regime tried to regain acceptance in society, but they failed.

On September 5, 1944, a spontaneous general strike and celebrations erupted nicknamed 'Dolle *Dinsdag*' (Mad Tuesday) after Prime Minister Gerbrandy announced via *Radio Oranje,* the Dutch broadcast from London erroneously that the southern city of Breda had been liberated. People danced in the streets.

Nazi supporters fled to Germany knowing that they would face an angry nation when Germany no longer controlled their destiny. The strike and celebrations lasted only a very short time. It nevertheless was a clear signal from suppressed people.

Reconciliation, possible in later years, remained impossible at a time when feelings and emotions were still high from fear, and uncertainty and above all enraged against those who supported an enemy that had taken our independence and freedom.

During a time of violence and fear, a little song composed in 1938 touched the hearts at both sides of the war as a sort of nostalgic hope for something tender and romantic in the harsh and cruel existence of violence and confrontation, a simple song with a girl's name: Lili Marleen. It was the only song we liked of the radio's propaganda.

Just as the tired, depressed soldiers had sung in the horrible cold and muddy French trenches of WW1, "There's a long trail a-winding into the land of my dreams." Neither words nor melody were of great importance, the song just expressed just an intense desire and nostalgia for a better peaceful world. But above the increasing maelstrom of activities and change was a growing certainty that soon we would be free again. Hope re-entered hearts.

But also fear for the price that may have to be paid.

On Desperation

Desperation can turn into irrational radical behavior when the future looks bleak and hopeless. As was the situation in Germany in 1919 because of the restrictions imposed by the Treaty of Versailles.

Desperation, despite some faraway uplifting events, had reached an all-time low on Christmas Eve of 1943 around us also because of the unusually cold and snowy winter without the means to protect us.

My father looked like a ghost with hollow eyes behind his glasses. There was barely anything to eat. It was cold in the living room. The only light came from an old car battery that slowly died. Its minuscule light would not last long. We had no candles.

My mother courageously tried to put up some Christmas decorations, but it is difficult to celebrate Christmas' Peace on Earth when you are afraid, destitute, cold, and hungry. The '*ersatz*' tea, a miserable brew, did not help much. The spirit of Christmas was absent and the mood somber.

At the back of the garage was a small room in which a German guard watched over the German military vehicles in the garage.

"Why don't we invite the guard over to be with us for a while," my mother suggested hesitantly. "It is Christmas Eve, and he is there alone."

She cared for others even though she herself badly needed to be cared for. My father shrugged his shoulders indifferently. He obviously did not like the idea of having a German soldier in our living room, who represented the despised enemy that caused our misery. But he would not oppose what my mother suggested. He seldom did.

My mother sent me to the garage below see if the guard would be willing to join us for a moment. I went down the stairs in the dark using a hand-operated light that gave a small ray of light as long as you kept pushing it down with your thumb against a spring, walked through the garage full of military equipment, and knocked on the guard's door that was opened after a while by a soldier with a suspicious frown. Before me stood what I thought was an old man, me must have been fifty or older.

I asked in my poor German of that time if he would like to sit with us for a short while. He nodded, surprised, hesitantly, but willingly.

Back in our living room, he greeted us solemnly and excused himself for having to bring his rifle with him which he placed in a corner of the room. He was German and did what he was ordered to do. Also, on Christmas Eve.

Words did not come easily. Heavy silent moments followed. What could be said? He knew he was part of a hated enemy.

The soldier sat down in an uneasy shadowy silence. When I looked closer at the man after some awkward Christmas greetings, I saw how his body started to shake, slowly at first, but then in deep shocking motions. He cried, deeply and emotionally, in this strange way our body reacts when our souls are hurt.

When he calmed down after a while, he excused himself. We listened to his story.

A farmer he was, a small farmer in East Prussia. He and his wife had two sons who were conscripted and missed in action on the Russian front. He knew that he would never hear from them again, where they died, or how. Missing in action, the report had said, somewhere in the endless Russian steppe.

Frozen to death perhaps like those who even clung to the tracks of tanks to find some heat in the frozen endlessness. Or as those who suddenly had collapsed when their brain had frozen under their steel helmet in one of the coldest Russian winters on record. He had not heard from his wife for six months.

The last time he did, the Russian Army was only fifty miles from his farm. And the Russians were known to be merciless after losing millions of their own citizens by German aggression.

All that was left, was a wretch without hope, just a bundle of desperation whose dream had been to farm his little piece of this earth with his sons and enjoy the simple ups and downs a farmer's life knowns.

There was nothing left for him. He gave up. The military demands of his environment did not even allow him to expose his obvious signs of depression, such as fatigue, loss of interest, the slacking of his shoulders, or tears, or any outward sign that would express his mindset.

In all his intense desperation, he was not permitted to surrender to his true feelings, the total and absolute absence of hope, of any events in the morrow that could lift his spirit, not even the slightest glimpse of joy or the gentle power of a smile.

When he entered a civilian's home, away from his military environment, he could no longer hide and control his true feelings and desperation.

Hitler and his followers may have had dreams of power and might and the creation of a superior race.

A lonely farmer was paying the price for the criminal minds of arrogant despots.

I learned a new insight about enemies.

He was the enemy, to be hated and destroyed.

This enemy was but a broken lonely soul without hope or the will to live after losing everything he loved and cared for, a man to be pitied, not a man to be hated.

After WW2, PTSD post-traumatic stress disorder was not recognized as such. The common approach after WW2 was the expectation to pull oneself together and make the best of the future. What happened in the past could not be changed or improved. Community support, education, and job availability were seen as the best way to help veterans deal with war experiences.

Our time is more sensitive. Professional assistance is available. But ultimately there is no alternative to desperation but to make the best of the circumstances one must face. A beautiful Greek song warns us: Not to keep sorrow and desperation as a chain around our necks.

These are empty words for the desperate soldier who lost all he once cared for and loved.

We were cold and hungry, but we still were together as a family.

Not this wretch who no longer had any purpose in life and continued living as a totally depressed, suffering human robot caused by circumstances far beyond the conditions he ever could have imagined.

Enemies are compromised by a variety of different people, some cruel and evil, some blind and ignorant, and many who never had any desire to be pulled into the life they had been forced to live.

Some lost everything they once cared for to the inevitable violence of war. And were desperate.

There was a lesson to be learned:

Enemies are the power-hungry, cruel, and merciless politicians and their fanatic often blind followers,

Enemies are not those who are pulled into war, violence, and service without their will, intent, or desire. They are mere victims of circumstances beyond their control.

A small farmer once had dreams to work the earth with his sons, hard work, honest attempts to profit modestly from their endeavors, milking their cows and play with their grandchildren.

This wretch now stared into black emptiness without any hope for a ray of sunshine.

War may bring victory and glory to some.

For most, civilians war means death, suffering, and the absence of dreams and hope.

And black desperation.

Liberation

"It will be a question of only a month."

That was what we could hear from the hidden radio between the awful cracking confidently from London! Our hopes and spirits were lifted high!

Field Marshal Montgomery's daring plan to outflank the feared German Siegfried Defense line by a fast operation through the Low Countries, to then enter the vital German industrial region from the less defended north side of the Rhine River in a pincer attack, was approved by Prime Minister Winston Churchill.

Supreme Commander General Eisenhower was put in a difficult position. Boisterous General Patton had stolen the limelight with his thundering tank attacks that had already gained a great admiration for the charismatic unstoppable general. General Eisenhower needed to keep peace and cooperation between experienced but egocentric generals. If the plan succeeded, a frontal action against the feared German defense lines could be avoided which would certainly save many lives.

D-Day had started with the expectation that the war would end by Christmas 1944.

But progress had been slow. Three months after D-Day, the Allies were ready to attack the territory of enemy Germany, as the Russians were from the East and the Allied Forces were now ready from the West. The Allies controlled the air despite occasionally strong German attacks with excellent fighter planes, but limited fuel.

Long columns of dispirited German troops had been observed and reported moving eastward back to their native country especially during restless nights out of sight of the dive bombers.

After France had been liberated as was Brussels and parts of Belgium, the Allies had to decide how to proceed. Along the German border was their highly respected and feared Siegfried Defense line. Any direct attacks would be at great cost.

To accomplish Montgomery's daring maneuver, multiple rivers and canals needed to be crossed while it was well known that all bridges could be easily destroyed by the retreating Germans making any advance exceedingly difficult.

The plan was to involve some 50.000 troops with four separate attack forces.

1. The British First Airborne Corps dropping at the furthest point at Arnhem to capture the vital bridge over the river Rhine.
2. The US 82nd Airborne to capture the vital bridge over the largest river Waal.
3. US 101st Airborne to allow the attack near Eindhoven clearing the crossing of several obstacles and canals in the early stages of the plan.
4. Montgomery's Second Army spearheaded by the famous XXX Corps to begin the heavily armored ground force attack via the only available road with the expectation to be north of the Rhine River in 48 hours.

The picture below shows the 1938 bridge over the river Waal before the start of Operation Market Garden. It was the largest bridge to conquer over the main river between the global harbor of Rotterdam and the industrial region of the *Ruhrgebiet* in German.

Operation Market Garden was authorized by General Eisenhower, who preferred a strategy of exhausting German resistance along their long frontlines, knowing that Germany was short of manpower and supplies, having to defend a very long frontline in the east against the Russians and in the west against the Allies.

Eisenhower assumed that this would inevitably lead to defensive weaknesses which could be to the advantage of the Allies who had a much greater supply of the needed manpower and supplies.

Eisenhower approved Operation Market Garden reluctantly.

Yet it started and we, civilians, were excited and confident observing that something very great was about to happen by the increased appearances of Allied planes.

The arrival of liberating Allied Forces had taken longer than expected. Many had assumed that the Allied Armies would advance with the same overwhelming progress as the German assaults in 1939 and 1940.

Was it true that the Allies were already in Brussels? We knew little.

Something was going to happen. And happen soon. Planes searching for German targets were everywhere.

September 15 and 16, 1944.

Disorganized columns of retreating German army units passed by with only one obvious objective, to return to Germany. Gone was the proud and overconfident attitude. The remnants were of what had been the perfectly operating war machine.

The convoys seemed to be disconnected parts from different military units portraying a great urgency to retreat to their homeland. During the night and cloudy weather, the intensity increased trying to escape from the swarm of planes that circled around like hawks looking for prey.

What was their aim? To re-organize in the defense on their native soil or to disappear into the civilian population, we wondered. In occupied nations, their accent would betray them when they changed to civilian clothing. But once on German soil they could more easily integrate into a chaotic society and try to stay out of sight of fanatic Nazi members who were known to be cruel and merciless!

What we saw as civilians, to our great pleasure and satisfaction, was but a miserable remnant of the superior arrogant army that had taken our freedom away and caused immense suffering. From the soldier's faces, hollow and tired eyes stared with only one strong urge to go home.

Gone was the arrogance; also gone were the impressive parades and songs of confidence and victory. There was no doubt in our minds any longer. The almighty Allied Forces would just walk over this totally chaotic assembly of disconnected units. How mistaken we were!

September 17, 1944. Small gatherings of people watched in awe at the skies filled with sheer endless formations of planes, with a mixture of excitement, elation, expectation, and caution. We still were in German-occupied territory.

Large numbers of the slow reliable C-47s also named the Dakota and Gooney Birds developed from the early 1930s Douglas DC2 and DC3, filled the air pulling their flimsy gliders and dropping countless paratroopers of the 82nd Airborne. Excitement reigned!

The largest airborne operation of WW2 had started!

The German army first used gliders on May 19, 1940 assault on France, Belgium, and the Netherlands pulled by the Junkers 52 and later in 1941 to capture the Mediterranean island of Crete, which resulted in horrible loss of life when General Student had ordered his men to jump without their arms to enable a faster way to leave the plane. But once down on the ground, the soldiers had to find their weapons.

Parachutes do not allow great accuracy during the landing. It left many soldiers without weapons and easy targets.

The use of gliders also failed in the Allied attack on Sicily when the slow and underpowered C-47s encountered heavy headwinds that caused many gliders to end up in the ocean instead of land.

The general perception was that glider pilots were looked down upon when compared to powered aircraft pilots. The following comparison will hopefully show this misconception.

	Military Pilots	
	Gliders	Powered aircrafts
Risk	Very high	High
Landing abortion	Impossible	Possible
Landing conditions	Very poor	Mostly runways
Enemy fire during landing	Expected	Seldom
Comfort	Poor	Adequate

Avionics	Minimum	Advanced for the time
Tower assistance	Not available	Available
Load at landing	Maximum	Mostly minimal (close to empty)
Braking at landing	Poor	Possible
Weather corrections	Impossible	Possible
Duty after landing	Infantry	Next aviation assignment

This comparison is, of course, far from accurate. Conditions, circumstances, terrain, enemy strength, and many other factors must be analyzed for every operation. Yet the conclusion cannot be avoided that the glider pilots had an extremely difficult assignment and deserve high respect for their courageous contributions. Glider pilots and paratroopers all came down with their arms.

Initially, the US credentials to become a glider pilot were set very high, but when General Arnold spearheaded the glider program, he increased the demand for glider pilots from 1000 to over 4000. As a result, the training began with volunteers who had no glider or flying experience at all.

The US mainly used the Waco CD-4A glider capable of carrying a load of a 13-combat-ready crew, a jeep, or an artillery piece. Only one instead of the intended two glider pilots were assigned because of a shortage of trained glider pilots.

Over 14000 gliders were made of steel and wood frames covered by fabric.

Some 6000 glider pilots had been trained. The massive airborne operation had to land in a partially tree-covered area, which caused many powerless and helpless gliders to crash.

Gordon L Rottman in his book about World War II glider assault tactics, wrote:

"Every landing is a crash-landing" was a glider pilot's catchphrase, "a planned accident." While pilots of powered aircraft looked down at GPs (glider pilots), they overlooked the unique challenges that glider pilots had to be faced. The GPs had no second chances of too long or too short an approach; they could not abort a landing and come around in another attempt.

Once released, they had to land at their first attempt and could not remain aloft looking for a better LZ. (Landing zone). They had to be good every time.

The distance a glider required to come to a halt was highly variable; it depended on touchdown speed which could not be powered back or increased as with powered aircraft, angle of approach, glider weight, surface composition-grass (wet or dry), bare earth, sand, rocks-and obstacles in the landing zone. Landing slides could vary from 50 ft to 200 ft and even more.

The basic difference was that GP could not land in carefully planned and designed airfields but instead, they had to land on unknown territory known at best from some photographs without knowing what the actual condition of the territory was.

Every landing was a 'belly landing'. Trying to control an often-overweight fragile glider made for only one operation and thus at a minimum cost of construction.

Pilots of powered planes would, under normal circumstances, land on friendly well-prepared landing strips aided by the support and instructions of an air traffic controller.

The glider pilot had to land mostly in enemy territory on rough landing terrain, often under enemy fire. After the landing, he then becomes a combatant if he survived.

Their courage and of their parachuted comrades made it possible for us to cry out:

We are going to be liberated!

Three thousand transport planes and gliders dropped 14000 US Paratroopers of the 101st and 82nd Airborne Divisions.

There seemed to be no German ability to resist this overwhelming force falling from the skies. Only continued columns of retreating chaotic German troops were seen by us moving hapless toward the border.

Yet the local civilians knew that the time had come to prepare for being in the thick of war. A short period only was expected.

Under our carriage house was a large basement, occupied by the Waalheuvel Manor gardeners, and a separated second small cellar for the private use of my family.

The larger basement had an outside entrance because the house was built on a slope. The gardeners used the basement to store tools and equipment for the maintenance of vegetable and flower gardens and two large greenhouses.

With neighbor Anton Smit, my father considered the possible collapse of our carriage house by bombs, a V-1, or artillery in four possible directions and decided that for safety's sake, a connection was necessary between the smaller cellar and the larger basement that would permit escape routes in more directions.

It was a hard job to work on the thick brick wall with a hammer and chisel; not a very large opening it was, but enough for someone to crawl through during an emergency. Even the rather obese figure of elderly refugee 'Aunt' Horst dove through it later with amazing agility when we came under direct fire.

Like a pike in the water, my father would later recall with a grin. Fear can make people do extraordinary things, even older people, and jump over an eight feet wire fence that would make an Olympian proud.

September 18, 1944

Against strict orders to stay close to home, I ventured upwards via the Holleweg, the small forest road that led from our village to the top of the ridge, to be closer to the area where the paratroopers and gliders, according to rumors had landed.

There I saw the first paratroopers, the first three liberators. When I came closer to a streetcar station on the ridge called Hengsdal, I stared at these first paratroopers of the 82nd Airborne, and I looked at them as if they were an apparition from outer space, tall, healthy, they were, dressed in a practical uniform with soft soled high boots, knives fasted to their lower legs, two round hand grenades banging on his chest, a revolver hanging quasi-nonchalant on their side while carrying an 18 mm Tommy guns (Thomson 18 mm submachine gun).

We were familiar with the German hand grenades with the wooden extension handle but had never seen the egg-shaped hand grenades of the paratroopers. One paratrooper surprisingly spoke Dutch and commanded that all civilians should go back and stay in their houses.

Inside the streetcar waiting station were three German soldiers who had apparently surrendered sitting quietly smoking cigarettes.

Before I reluctantly turned toward home as ordered, my eyes caught an approaching paratrooper walking behind another two German soldiers who had obviously also surrendered holding their hands on the back of their heads. The paratrooper pointed to a large stockpile of German rifles and other weapons near the entrance of Sint Maartens Kliniek hospital.

What I observed reflects the opposing moods of the German soldiers. The younger German soldier took his rifle and threw it on the pile, angry and frustrated. All the expectations and illusions he must have once believed in had come for him to an embarrassing surrender.

The older soldier went slowly to the six-foot-high pile of all sorts of enemy personal weaponry. He stood still for a moment as in a brief meditation, to then softly lay his rifle down on the pile expressing hopelessness but also a tired relief that all the fear, destruction and death had also ended. At least for him.

I looked at the paratroopers in amazement realizing how miserable we must have looked compared to these well-nourished Americans. But when everyone is looking miserable in the community around you, it becomes the norm. Only when seeing how humanity could look did the truth of our situation become obvious.

Excited to bring the good news to family and neighbors, I ran down the Holleweg on my way home.

Only to see in the distance a German half-track slowly approaching, stopping from time to time and searching. The sight of the reappearing Germans caused the immediate retraction of the Dutch flags that had come out of hiding, as were the orange asters people were wearing.

Too well was it known that the Germans punished every provocation ruthlessly, even more cruelly so in a war zone!

Back up the hill I turned and ran to warn the Americans with my inadequate English that Germans were coming their way. They understood and took a defensive position and listened attentively but remained very calm, seemingly nonchalant.

Half-tracks, just as tanks, are very noisy when they move thereby announcing their position. But halfway up the Holleweg, the half-track stalled and turned back.

I learned an important lesson. Other than the common perception of a clearly defined frontline where each side was located, this type of war was different and confusing. At least, in the beginning, the Americans did not know where many Germans were and vice versa.

To clarify the local situation the map is shown from the book 'De *Gemeente Ubbergen in de Frontlinie*' (The County of Ubbergen in the frontline), published in 1945 by HARK, *Hulp Aktie Rode Kruis (*Red Cross Aid Action).

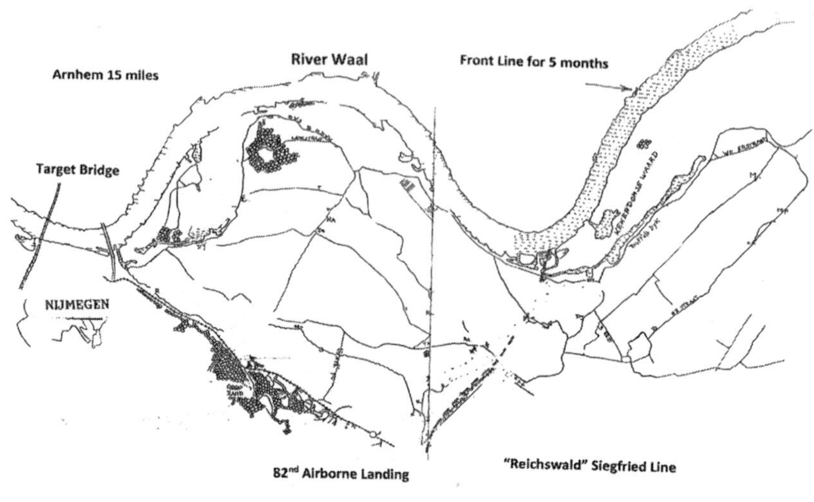

County of Ubbergen 1944/1945

The map shows the situation as it was in 1944. On the left is the town of Nijmegen known as Noviomagum in the Roman era, with its two bridges across the river Waal. The river that was the main shipping route between the German industrial *Ruhrgebiet* and the world's largest harbor near Rotterdam on the North Sea.

The bridge on the left was the 1879 constructed railroad bridge captured by the 82nd Airborne but destroyed by German frogmen on September 28. The vehicular traffic bridge on the right was the main operation target as the only gate to Arnhem some 15 miles further north.

Capturing this bridge was essential to allow the XXX Corps of the Second Army to contact and support the isolated British paratroopers in Arnhem.

From the location where the 82nd Airborne landed near the villages of Groesbeek and Berg en Dal in the County of Ubbergen can be seen that just a few miles east was the main German defense line, called the Siegfried Line, a major concern for General Gavin. The commander of the 82nd Airborne, who had to anticipate German attacks from this Siegfried Line while moving his troops in the opposite direction toward the bridge.

The area between the river and the ridge was inundated in February 1945 by the Germans to make an assault via the low region practically impossible. It took the French-Canadian forces, who had successfully held the low polder area for over four months, by surprise and urgently required amphibious equipment to rescue and support them.

Along the river were brick factories that used the clay deposited over centuries of flooding, to fabricate bricks. Most regional houses were constructed with brick walls.

The German/The Netherlands border was as shown on the right. This borderline was changed after the 1945 peace agreement and straightened with the Netherlands gaining land.

All citizens were forced to evacuate in the yellow area except for the few who lived in Ubbergen where it says Waalheuvel and where we lived.

The red line shows the stagnant front line for over five months.

What happened during the following days after the landing on September 17 seems now so unrealistic. Some Germans were still trying to escape across the border.

Standing with a group of neighbors under the majestic brown beech in the center of the village, we observed with great satisfaction how disorganized German units tried to escape toward the border on the main road below us.

Hearing a rustle behind us we turned around and saw to our surprise how a smiling and gum-chewing paratrooper stood behind us also observing what was going on. We were stunned. He quickly disappeared as silently as he had come.

Aided by the Hitler Youth the Germans regrouped and formed counterattacks. In our region, the attacks came from the low side of the frontline. Germans will not tolerate chaos.

A paratrooper motioned to us to open all our windows. We had no idea why. But we did quickly what he recommended. When the German half-rack approached nearby, the paratrooper hid below a low concrete wall and threw a hand grenade into the half-track which blew up in a horrible explosion turning young men into black ugly puppets.

"Now your windows are still undamaged," he said.

An unusual show of care during life-threatening operations. It was only a matter of time till the windows were broken, nevertheless. Only after the war did we understand that asking for windows and doors to be open was often demanded by Canadian troops to ensure that no Germans were hiding. This led to an unfortunate death when in the street, called the Fennenoordseweg in Deventer where my wife's family lived.

All people complied with the order except for a middle-aged woman who was hiding with her elderly mother in the basement unaware of the order. When she later opened her front door, she was immediately shot. The Canadian soldiers could not take any risk after so many of their comrades became victims of German soldiers hiding among civilians.

We, civilians, had no idea what was going on; we had absolutely no clue. What we knew was that the main paratroopers and equipment had landed on the ridge in the Groesbeek region, just a few miles from the German border.

We also understood that their objective was to overtake the vital bridge across the river Waal, the last bridge before the 'Bridge too far'. The most direct path toward the bridge would be on the high side of the ridge and not along the low-positioned road between our village and the Nijmegen Bridge.

German troops and tanks had been observed in the low Ooi Polder area which bordered Germany. (A polder is a Dutch word that identifies low land area protected by dikes and is often below sea level). The greatest threat could come from the East German side and could prevent paratroopers from reaching the bridge.

Several days later, the ridge area became in the hands of the 82nd Airborne after changing a few times back and forth in the confusion of a still undefined frontline. As far as we could observe from our hiding places. With several arriving refugees, we waited in the basement and did not know what was going on outside.

All we could do was try to listen and interpret what we heard as well as we were able to. Only sporadically would one carefully glimpse outside to find out whether we were in German or Allied territory. Truth was, we did not know most of the time. But after several days it became clear that we were indeed in Allied hands. For now.

Staring with utmost admiration at a paratrooper I was just totally taken by their calm almost inhuman posture and spent all the time I could with them when the fighting allowed being outside for a while.

The 82nd Airborne paratroopers looked and acted so differently compared to the military forces we came to know. Their uniforms seemed very comfortable.

Greater freedom was allowed when I saw pictures of girlfriends on their weapons, also Bibles texts were visible on some. But the main difference was that to us they made an impression of an organization existing of a well-trained, calm individualists, acting alone and even outside their orders as the situation would require.

In every way, they contrasted with the loud German approach with their steel nob boots. The paratroopers instead had long flexible silent rubber boots. You did not hear them coming. Or going. A totally different style of a military army.

Almost nonchalant they seemed while smoking or chewing their gum. It took us a while to find out what the difference in rank was. They all seemed the same.

Another difference between the German military and most European military organizations where officers looked, dressed, and behaved differently and were of a different class. The US Constitution claiming that all men are created equal seemed to be practiced in the military also.

Standing on the beautiful mosaic terrace surrounding the Waalheuvel Manor, I saw a French Peugeot with German army colors moving at high speed on the narrow road across from the creek Het Meertje in the Ooi Polder at the bottom of the ridge, obviously trying to escape to Germany.

With a mixture of amazement and curiosity, I saw how one of the paratroopers calmly put his cigarette aside on a railing, called his buddy, put a bazooka over the other soldier's shoulder, aimed the weapon and the Peugeot was no more, and with it a certain death of the occupants. Calmly the soldier who had fired the bazooka picked his cigarette up and continued smoking. War can be indifferently cruel.

A most welcome change was the sudden plentiful availability of cigarettes to the great enjoyment of my father.

The superior strength of the Allied Forces would soon end the war in our region we assumed very confidently and for good reasons. Most of all because the Allies had complete control of the air and seemingly unlimited supplies while the Germans were lacking everything, especially ammunition and fuel.

Before dust set in, a German dive bomber would try to destroy the main bridge across the Waal River after the bridge was conquered in only lightly damaged condition. We would hear how the multiple anti-aircraft fire would suddenly burst alive and fill the air with tracers even before we could hear the plane and anticipated the rain of shrapnel that would come soon thereafter.

A large hole in the bridge deck was somehow caused by German activities which was quickly covered by the engineers and caused no delays. I thought that the hole had been from one of the many air attacks. But I read in British commentary that it was the work of a frogman.

When the Germans had failed to destruct the bridge, numerous efforts were made with submarines, mines, and frogmen moving downstream from Germany. Seventeen submarine attacks were recorded and about 240 mines were counted by January 1945.

To protect the vulnerable but so important bridge, net barriers were installed upstream, and no further damage was done thereafter. Since the bridge deck was high above the river as the main artery between the harbor of Rotterdam and the German *Ruhrgebiet* industrial region, it seems unlikely to me that frogmen could have caused the damage by climbing onto the heavily guarded bridge. Yet in war the strangest things are possible.

We never understood why the attacks came always at the same time of the day before dust set in.

Impressed with the total control of the air and the confident demeanor of the paratroopers, we anticipated that the war would be soon over in our region. Soon, the mighty forces of the Second Army would connect with the paratroopers and then advance north.

But it turned out so very differently.

September 20, 1945

In front of our house, two paratroopers had dug a foxhole behind a concrete and steel grid fence shown on the carriage house picture apparently expecting the danger coming from the west toward the target bridge across the river Waal. Fascinated by their appearance and language I tried to observe their activities from a respectful distance.

They tolerated my curiosity very pleasantly and even at times conversed with me making a gallant effort to understand and correct my poor English. Calm yet very alert the two paratroopers completed their digging.

This picture shows another foxhole dug on our street as was in front of our house.

The initially relatively calm time came to a sudden end when unexpectedly the alarming rattle of approaching tanks was heard coming from the west and bridge side where fierce battles were raging.

It was not known yet if the Second Army had already contacted the isolated paratroopers. The tanks could very well have been German on their way back into Germany or in support of the ongoing battle for the village of Beek.

The casual attitude of the paratroopers suddenly changed into focused serious soldiers who immediately got their bazooka ready, assuming that the tanks could be German from where the fierce battle for the bridge was raging. The bridge was assumed to be still in German hands.

Tanks have besides their destructive power a frightening sound of doom when approaching. When the tanks turned at full speed around the corner at the bottom of the hill of our street, their bazooka was ready to explode.

I ran as fast as I could back to our supposed basement safety seeing in a flash the two tanks approaching. But I stayed outside from where I could still observe the actions of the two airborne troopers who were ready to face whatever would be required.

As soon as the two tanks appeared at the bottom of the hill, they were immediately identified by the soldiers as Allied Sherman tanks. The bazooka was retracted with a relieved sigh.

It was not the end of the story. Before the paratroopers could even had a chance to warn and signal the tank drivers, two explosions were heard within seconds of each other when both tanks ran on land mines the paratroopers had placed on the road just beyond our house at the intersection of the Holleweg leading to the top of the ridge. War is chaos I learned again.

How did these two tanks get there, where did they come from? Only later we understood that the tanks were from the arriving XXX Corps and may have been part of the thirty that were lined up by Lieutenant Colonel Giles Vandeleur of the Irish Guards to destroy everything within sight on the northern shore of the river Waal before the high-risk assault across the river by the 82nd Airborne to take the bridge.

These two tanks must have been sent to check out if German attacks could come from the low eastern road along the ridge that led directly to Germany.

The tanks did not encounter enemy resistance thus far but were lamed by friendly devices. There were no injuries, but the tracks of both tanks were damaged making them sheer immovable heavy objects blocking the main road. How do you move an object weighing some 36 tons? But I learned that human ability and motivation can lead to extraordinary accomplishments during emergencies.

Action was urgently needed because we learned that twelve Sherman tanks were ready at the top of the Holleweg to reinforce the defensive forces in Beek that were trying to hold off the German counterattacks from the *Reichswald* Siegfried Line as it had been more south near Groesbeek.

From the serious faces of the Allied Forces, we understood that the situation became critical, even though we could understand by the arrival of the tanks assured us that the Second Army Allied Forces had had made contact with the 82nd Air Force.

What I learned from what followed was that human capacity is sheer unlimited when strongly motivated. With the combined power of soldiers and civilians, and with the help of manpower, car engines, and horses, the two tanks were shoved and pulled far enough aside so that the waiting twelve-tank reinforcement could pass.

The combined desperate effort continued despite the continued frightening and exploding enemy grenades nearby. The tanks were much later loaded and transported away on huge tank transporters.

But the Second Army had arrived!

The war would soon be over, we thought! The mighty Allied Forces would just roll over the disorganized and discouraged parade of a defeated German army that had passed each day! The radio news from London still predicted the war would end before the year's end.

We were free and liberated, thanks to the overwhelming power of the Allied Forces!! The once seemingly unconquerable German war machine would be destroyed.

It would indeed, but not yet. The optimistic London assurance that the war would end by 1944 still underestimated Nazi capability. Operation Market Garden (Market for the paratrooper's actions and Garden for the advancing land forces) became one of the greatest setbacks suffered by Allied Forces, as so well described in Cornelius Ryan's book *A Bridge Too Far* and the subsequent film.

His excellent book covered what happened between September 17 and 28, 1944. But that was not the end of the battle, only the beginning.

While those dates were crucial, the stalemate did not end there; it was only the beginning of five months of a stagnant frontline war. And for the civilians who were not evacuated, living with the constant shelling and bombing at unpredictable times during day and night.

Ryan's book especially described the desperate and courageous battles in and near Arnhem and the bridge over the river Rhine. Assaults from the east around the Ooi Polder toward the bridge over the river Waal were not mentioned. The focus of the book was on the battle in and around Arnhem. Fighting in the regions continued for five months till the final attack on Germany began in February 1945.

Far be it for any civilian to judge who was right in the controversy between Generals Eisenhower and British Field Marshal Montgomery. We had no idea what was going on at the Allied Staff levels and had neither the competence nor information to make a fair evaluation.

This did not prevent us to believe that it was an irrational assumption that some eight undamaged bridges could be taken since it was well known that all bridges were loaded with explosives and could be blown apart at any time by a retreating German army on just a brief command which would stall the Allied advancement and allow German forces to regroup and concentrate on their defenses.

Moreover, the entire success depended on capturing and controlling one single road with no alternative possibilities, which allowed the German defense an easy target to concentrate their firepower.

Who saved the all-important bridge across the river Waal, the strategically critical and important last bridge toward the isolated British paratroopers in Arnhem?

Two days after the paratroopers came down, they made a most daring assault across the river ad captured the all-important northern end of the bridge toward Arnhem mentioned as the 'Second Omaha Beach', a great daring military success, at the cost of 134 brave young men.

Advanced units of the Second British Army took the southern end against fierce SS German defense, and their tanks rolled across the bridge while snipers hiding in the bridge were eliminated. Soon contact was made with the Americans at the north end. Reports say that 180 Germans had been hiding in the bridge structure which I dare to question.

Numbers can be, just as statistics, flexible. Or pliable, as Mark Twain said. There is no doubt however that many German SS soldiers and young members of the *Hitler Jugend* had been willing to sacrifice their lives in assignments they knew could only end up in death.

The Nazi fanatic propaganda machine had been successful in brainwashing many young Germans. The number of 180 snipers hiding in the structure of the bridge seem however unusually high for such a structure.

The fact is that the tanks of the English XXX Brigade rolled over the bridge first. Reports and opinions differ about what prevented the bridge from being destroyed, failure of the German explosives, heroic efforts by Lt. Tony Jones of the Royal Engineers who stoically and courageously disarmed the multiple and cleverly hidden explosives, or the actions of resistance member Jan van Hoof.

Every one of these military and resistance members contributed with their incredible life-threatening courage, and unfortunately many paid for it with their lives or life-long invalidity.

Some reports express doubt that it had been resistance member Jan van Hoof who saved the bridge. The most factual and detailed report I found was from Jan Bos' excellent report 'The Battle of Nijmegen'.

"Dutch resistance fighter Jan van Hoof crept on the night of September 18 beneath the bridge's structure and with his knife cut the cables that were connected to the explosives on the bridge. By cutting the cables, van Hoof saved the bridge from destruction. He went back and guided the Americans through the maze of city streets avoiding the German positions."

"Led by van Hoof sitting on a Humber, a British scout car, American tanks, and half-tracks were creeping through the streets with paratroopers riding in the tanks. Soon the Shermans and armored cars came under fire. The Humber raced toward the railroad bridge. In the scout car were an American paratrooper, van Hoof, and the two-man British crew. A German anti-tank gun destroyed the car, wounding van Hoof and killing the others."

"Several Germans approached the smoldering Humber and seeing van Hoof still alive, shot him in the head. During a lull in the fighting, the four men were buried by Dutch civilians in the garden of a house. An official investigation into van Hoof's role in saving the bridge was held."

"Both Dutch and American reports gave Jan credit for his part in the capture of the bridge. By Royal Decree, Jan was posthumously awarded the Military Willems Orde, fourth class, the highest Dutch military award."

These annals of Jan Bos appear to be credible. The American paratroopers did of course not have Sherman tanks and half-tracks; only the XXX Brigade had.

It does not matter who did the most or who was the most courageous and successful. Not anymore. All battles are chaotic, and details are often vague under such confusing circumstances. Time has erased many of the wounds of the heroic stand of the British and Polish paratroopers who took the third bridge in Arnhem over the Rhine but could not hold it.

But whether Jan van Hoof did or did not save the Waal Bridge remains an unsolved controversy. It will never be known since his death prevented any exact knowledge of what happened during the confusion around the battle for the last bridge that had to be taken before the 'bridge too far' could be reached.

Whatever the truth may hide, the fact remains that he tried and became a young man who died for what he believed he had to do regardless of the obvious fatal consequences. He deserves respect and should be remembered by future generations to let them know how high the quest for liberty can be!

Did intelligence and resistance information fail to detect German military movements near Arnhem? Was intelligence data ignored? Had strategic battle plans fallen early in German hands as it was rumored? Or was the arrival of the main force delayed too long by a blown-up bridge back over the Wilhelmina Canal near Son in the Province of Brabant?

Whatever the reason, all circumstances were against the trapped British and Polish paratroopers who had come down to take a too-far-away bridge. The plan to reach them within 48 hours or even later had failed.

Intelligence about local military strengths was of paramount importance for all strategic planning. The D-Day location was at least partly determined by French resistance intelligence.

Such information could not be totally reliable because of the difficulty of determining military movements from random observations while German communication interceptions were at times fake when infiltrated by German counterintelligence doing all it could to cause confusion with false information.

Did the resistance know that the 10th SS Panzer Division '*Frundsberg*' had moved north through German territory all the way back from von Rundstedt's Headquarters west of Koblenz on 5 and 6 September? Or that the 9th SS Panzer Division '*Hohenstaufen*' had been hiding in the sparsely populated *Veluwe* region? The courageous members of the resistance provided essential information. But the reliability was questioned or ignored.

Whatever the reason, either clever German strategies or insufficient trust in the reliability of the intelligence, the operation failed.

I saw a few of the men returning from the Arnhem battlefield, only briefly, these totally exhausted young men with hollow eyes, apathetic after having lived in an endured hell, totally drained physically and deeply mentally hurt by seeing the heroic actions of their comrades and friends end in death, painful wounds and defeat.

Even as non-military educated civilians, we questioned if it was strategically clever to attack in the low delta between two main rivers called the Betuwe in the Netherlands and 'the island' by the Allies, where tanks could not leave the roads because when they did, they would immediately be bogged down in the soft clayish lowlands?

The only road was under heavy German fire and became a tank commander's nightmare. When the Irish Guards units of the Second Army began their offensive on September 17 at 14:30 hours, the first nine vehicles were immediately destroyed by German anti-tank units who had an easy target on single roads. The offensive did 'only' twenty miles that day.

Several weeks later we befriended two British soldiers, Noman Lee of Nottingham and Tony Sutherland of the Orkney Islands, part of a British tank crew who visited us in our temporary basement shelter. They told us of their struggles to move their tank around on 'the island' they were assigned to from time to time to the front lines in the river delta.

When the Germans had the major 12-mile road between Nijmegen and the encircled British paratroopers in Arnhem under fire, it was impossible to advance. They told us that starting their tank engines was immediately followed by German fire.

Whatever the main reason may have been, the reality was that the operation had failed and that the frontline remained static, the Netherlands was divided by the Germans in the north and the Allies south of the rivers.

Initial jubilation was fading fast. Fear of the Nazi occupiers and the lack of food was no longer our main concern any longer, survival was now the war had spread its grip over family life. We came under heavy German fire that set the woods in front of our house aglow, which luckily burned itself out because there was nothing we could have done to extinguish it.

Frightened and stunned, we huddled in the basement listening to the projectiles flying and crashing down. Every impact made your body shiver, and we were relieved when it was not too close while guessing where the impact would come down. Most fell aimed at the higher ridge level called the Kopsenhof, an open area without houses or buildings.

Not far from our village, in the Ooi Polder, was and still is the hamlet of Persingen, consisting of a farm and a church, and its claim to fame was being the smallest village in the nation. Village rumor said that the farmer may have milk to sell. With all the courage I could muster, I went there on my bike without tires via the village of Beek to Persingen farm.

Madly paddling, I progressed while gun and rifle fire was exchanged between German soldiers and US Paratroopers at opposite sides of the flat open road from Beek to Persingen. Did the combatants have mercy on the young man on his bike? They must have.

I was of course no threat to anyone. The farmer's wife was kind but said she was out of milk already. She looked as if in a daze and must have had pity on me. I experienced the power of fear when I paddled back. When you are hungry, you risk your life for the half a quart of skim milk I returned with to our shelter.

Even during the most fearful hours of fighting, often defying routine activities are irresponsibly continued.

Cornelius Ryan included in his book an episode during the fierce fighting for the targeted Nijmegen Bridge between attacking American and British soldiers and fanatic German SS Units as defenders: "In the middle of the war action Private First Class John Keller heard a low pounding noise. Going to a window, he was amazed to see a Dutchman on a stepladder calmly replacing the shingles on the house next door as though nothing was happening."

I can relate to that. Common citizens do irrational things, whether out of a deep urge to hold on to what they have, to find food to survive or from a fundamental notion and instinct developed over multiple generations that if something needs to be done, you do it, regardless of the circumstances!

Near our little plot of land across from the Het Meertje where we grew our potatoes, vegetables, and even tobacco, a lone German soldier, who must have been hiding in the woods, tried to escape by swimming and wading across the creek.

Two paratroopers saw him and urged him by cries and motions to halt his desperate escape attempt and surrender. But the German soldier pulled his pistol shooting irrationally at them from his unprotected position. Hitler's brainwashing made another victim '*Befehl ist Befehl*' You follow orders even when it makes no sense.

The two paratroopers unloaded their Tommy guns from the other side of the creek and the German soldier was no more. He was buried where he was found, and a simple wooden cross placed over his grave. Later the area was inundated, and the cross washed away. Another soldier was added to the list of the unknown, the 'missed in action' and known but to God.

Fascinated by the nonchalant confidence of the 82nd Airborne troopers I spend as much time with them as possible trying to upgrade my struggling English when the fiercest shelling had diminished. They were the liberators, the angels fallen from the sky to allow us to be free again. All Americans seemed very healthy, and we thought, had to be rich.

The expected arrival of the Allied ground forces was delayed, and the Germans reorganized and counter attacked. Fighting increased. Fears also. The bombardments of arriving German Tiger tanks made being outside extremely hazardous.

Our neighbor Anton Smit was killed by an erratic fired grenade, as were so many. A very pleasant talented young man, a neighbor enjoyed and respected, a bank employee in Nijmegen. During one of the unpredictable pauses in the shelling suddenly a grenade fell, only one, seemingly without any purpose or a nearby target.

Anton had barely survived the bombing of February 22, 1943, witnessing the horror of people jumping to their death from burning buildings across the street. He was engaged to be married to a very attractive young woman. We missed his optimistic outlook even during the darkest moments, his mild manners, and his kind humor.

Somewhere an artillery or tank commander ordered a shot into nowhere and never knew that it destroyed the lives of a talented, pleasant, and hopeful couple. His death increased our anxiety and the awareness of sudden death that could occur at any moment any time.

After the Second Army had arrived, every twenty-four hours twelve tanks came down the Holleweg to replace the ones coming back from the front line. Sometimes twelve came back, sometimes less than ten.

One time only seven. It would not necessarily mean that the non-returning tanks were incapacitated during war operations. We later found out that some had to be abandoned when bogged down in the often-soggy soil.

At the bottom of the Holleweg, the tanks had to make a ninety-degree turn around the Waalheuvel Manor. The grinding movements of the tracks combined with the unusually heavy weight of the tanks proved to be too much for the brick road.

The motions of the tank tracks twisted the road to destruction. Bricks were flying through the air as propelled by rockets from the turning motion of the tank tracks making it increasingly difficult for the tanks to round the corner on the now soft-milled underground. What to do?

Village heads were put together and to the woods everyone went. Trees were cut to a measured length and installed side by side in the section of the road where the ninety degrees turn had to be made and all bricks were gone. We were amazed how long the tree-filled road lasted. Long enough to hold up during the five months of active war conditions.

It was obvious to us, civilians, that to provide support to the defenders of the bridge over the river Waal the Germans could not advance via the high ridge where the 82nd Airborne had landed.

The most obvious choice would be via the road along the bottom of the ridge via the villages of Beek and Ubbergen. The battles in Beek were fierce and the village changed several times from German or 82nd Airborne control.

Confused villagers grouped together after their houses were totally ruined by the fierce fighting. Some fifty people under the leadership of the local constable who was waving a white bed sheet tried to walk toward Nijmegen further inland but were stopped by the soldiers and urged to spread out and hide because the road ended at the Waal River Bridge where a battle raged that would cause a certain death threat to exposed civilians.

Three days after the day the paratroopers entered landed an elderly couple from nearby Beek came to our house forlorn and in a state of shock. Mr. and Mrs. Horst (not their real name) we knew from attending the small chapel in Ubbergen.

Mr. Horst was a rather stubborn and difficult man. With his closed carriage pulled by his beloved mare Lieske, he delivered and returned laundry to and from Nijmegen. He had just entered a hotel near the railway station, when the bombs of February 22, 1943, had rained down destroying his covered wagon and killing Lieske. The event had made an already quiet stubborn man even more introverted.

Mr. Horst wanted to return to his destroyed house, against all warnings and objections.

When entering the village of Beek from the west, there was on the left side a road to the Ooi Polder. On the corner was the village municipal hall and across the road on the right-side café/ hotel /restaurant *De Oorsprong* (the fountainhead or source) that included also a gentlemen's club.

Attached to the backside of this multi-purpose building was the Horst family house. When fights started near their home in Beek, Horst had dug an emergency trench in their garden following the basic human instinct that the safest place to be when in danger threatens, is below the earth's surface.

It saved their lives when their house was hit by several grenades for some unexplainable reason since there were no military installations or troops anywhere close. The grenades must have been intended for the main *'Oorsprong'* building which was only slightly damaged.

Without a livable place, Mr. and Mrs. Horst fled and came to our house. My parents invited them to stay with us, reluctantly, because we did not have any spare rooms and we also knew Mr. Horst as a rather difficult stubborn man.

A day later Mr. Horst insisted that he wanted to go back to his destroyed house despite the ongoing fighting and rescue whatever was left in his house, an understandable desire, but irrational and extremely dangerous being in the middle of the fighting while we had no idea what was going on.

Initially taken by the airborne troops, the Germans had reorganized and attacked the village where fierce fighting was ongoing. Many houses were destroyed, and soldiers were wounded and killed on both sides.

The importance of the German attacks via the villages of Beek and Ubbergen was evident: the Germans Generals knew that any attempts to retake the all-important bridge via the high ridge were impossible because of the terrain and a large concentration of Allied troops. The only possibility to reach the bridge was via the road along the bottom of the ridge.

We experienced the battle from a civilian point of view. The reality is better expressed from the American military side as the following accounts of the situation as recorded by author Jan Bos in 'The Battle of Nijmegen' (abbreviated):

Harry Roll, Company H, 508th PTR (Parachute Trooper Regiment): After the order to pull back I went over to the foxhole of a buddy Cecil Bledsoe to give him the word only to find Bledsoe shot through the head.

Tom Horne, of Company H, said that his company was involved in a heated skirmish in the streets of Beek. They were throwing grenades and firing from everywhere. I was in a kneeling position firing my rifle when I got hit and knocked flat on my back.

Harry Roll was behind me and he said that I was hit in my midsection because blood was coming out. This ended my Holland campaign. Hospital life was more to my liking.

Another company H Trooper Ollie Griffin returned to Beek on September 20 after pulling back the night before and jumped in the trench they had dug on the 19th. Sergeant Curtis Sides was in a hole about ten feet away from me. Bill Kurzawski was in another about ten feet in front of Sides.

The first shot hit Kurzawski in the head, killing him. The next shot hit Sides' rifle. He turned to me and said that he could not use his rifle. I said to get down but should have said, "Let's move." The next shot also hit Sides in the head and killed him.

Griffin got out of the killing zone in small woods. Where he was joined by Frank Bagdonas. We observed the closest house when out of the door walked a tall German soldier as if no one was within a hundred miles. Frank and I decided to count to three and both would shoot. We did and he went down.

We were going down a small alley with eight men when a German machine gun opened up and got five out of the eight. Frank Shimko, R.J. Brown and I managed to duck into a small building. I saw a German sticking his head out of a window.

It took me one shot to get him. Throwing all our grenades down the street we must have gotten the machine gun because it stopped firing. Then we got orders to withdraw. The next day we took the village without firing a shot.

So far, the stories of these brave men that give a realistic account of the situation we were going to experience in Beek.

The area changed several times from German to Allied control.

Against the backdrop of the fighting described before, Mr. Horst insisted that he wanted to go back to his destroyed house and have me go with him to pull the heavy cart with the collected damaged remnants of his house about half an hour's walk from our home.

My parents, bewildered by the uncontrollable and confusing events, reluctantly agreed to avoid more stress and tension and allowed me to go with Mr. Horst and a converted former firehose cart. Everybody was under great stress and did not know anymore what one should or should not do. Nobody did. We set out on a journey I will not forget.

Arriving at what was left of the village of Beek two dead German soldiers lay next to each other behind a machine gun in the front garden of a house on the north side of the road. The finger of one soldier was still on the trigger. I looked at them but somehow did not take it in. The world around me seemed surreal.

Nothing we saw had any relation to the routine life we once knew. For a moment, I halted near the two dead soldiers who looked still very real as if they could come to live at any moment. There was no blood, no detectable injury. They were as if ready for immediate action. The soldier on the side of the machine gunner had his hands around a string of ammunition.

They must have been dead only for a very short time. Two only of millions. Of no consequence. Somewhere, much later, a devastating message would arrive proclaiming their death to their family, probably without any details about where or how they died. It was still too dangerous to bury them.

But not too dangerous to remove some damaged and worthless goods from a destroyed house? I looked at them in a daze without taking it in. The entire world seemed unreal. Like two mannequins in a showroom, they seemed, motionless, they must have been killed quickly with two bullets from the back. Their helmets were in place, and they stared forward as if in a trance from still-open eyes.

The *Oorsprong* building, which was demolished in 1967, may have been the target of the grenade attack. The Horst domicile, attached behind it, was in a state of total ruin with the upper floor totally open and damaged and the roof completely gone. I climbed on what was left of the damaged and very unstable stair with great difficulty.

The stairs was only attached to one side and moved dangerously with every step I made. I soon saw that there was nothing left worth saving. I moved cautiously since the entire structure was shaking and close to collapse. There were large holes in the floor through which I could see Mr. Horst who stood surrounded by what was left of his family room furniture on the ground floor. He instructed me to throw down what was left in a clothing cabinet.

I argued that it was useless because the cabinet and all the clothing therein were complexly riddled with shrapnel holes. But in vain. He wanted what was left in it. People cling to familiar things in desperation even when it no longer makes sense.

Grenades were whistling by me, there was a constant rattling of rifles and machine guns in the air, and I saw how from my elevated position how Allied soldiers were hiding under a truck. My urging to discontinue a useless operation met a brick wall and I was told to continue throwing damaged clothing down.

I complained, wanting desperately to advance toward safer places. But to no avail. With a cart loaded with worthless, damaged goods, we started to my relief our return, Mr. Horst at the handles of the cart and I pulling a rope.

We were halfway on the first hill toward an elite Catholic school for young girls called *Pensionaat* when we heard the strange noise coming from a low-flying airplane. I had no time to see whether it was an Allied or enemy plane and threw myself behind a low brick wall. The noise I later was told had been from a chain bomb.

I did not know if they existed or what they were. I still don't. The bomb or bombs fell about a hundred yards away from us in a meadow without causing any damage. Were they intended for us? We will never know.

Soon after, on about October 3, the area was evacuated, and no civilians were allowed there any longer for months to come. Some returned, if they still had a home, some seven months later in April 1945.

I never was happier to arrive home where my father was not pleased because he did not know what to do with the useless stuff we rescued at great risk.

Several days later we heard for the first time a strange unidentified noise in the skies coming from what turned out to be a Messerschmitt 262. The first jet plane it turned out to be, but we did not know that they existed or what they were, so very different from the familiar propeller-driven aircraft sound. An eerie and foreboding sound it was to us lasting only a moment.

The ME 262 *Schwalbe* (Swallow) or *Sturmvogel* (Storm Bird) was the first jet engine-powered aircraft and was introduced in April 1944, too late to have a great effect even though over 500 Allied planes were supposed to have been shot down by this advanced technology plane that was eagerly studied by several nations for its capabilities and influenced the design of several jets including the US F-86 I later became very familiar with.

The axial compressor engine concept was in later years replaced by centrifugal designs. German fuel shortages hampered the effective use of their advanced military technology.

After the Second Army forces arrived, the paratroopers left and were missed. There have been some questioning reports written about the effectiveness of their assignment. From our civilian point of view, they were magnificent. And always will be for me.

As civilians in a war zone, we were surprised that the German army with all its undeniable capabilities and strategic planning, overlooked a simple tool in the hands of the people they suppressed: the telephone. They focused on the known resistance activities, people in hiding, sabotage, etc. but overlooked a perfect communication system.

Even though telephones were not as abundantly used as in later years, there were enough phones available. It would not have been difficult to make telephone centers inoperative. In several cities, people who were still located in occupied territory, phoned their friends who were already liberated and gave them information about the strengths and locations of the German defenses and equipment.

And so, it was in our area where doctor van Hasselt in the village of Beek, still under German control, transmitted vital information to friends in Groesbeek who were already liberated. The paratroopers were then informed where the German defenses and locations were, vital information during a war.

It would not surprise me if the two dead German soldiers I saw laying in a defensive position were the victims of this information. They could only have been killed from a backside unless someone knew where they were in their well-camouflaged position.

The excellent article 'The Battle of Nijmegen' by Jan Bos allows an approximation of the high casualties to the Allies in Operation Market Garden.

Killed, wounded, or missing in action were:

British Airborne Corps	7,212
82nd Airborne	1,432
101st Airborne	2,118
Polish Paratroopers	379
Glider pilots	122
Transport Crews	596
XXX Corps	1,420
Total	13,279 out of a total of 50,000 (26%)

How many citizens died from this war violence? It is not known. Evacuation and the general chaos of war made it impossible to come to a reliable summation. Yet also in this phase of the war, the general experience that more civilians died than military combatants may well apply.

And how many Germans? This is also unknown but because of the total Allied control of the air and limitless use of ammunition, their casualties must have been considerably higher.

The unofficial numbers from the Red Cross can give an impression of the effect the war had on the County of Ubbergen.

1944 inhabitants	6,200
Evacuated citizens	5,700
Remained in war zone	500
Totally destroyed houses	141
Heavily damaged houses	125

Medium-damaged houses   334

Houses with glass and roof damage   447

An estimated 3,500 cows, 650 horses, 2,500 pigs, and countless poultry were killed or drowned.

The picture below gives an impression of the conditions evacuated citizens encountered upon their return to Ubbergen County.

Five Months War Zone

October 1944

Optimism faded during weeks of continuing fighting. There were no signs of an imminent advance to the north across the rivers to liberate the northern Netherlands nor eastward into the German Siegfried Line.

After Operation Market Garden had failed, the Allies had to reconsider their options. They controlled the air and the bombing of German industrial centers infrastructures, military targets, and cities continued relentlessly.

It was expected that the German military would be highly motivated to fight for every square meter of their native soil and had constructed massive underground bunkers long before the war began. Even civilians could understand that the Allied Command Center had the difficult task of deciding how to proceed!

Going north would be sheer impossible because of natural barriers of rivers and boggy lowlands that restricted the use of mechanical vehicles such as tanks and artillery units. The only other option was a straight attack toward Germany's strongest defense, the Siegfried Line, at the high cost of manpower, equipment, and s supplies.

Yet time pressed because the Russians advanced rapidly. The Allies still mistrusted the totalitarian Communist Regime also after the Yalta Conference between Stalin, Roosevelt, and Churchill in February 1945, had produced an agreement about the division of post-war Germany including the unfortunate 'island' separation of Berlin which caused so many problems and anxiety during the cold war in later years.

Communal living in the former basement and gardener's abode became more established in Ubbergen the only village in the County that was not ordered to evacuate and where people lived 'underground', unaware that five months of frontline existence was ahead for them, exposed to random danger that made protection difficult.

Sporadic grenades or bombs could come at any time without a known or expected warning. There may be a chance to protect oneself if it is known from where danger may come. But during the frontline months, it was never known from where or when danger would come and thus tried to restrict any appearance 'above ground' and in the open to the necessary.

Tired, frightened, and often dazed apathetic refugees had stumbled in, exhausted after a lack of sleep and seeing their houses and belongings destroyed but thankful to hide where it was believed relatively safe. I do not recollect all who came and left. Some families such as Dirk and Martha Broers lived in this shelter for over a year.

The basement and cellar under our carriage house were deemed to be a good shelter as far as it could be judged. Conditions were not expected to improve any time soon. Since the house was built on a slope, the south and west sides and fifty percent of the east side were underground.

On the north side were two double walls and a covered pigsty that could be entered via three narrow steps. The outside double door was on the east side from where the main danger was anticipated. From steel plates, a vertical defense wall was erected about a meter before the doors intended as protection against shrapnel but was not expected to withstand any direct hit.

Inside the basement, the air was stale and smelled of garden tools and equipment, wheelbarrows, spades, rakes, and so on. In the middle of the basement was a supporting structure forming an enclosure for smaller tools. The stale air had a heavy, unpleasant smell from a milky substance used to spray trees and plants against insects.

The backside was dark and exposed multiple spin webs. The floor consisted of roughly placed uneven bricks. A good place for garden tools and equipment. But not as a living quarter. A cleaning operation started including children above about six years old. With garden reed mats used to protect plants from the sun or frost, sections were established to give families a minimum of privacy.

People who had in pre-war times known the privilege of common utilities such as electricity, water, and heating learned to cope without them or with only sparse and interrupted supplies, adapting to the reality that humans can survive with a minimum of food and comforts. Humans have an amazing ability to adapt when necessary and when united under a common threat.

More permanent solutions needed to be found. How do you maintain order and livability among families huddled together in a dirty garden basement?

The answer was twofold, first, the willingness to cooperate and survive, an immensely strong fundamental human instinct, and second, the natural talents of my mother who without ever raising her voice began to organize and adapt to the conditions given.

How to cook? Well, the answer was simple, cook for everyone on a makeshift outside fire and later gas heaters left by the American paratroopers. The question was rather what was there to cook? Some potatoes were still available and the vegetables my mother preserved in glass containers in a process called Weck.

Allied Forces leftovers were received and very welcome. Add to this horse meat and rabbits. The cooking was basic but adequate.

An unused and neglected toilet near the pigsty was cleaned and disinfected. At least, there we had a toilet and learned how precious toilets are! In the evening small groups would gather with the light of a candle waiting for each other's turn. During the night, buckets were used.

A sort of routine was established, and we got used to each other's habits and ways of life.

I became used to hearing the Rosary and Hail Mary prayed by our Roman Catholic kneeling neighbors. Every night but also when things became critical from nearby fighting or exploding shells. It disturbed me because I wanted to know what was going on but could not hear it because of the beseeching prayers.

After the arrival of the first evacuees, mostly those who wanted to stay close to their houses and property instead of being transported away to regions beyond the reach of tank and artillery fire, my mother's kind but firm talents went into action.

Garden equipment and tools were stored in the greenhouses, and the small tool storage space was cleared to place valuables people had taken with them. Mattresses were assembled from somewhere, blankets were brought in from somewhere, everyone contributed and there was never an argument to whom an object belonged as long as it was needed.

A miserable, afraid and confused cross-section of society huddled together trying to encourage each other and gain the comfort of each other's presence. Gone were the separations of a class-oriented society, for the moment at least.

I slept with my little dog Meta on straw behind the storage enclosure of the basement. A small outside room with a coal-fired furnace to heat the garage was cleaned and converted to a wash and cleaning room. No showers, of course, just water and soap as long as the supply would last.

To enter or return to the temporary bathing location a group of people would first stand and listen if grenades were fired, to then run quickly to the imagined safety of the temporary wash location.

Civilian assessment and knowledge of war activities came mainly from the sounds we heard since from our hiding places we could not observe what was going on outside.

After a while, we became amateur experts in judging when a grenade attack would occur. First, a distant soft explosion could be heard from artillery or tanks. Followed by the whistling sound of the projectiles and the loud impact when the grenade exploded. Or occasionally did not explode. From the sound, we tried to estimate where the impact could have been.

When close by, everybody would shake as if making instinctive protective gestures when the grenade would explode on its target. If there indeed was a target. To us, civilians, most grenades landed at totally senseless locations. Most ammunition in a war, we learned, is wasted. After this experience, fireworks in later years did not appeal much to us anymore.

Sometimes, the firing could not be heard because of wind direction or when fired from remote distances, but we were aware nevertheless of what was coming by my dog Meta's soft whining. She could hear what we did not. And let us know.

Anti-aircraft sounds came from either the high pitch repetitive four-barrel guns or the heavy sound of the large guns that targeted high-flying airplanes.

Frightening also was the death cry of the damaged and often doomed planes desperately trying to stay controlled and survive. We saw many, far too many. Damaged planes had to release the bomb load randomly to keep control, resulting in a very unpredictable danger for the civilian population.

With the departure of the 82nd Airborne, the supply of cigarettes diminished such as Lucky Strike, Chesterfield, and Camel, later replaced by English cigarettes such as Pall Mall and Graven A. Cigarettes became the main barter medium.

The fake occupation money was worthless. I bought new pants after the war with cigarettes and never smoked. It did not make sense to let your valued money go up in smoke. Some temporary paper money appeared from the Allied Forces, but cigarettes remained a strong barter medium.

French Canadian regiments replaced the departing 82nd Airborne, the Regiment de la Chaudière and the Regiment de Maisonneuve. The cold rainy winter made their assignment miserable and depressive during patrols and fights in a cold, rainy miserable winter.

Shivering and always exposed to sudden attacks from Germans who were more familiar with the region, added to their unhappiness. How often they must have questioned why they ever volunteered to leave the far away peace and beauty of Quebec.

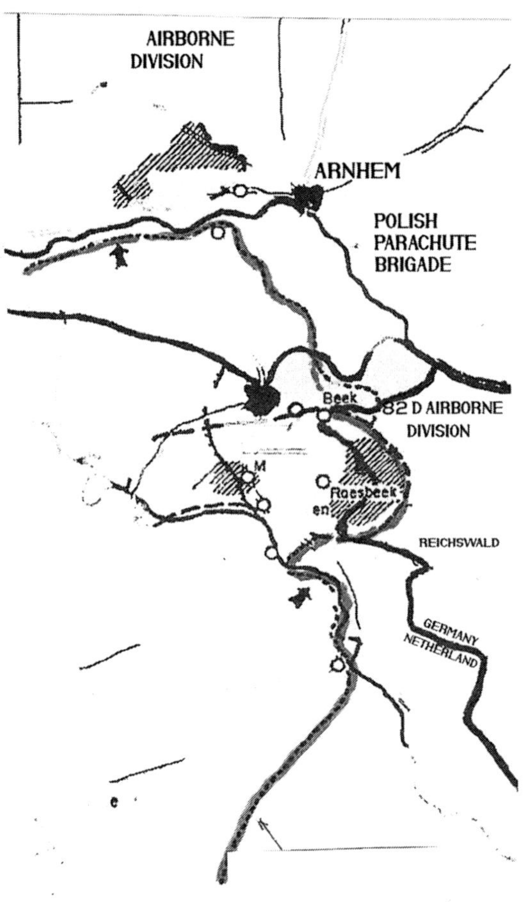

The above sketch portrays the 'stalled' frontline. The village of Ubbergen located between the city of Nijmegen and the frontline was the last village that was not evacuated.

Frontlines were not static but changed with military action from both sides, especially in the lower region.

Before the assumed attack eastwards toward the Siegfried Defense into Germany in February 1945, a young soldier hang himself next door in the former youth hostel. We do not know why. It could have been personal but also caused by the horrible conditions.

On top of the ridge in an area called Brakkenstein, an airfield came into being by bulldozing an area flat and by putting pierced steel interconnecting planking or grating sections for the takeoff and landing strip.

Soon after, a squadron of P-40 Warhawk or British Hawker formidable ground attack Typhoons arrived. I am not sure which of the two fighter/bombers were used, but believe, that only the P-40 had the painted open dragon mouth. We could follow them from takeoff and see them dive and return on very short sorties.

Relations with the French Canadians were more distant. They did not seem happy to be assigned to the cold and miserable tasks of patrols in the damp, dreary weather and the unpredictable sudden German attacks, for good and understandable reasons. Communications were also more difficult because of a greater language barrier. Their French-Canadian French accent differed from our school-taught French.

Standing next to them when they fired their mortar shells in front of our neighbor's house, hand over my ears as they did when firing, I wondered how they knew where or what their targets were. Settings were adjusted without receiving any apparent communications or instructions.

Although I had several years of French in school, conversations were limited. English seems to come more naturally to the average Dutchmen; English is even easier to learn than the language of neighboring Germany. French, however, as a Latin-based language is more complicated.

It is an established fact that the Angels and Saxons immigrated to England. But they probably had to go through the coastal territory of the Frisians to sail for England. Because there are so many identical words for common objects in the English and Frisian languages, many Frisians may also have been among the invaders from Northern Europe into England.

Maybe, this is why the English language comes more naturally to Dutch citizens just as it is for Scandinavians. Friesland is located on the North Sea coast of the Netherlands and Germany.

With the Canadian troops came Sten guns, a primitive gun that cost about $10 in 1942 to manufacture. The name was an abbreviation of the inventor's name Shepherd and Turpin and the Manufacturer Enfield. When the Canadians could find a 9 mm German Mauser, the Sten gun was just thrown away. I had one. It could at best be used for close combat because it was not very accurate.

With the Canadians also came the British Universal Carrier, a light and fast-tracked open vehicle better known by its name Bren Carrier. The word came from Bruno, a Czechoslovak city where the initial design was made in the early 1930s, and Enfield, where the light machine gun was manufactured.

I have, of course, no idea how successful they were in combat. But they were much fun when the driver would block one track and let the other one run at high-speed making it a carousel driven by the Ford V-8 engine.

Besides the ravages of war, other human frailties remain the same, as for instance the attractive sensuous young daughter of very dedicated conservative Roman Catholic neighbors. She found that she was pregnant, a rather frequent happening before birth control became common in society.

The search was, of course, for the alleged father. But all she could say was that he had a plume on his cap. The trouble was that all the soldiers had plumes on their caps. Was she to blame? The liberation had an intoxicating effect on the population; a deep urge was felt to give the liberators whatever they desired as a reward for their courage and our regained freedom.

The young soldiers were handsome and in good physical condition. They saw their friends die and knew the impact of fear. Can they be blamed for seeking a moment of tenderness and female warmth while living in a cold world of misery? The baby was born and given to an orphanage. So sad. Another war victim.

Being in a war zone means becoming familiar with war equipment without having any idea about efficiency or capability—especially the tanks. We soon learned that tanks were wide, unmovable, and dangerous. You better stay away and give them the right of way and more.

A collision with a massive M-4 tank killed the best friend of my youth Pietje Heinen while right in front of our house, a Sherman tank collided with the horse-pulled car of a refugee farmer from *Groesbeek*.

Village roads were narrow and not designed for heavy tank traffic. Although the Sherman tank was not as wide as other tanks used in the region, tanks are not very agile and difficult to maneuver on narrow country roads.

One of the metal shafts on the horse's side broke, and a piece entered the shoulder of the horse. Since we had a very nice, enclosed stall in our carriage house, the crippled horse was moved there in the hope of recovery. I often visited the horse listening to its snorting expressions of pain, trying to encourage him with soothing words.

The wounds infested and swelled. When a veterinarian dared to come some weeks later, he cut the wound open, making the pus come out as the spray from an opened water hose. After weeks, the wound healed, but the horse remained crippled and could not be of any further use to the farmer. When he came to claim his horse weeks later, we asked what the future of his horse would be. The farmer softly stroked his horses' manes and said quietly:

"I, unfortunately, cannot use him anymore. But I will give him a year of leisure and recovery, after which he must go to the slaughterhouse."

Horse meat is popular in Europe.

Ignorant as we were about military technology, some knowledge was nevertheless obtained from observation and later obtained information.

The name 'tank' is based on a misconception. When the Allies surprised the German military in WW1 by introducing the first 'mobile canon', the Germans initially assumed that they contained water or other fluids as a tanker. Thus, the word tank was born.

A brief overview of the tanks we became familiar with:

	Weight	Width	Speed	Number produced
Sherman	38 tons	9'	30 mph	Over 49,000
Churchill	40 tons	10'8	15 mph	5,640
Tiger 1	62 tons	11' 9"	28 mph	1,300

These numbers are approximations and vary with the type and special application. The Sherman tank, officially the 'Medium Tank M4', was most familiar to us with its crew of a commander, gunner, loader, driver, and driver/bow gunner.

It was a fast and agile tank that was able to fit better into the narrow roads of our village and fitted nicely in the early days of combat, hiding in a small cove across from our house. The Sherman tank has been the subject of debates and myths about its quality and efficiency compared to the Russian T-34 and German Tiger tanks.

It's up to military experts to evaluate, although even the experts seem to have different opinions. For what it was worth, we, as common citizens, thought that the Sherman tank seemed to be more maneuverable.

The Tiger tanks were, according to post-war experts, a superior tank. Only Tiger 1 was known to us. The advanced Tiger 2 developed late in the war was mainly seen in France and on the Russian front.

All we knew was that these tanks were our main enemy with their long-range capability to kill and threaten for many months without any notion of where they would strike aimlessly and uselessly was all that we could apprehend. The only guidance we had was that most barrages came for some unknown reason in the late afternoon before the dust set in.

There was only a very limited possibility for the Germans to put the Tiger tanks into action in the 'Ooi' Polder where the heavy weight of the tank turned out to limited use in the soft soil conditions.

These tanks were nevertheless a great threat for some six months by their unpredictable random shooting toward our village and the town of Nijmegen. Shortages in fuel, trained crews, and ammunition prevented the Tiger tanks from being the threat they could have been.

One of the German Tiger 1 tanks that threatened our lives for five months.

This picture shows how one Sherman tank became the victim of the soft ground in the Ooi Polder.

Churchill tanks appeared later in the scene. Churchill tanks were called 'engineering' tanks which means that they had several adaptive applications. The two different versions we saw were different from the usual turret guns type, one type had a rotating roll installed on the front with steel balls on chains, obviously to clear roads and fields of landmines, and the horrific fire-spitting 'Crocodile' pulled a small cart with its deadly fuel behind it.

The slower Churchill tanks had a great capacity to climb on steep slopes, a much-needed ability to advance in the totally devastating region with many tank trenches and a rough terrain after the twenty-four-hour artillery barrage, according to rumors by 1800 tanks and artillery.

The truth of this number may be questionable, but there was no doubt that it was thundering and deafening twenty-four hours from artillery and air strikes that destroyed the region just across the border. Yet the advancing forces encountered stubborn and fierce opposition that took several days to overcome at the cost of heavy casualties.

Impressive were the supply convoys once the Second Army had arrived using Mack 10-ton trucks driving at high speeds. Disabled trucks even for a flat tire were just shoved aside. Nothing seemed to be able to stop this rolling thunder. The most dangerous jobs were the motorcyclists who had to ensure that nothing and nobody was in the way of the speeding convoys. They sat straight up, not in the saddle but on the tank of their Harley Davidsons wearing large leather one-foot-wide belts.

Against kidney movement, we were told, but do not know if this was the reason. To halt cross traffic, they had to move to the front again when one crossing was cleared to the next on often very narrow roads passing the large heavily loaded trucks. Not a job for scared souls!

The chaos of war creates unprotected access to goods and equipment and those who profit from it. In a war zone, there is no time for clean-up and orderliness. Weapons and equipment were lying for grasp everywhere and some may have become wealthy because of it.

December 1944

Against all hopes and expectations, the situation became worse and frightening increased when Christmas neared. On December 16, German Field Marshal von Rundstedt began his feared attack in the Ardennes with as a goal the supply port of Antwerp.

If he succeeded, the Allied Forces in our region would be cut from supplies and in a very desperate situation. The worrisome faces of our liberators made the seriousness of the situation very clear.

Much has been written about what was called the Battle of the Bulge. The cold snowy time of the year made the condition of the Allied Forces close to impossible. A word was later added to our American English slang called 'Nuts' as the response of the US Brig. Gen. Anthony McAuliffe to the German demand for surrender on December 22, 1944, near the City of Bastogne.

This WW2 episode about the defense of Bastogne illustrates an interesting clash between two different cultures. When the surrounded American position became desperate, the Germans demanded surrender. A German delegation came with a formal written letter, shiny boots, and every detail of their uniforms correct and prepared.

Knowing that they would not be allowed to see the American local headquarters and defenses when guided to one of the American Commanders of the 101st airborne defenders of Bastogne, they even carried their own blindfolds with them. They were prepared in accordance with their standards of behavior and military etiquette.

Colonel McAuliffe's response of 'Nuts' was typical for a culture where not etiquette, but down-to-earth reality counted. The Germans must not even have understood what nuts meant as an expression. To them, the answer must have been insulting and unacceptable behavior. The American response did not care about feelings or behavior but about clear understanding and factuality.

German culture values correct and good manners. American culture evolved from the hardship of early settlers where only reality and results count.

Christmas 1944 was depressing and frightening which made its intended moment of light and peace a mere faraway dream.

The battle is history now. All that is left are memories and statistics of some 75,000 casualties (US Army Center of Military History), the 19.000 who were killed and 23.000 who were missing in action, horrible cold approximate numbers of young people who died in a cold hell far away from family and home.

German casualties are estimated to be between 80.000 and 100.000, numbers of questionable accuracy. Many died horrible deaths in a cold snowy world that so often romanticized white Christmas. For them, the white Christmas was not a white dream but a white hell. Many wounded soldiers were without medical help. How immensely high can the price of freedom be!

Clearing skies allowed a superior Air Force to change the tide and halt a frightening offensive that almost succeeded. It ended on January 25 after a month that seemed never to end.

The initial Allied plan had been to begin the attack from 'bridgehead Nijmegen' and the southern region on January 1, 1945. But the Battle of the Bulge had delayed the offensive into the *Reichswald* Siegfried Line.

It was a miserable winter with continuous cold rain, and it is no wonder that it did affect the morale of the French Canadians whom every day crossed a quickly build bridge over *Het Meertje* on patrol to face a dangerous and treacherous enemy under the most miserable cold and wet weather imaginable.

For us, common citizens, obvious realities emerged.

It became obvious that there would not be any advance for months to come to liberate the northern half of the Netherlands or eastward to Germany. Certainly not during difficult weather conditions, from what we could observe, there seemed no effort was made to prepare for any attack soon.

The reality was that we would still be in a war zone for an unknown time to come. The fighting would continue for months to come.

Uncertainty about when or if progress led to anxiety but, even more importantly, reduced the confidence that was so reassuring when the first liberating paratroopers fell from the sky.

Somehow a more routine of war set in. Humanity is very adaptable, even during adverse conditions. Being in a war zone for more than five months has its expected consequences. Fear and anxiety cannot be avoided. Not even the often-unpredictable deaths. Yet people have an amazing ability to adjust to circumstances. Life continues.

War zone life continued without any idea when or how it would end. There were periods of relative quietness, but the anxiety remained because grenades could suddenly explode at any time.

On the low and polder of the Ubbergen village was a strip of land that was inundated in the winter to be turned into an '*ijsbaan*', a skating rink during freezing weather, attracting even visitors from the nearby town of Nijmegen. During pre-war winters a loudspeaker would blare the same records such as the 'Penny Serenade' and 'Little miss echo how do you do'.

A few Nijmegen youngsters, tired of being for months banned in overcrowded cellars and hiding places dared to escape to the skating rink during a supposed lull in the fighting. Till a grenade fell in their midst and ended with the loss of life and injuries. A grenade on ice worsens its destructive impact.

How many civilian lives were lost during the interim period fighting between September 17, 1944, and February 8th, 1945? No statistics are known.

Field-Marshal Bernard Montgomery did not accept responsibility for the catastrophe and failed effort to encircle the enemy from the north. He later blamed bad weather and inadequate supplies.

The reality was that Operation Market Garden had failed and that a stalemate had started of unknown duration.

The only actions northwards continued in the far west of the Netherlands, where Canadian regiments had been assigned to free access to the critical seaport of Antwerp, by capturing the islands along the access river Schelde even though it was known that the Canadians were short of manpower and supplies and the Germans had adequate time to set up defenses.

To attack the islands there was practically no way to protect and hide, it was extremely difficult, dangerous and calamitous. They succeeded but suffered immense losses.

We had no idea, of course, what was in the minds of the Allied generals but doubted that they would try again to attack across the river delta at a high cost what had failed before. Rivers and the soggy lowlands were even for modern warfare's difficult obstacles. The cold, wet, harsh winter made conditions even worse.

It also became evident that many civilians had to be evacuated from the war zone on both sides during the stalemate.

Those who lost their completely destroyed houses or were so badly damaged that they were no longer habitable had to be the first to be evacuated during assumed or real impasses in the fighting. Later, those were added who were living in the inundated lowlands after the Germans blew up sections of dikes upstream of the river Rhine and were shut off from common access and supplies.

Some authorities, whoever they may have been during confusing war times, civilian or military, had drawn an evacuation line just beyond where we lived. There were already so many refugees for whom shelter and refuse needed to be found away from the ravages of frontline war beyond the far-reaching artillery grenades.

Available capacity was limited. The order was received with mixed feelings. We were relieved that we could stay in the basement of our home but also concerned that were had to remain in the dangers of a war zone.

The County of Ubbergen, with its about six thousand people, consisted of several smaller villages and hamlets that were torn apart by the frontline fighting.

The villages of Berg and Dal, and Beek, located on and against the ridge, came immediately after the paratrooper's landing under German fire and suffered greatly during the fierce first days of fighting. Houses were burned and shot into ruin. Some inhabitants had dug trenches believing that they were safer there than in their houses, a mindset that grew after horrible experiences during the February 22, 1943, bombing in Nijmegen.

An elderly couple in Beek died a slow death in their trench when a German soldier threw a hand grenade in the trench. Did he believe that it was occupied by the paratroopers? We will never know. But it became very obvious that all citizens had to be evacuated, where and when possible, on both sides during the ongoing fighting.

The villagers of the hamlet of *Kekerdom* in the Ooi polder had put the crew of a British bomber that crashed in their local clothing and brought them to safety southward in an effort for them to return to England via France and Spain.

Located closer to the German border, they endured the first fierce fighting but ended up into a German-controlled area and were evacuated north to the German occupied region called the Achterhoek on October 20.

Being in an agricultural region there were many cows in the meadows that could not be milked anymore. Sullen and gentle cows, frightened by the explosion around them, formed herds again and stampeded. Most drowned when the area was inundated.

The nearby hamlet of *Leuth* was liberated on September 20, thus only three days after the beginning of the offensive. All villagers also had to be evacuated because of the ongoing fighting on October 3 but they had the good fortune to be transported south to the liberated regions close to the Belgium border.

The only people left in the war zone were those living in the village of Ubbergen itself where people lived packed in basements and temporary shelters with refugees who had not been transported north or south and were exposed to just as the villagers who lived there, to shelling, gunfire, bombes from wounded Allied bombers, erratic V-1's, and shrapnel from hundreds of anti-aircraft guns, from September 17, 1944, till mid-February 1945.

On the German side evacuation was also ordered for the town of Arnhem the capital of the Province of Gelderland and its surrounding villages of some one hundred thousand people that were only allowed to take with them but what they could carry, many to end up with people who did not have enough to eat themselves.

During times of distress humanity's most noble qualities can surface by caring for others while they did not have enough themselves.

The evacuation situation on the Allied side was less populous but just as urgent. People needed to be evacuated from within the front lines where most houses were damaged. Families could not stay without the possibility of the needed supplies which were impossible in a region of fierce fighting that changed control back and forth between the opposing armies.

It is a natural human instinct to go underground to protect themselves from the dangers above ground as the people in London did on the Railway Underground and the way everyone was hiding in basements and cellars.

There can be drawbacks to hiding underground, however. After February 22, 1943, bombing of Nijmegen, people were rescued as much as three weeks after their houses collapsed barely alive after consuming whatever could still be found.

If not, a slow death of thirst and hunger followed when buried alive. Water lines often ran through basements, and were often leaking and damaged, causing people to drown when they could not dig through the collected rubble of their collapsed houses, as happened with people hiding from tornados.

In the village of Ubbergen, a communal shelter was erected in a valley of the Waalheuvel forest by all in the village who could participate. No permission was asked to enter the private property. During imminent danger, one does what is deemed necessary regardless of normal respect for the law and expected behavior.

On top of the wooden structure roof, a foot of sand and earth was placed. The entrances on both sides were protected by a vertical barrier. I spent only a day there when we were forced to evacuate. It felt safe but uncomfortable with an anxious mind about what was or could happen to our house and belongings. People are hesitant to leave their homes if it can possibly be avoided.

People come together when faced with danger. The common irritations and conflicts faded. Neighbors got to know each other better than during peaceful times.

Having no perception of what was going on, our greatest concern was that a German counterattack would succeed and bring us back under the feared regime again that had suppressed our freedom before. And was now even more feared because we had, with great enthusiasm, celebrated the arrival of Allied Forces.

Relations with the American soldiers were completely opposite to the way German troops had been encountered. They were the liberators, the daring heroes falling from the sky to give us our blessed freedom back. Kind and supporting these liberators were. They also generously shared food and cigarettes with us during the short period before the Second Army arrived, till the paratroopers also ran out of supplies.

During assumed lulls in the fighting, they did occur from time to time, even though we had no idea when they would start or how long they would last, the evacuation had begun. It may be difficult to understand but even during the war, there are moments of relative quietness. How to judge when such lulls occurred and even more how long they would last was just a total guess.

Had the weather during the first month been pleasant and occasionally sunny, with the arrival of autumn, the typical dreary and rainy, and overcast days began. And with it, our hope declined. Where were the overpowering attacks that would put the Nazi regime to its knees?

We understood that during overcast cloudy days, the Allies were not able to effectively use their superior control of the air, in quantity if not in quality, because the German military aircraft were at least equal to that of the Allies but were certainly lower in number because of the German lack of fuel. In later years, the Focke-Wulf 190 was judged to be the best fighter plane of WW2.

The situation we found ourselves in was so different from the expectations we had before when mighty Allied Forces had fallen from the skies. Our confidence declined. German Tiger tanks had apparently arrived by what we could construe, and they were feared. Superior control of the air would be of little help during many dreary cloud covered skies, but absolutely needed to ensure success on the battle field.

The Arnhem debacle had shaken optimism of an early end of fighting and the confidence in Allied superiority. Citizens became aware that the situation was very grave. Christmas was still celebrated with hope under miserable conditions in a shelter, but also with great anxiety of what the future would hold. Peace on earth seemed so far away but prayers for peace were more fervent than ever before.

We did not know why we were not forced to evacuate. Because of the massive number of civilians for whom a temporary shelter had to be found, the absorption capacity was limited. Another reason may have been to keep the area open because of the Waalheuvel mansion's temporary role as an emergency hospital.

The Netherlands is a nation separated by rivers. As in the days of the Roman Empire, the river Rhine had divided Europe.

When Operation Market Garden started, the Dutch Government in London had called on Dutch Railway employees to go on strike to make it more difficult to move German military supplies to the front lines, in expectation of a brief and successful operation. That had been the plan.

When the liberation of the northern half of the nation had failed, the strike left the Dutch northern half without transportation to supply needed food and especially the north-west region with its major cities of Amsterdam, The Hague, and Rotterdam, resulting in the 'hunger winter' of 1944/1945 during which many people died of starvation.

The courageous life-saving initiative of the Swedish Red Cross and others cannot be overemphasized by arranging in the middle of fierce fighting a truth to allow the bombers that threatened life one day, to come back the next day, flying very vulnerably low the next day to drop food from England.

The German authorities and commanders must be credited with allowing the low-flying enemy bombers to drop their life-saving loads. Since bombers were enemy warplanes, the slow and low-flying planes, even as low as 100 yards, could have been easy targets. They were the bombers that caused German cities to become flaming infernos that killed their families and friends.

It must not have been an easy decision to make, but a morally right one. According to detailed post-war studies, about 22,000 people died from malnutrition, and many more suffered from life long-illness also as a result of malnutrition. Among them was famous movie star, Audrey Hepburn, who lived through the devastating winter and had to cope during her life with medical repercussions such as anemia, respiratory problems, and edema.

Her mother was Dutch Baroness, Ella van Heemskerk, and the reason why she was in the Netherlands.

***

Meanwhile, the grenades continued to make being outside dangerous. Where there actual targets? We could not identify them. The grenade impacts seemed to be fired at random without pattern or purpose which made it even more unpredictable where to seek protection. Unexploded bombs formed another very hazardous reality to live with for years afterward.

The people ordered to evacuate could only take with them that they could carry, a most difficult decision. What do you take with you? Stunned and apathetic from the sleepless nights and continuous fighting and people began to accept their fate more quietly without outward signs of anxiety.

Most evacuees were transported further away beyond the reach of German artillery, but some remained nearby and tried to find a temporary stay close by so that the return would be quicker when allowed.

When people share a common danger, they get along and accept each other's idiosyncrasies. No one would pay any attention when the widow of a former mayor, and thus belonging to the elite, loudly peed in a bucket during the night. An older couple that lived just beyond the evacuation line escaped with their two most precious possessions on a wheelbarrow, an accordion, and a bedpan.

In the film A Bridge Too Far, there were scenes of total silence. My experience was different. Next to the basement shelter was a brick wall that connected to the greenhouses. Before the wall was a heap of sand, I could stand on to look over the top of the wall.

In the distance, there would be a constant rattling of machine guns throughout the night and explosions from grenades. Flares filled the air to locate enemy positions. There seldom were moments of silence.

There were several close calls. My sister entered the basement shelter when one of the house windows was blown out by a nearby grenade. She ran inside. The glass window missed her by about a foot and fell with a thundering clash apart and would have instantly killed her if she had been one step slower.

The airborne troops used large walkie-talkies but stretched communication cables everywhere also along the front of the neighboring youth hostel and our house. When tank artillery shells fell in the woods in front of our house, I ran as fast as I could to the basement but stumbled and fell over one of the cables on the road, injuring my elbow.

One of the nuns in Waalheuvel put a bandage around my arm. That night I suffered badly. There was no possibility to go to a medical unit during the night where all unidentified movement was immediately targeted.

When we were able to find a doctor during a presumed pause in the shelling, he took of the bandage and declared stoically, "You are lucky. Another hour or so and you would have lost your arm. The bandage completely restricted your blood flow."

The elbow healed eventually.

We escaped another disaster. Mr. Horst our refugee and a stubborn elderly man had an object in a vise on my father's workstation in the garage and intended to open it with a chisel and hammer.

My father saw what was happening from a distance and rushed to him pulling the hammer backward out of his hand and arm that was heaving upwards to strike the chisel and thus open the object.

Mr. Horst was not happy.

"What are you doing?" he angrily objected. "There is oil in there I want to have!"

"No oil, Horst, my father responded with a deep sigh of relief."

"You were trying to open a landmine."

Weapons and ammunition were just for grasp anywhere. When a year after the war my family moved back to Deventer where my father became responsible for the cars and trucks of the Noury & van der Lande Corporation headquarters, he noticed that the floor in the former guard room next to the garage must have been opened.

To his surprise, he found that there was a 9 mm colt revolver, a Tommy gun, and a Sten gun hidden under the floor, with an ample supply of ammunition. It did not take long to find that it was his son's collection. I sold the revolver and just left the rest behind. No weapons moved with my family to Deventer.

Schools were closed for one year.

The time I did not spend with the troops to improve my English and out of curiosity, I assisted the local carpenter in making coffins. He had set up a temporary shop at the backside of the garage. The coffins made were just rough unfinished wood that was available.

At one end, where the head would be placed, just a piece of plain paper would give the coffin a small touch of respect. Mr. Hendriks, the carpenter, was very busy.

On the riverside of the Ooi Polder factories had been making bricks for centuries from the rich clay accumulated over many years of inundation. Horses were brought presumably from Russia to pull the brick-loaded railroad cars instead of gasoline-powered tractors.

Gasoline was not available since the invasion by the German army. When the shelling started, the horses huddled together and formed herds again. Several were wounded from shrapnel.

One afternoon during the early days after September 17 we heard a herd of horses coming from afar into the village before the inundation. A herd of galloping horses is very imposing! Their eyes and nostrils were wide open and their ears backward. Yet some of the paratroopers must have been cowboys because they were able to calm the herd down.

One horse was shot and slaughtered when considered beyond help. The horse was hung on an engine tackle in our garage and the meat was distributed among the villagers. One of the airborne soldiers rode a while around on an unsaddled horse. The horses later moved away, and I do not know what happened to them.

It became obvious that the situation would not change during the winter months. The expectation of a quick end to hostilities faded. There were no indications that an offensive to liberate the desperate northern half of the Netherlands was imminent.

On the contrary, we feared that the once superior Allied Forces would not be able to hold the present lines.

A certain routine had emerged nevertheless even in a war zone. Till another frightening event happened. I do not recall the exact date, but it was shortly after the courageous fought Battle of the Bulge with its heavy cost in human death and suffering.

Having failed to take Antwerp's important harbor, the Germans tried to destroy the strategic port with a barrage of V-1 pilotless rockets and devastating explosives. Some twelve thousand V-1s were targeted for Antwerp and nine thousand for London.

We became used to its loud pulsating jet engine that could be heard and seen up to ten miles flying at about two thousand feet. The German propaganda machine had predicted glorious success leading to an Allied truth or surrender which common citizens took with an indifferent shrug of the shoulders.

Too often the unrealistic boasting had been found to contradict what had been seen and heard. Pipe dreams they were that had lost their effect after trying to pretend that the defeat of the German invasion of Russia was a victory.

As long as the noisy pulsating noise could be heard the V-1 rockets would fly elsewhere. But when the engine stopped, an immediate cover had to be found. The V-1's distance to its target was measured by the rotation of the propeller, simple but unreliable.

It was about three or four o'clock in the morning when the families that crowded in our basement were suddenly rudely awakened by an enormous loud explosion that shook the ground and the building on its foundation. Dust clouded vision. Cries of horror and prayers came from people whose nerve systems were already shaken.

Since there was no electrical supply, candles needed to be lit to show a limited view because of the dust in the air. It took a while to realize that a V-1 had exploded about fifty yards behind our house identified by a huge crater. A close call, a very close call. Fifty more yards and we all would have succumbed. Besides windows and roof tiles no other damage was experienced.

The next days I had to help to put undamaged roof tiles back in place and was very scared to work on the roof without any safety gear or protection, standing on light gutters or holding on with one hand on the roof edge trying to replace the heavy tiles with the other hand about three floors high above a brick covered area below. When needed, people can do what they would never have imagined that they could.

The V-1 often called 'doodlebug' or 'buzz bomb' carried about 1000 kg of explosives. Called V-1 after the German word *Vergeltungswaffen*, meaning vengeance weapon for the destruction of the German cities.

They were obviously unpredictable and made of cheap sheet metal. We do not know of course where the one that came down behind our house was heading. Antwerp perhaps. It would have been within their range of a maximum of 148 miles. Or was it intended for the critical nearby bridge over the Waal? Who knows? The gyrocompass-operated autopilot proved to be unreliable.

Treacherous they also were since some were equipped with a time-fuse which could delay the explosion as if it had been a dud and not exploded when it came down. Some were also launched from Henkel 111 bombers.

Fighter pilots discovered that when they were able to tip their wings under the short square wings of the V-1 they would immediately get out of control and crash preferably over the Chanel before reaching the English coast. The V-1's speed was about 400 mph, the North American Mustang's maximum speed was 437 mph, the Hawker Tempest 432 mph, the de Havilland Mosquito 380 mph, and Super-marine Spitfire 378 mph.

The Germans soon found this out and restricted their launches to weather conditions unfavorable for the fighters to attack. Hence the timing of the bomb behind our house was launched during the night.

There were other problems for our family. Since the city of Nijmegen gasworks hired my father after his employer died in 1943 during the occupation he was dismissed after the liberation. To earn some money, he worked on cars hidden under haystacks and other such places to avoid being confiscated and make them run again after four years. Not an easy task.

Thereafter, he had a job working in a garage in Nijmegen mainly working on German cars that individual American soldiers had captured and taken for their private use.

One evening when he came down from the ridge on his bicycle, a bomb exploded just ahead of him on a barn next to the septic tank service farm in our village, annihilating the barn. There had been no alarm signal. We assumed that the bomb probably was released from a plane in an emergency since no air battles were ongoing. There always were planes in the air.

The event was not so unusual. Unexpected things happen regularly in a war zone. While the barn and everything in it were destroyed, a goat in the barn stood blaring arrogantly in the bomb crater. Explanation? No idea. The only possibility we could come up with was that the air pressure from the explosion must have thrown the goat high up where he landed after the explosion's main damage was over.

Strange things happen during wars.

Lacking access to a much-needed cemetery, a temporary cemetery was established at the *Pensionaat*, our village's elite girl's boarding school.

Soldiers were buried where they were found, and it took years to move all to the impressive, very well-maintained cemeteries except those who remained buried at local cemeteries at the request of the local populate as a reminder of the sacrifice these young men made so that others could be free.

The atmosphere was one of fear and uncertainty from unpredicted events such as grenade attacks or from bombs released at random from planes that were en emergency. Danger from a V-1 could be seen or heard allowing some ways of protection or escape.

Severely damaged bombers also could be heard or seen too often followed with heavy hearts during their desperate attempts to keep the damaged plane under control. And there were many. Most bomber groups on their way to Germany flew over the Netherlands. There are many statistics that show the horrible losses.

US Air Force bomber casualties	9,949
US Air Force fighter losses	8,420
US Air Force crews losses	79,265
RAF bomber casualties	11,965
RAF Fighter losses	10,045
RAF crew losses	79,281
Total airplane losses	40,379
Total crew losses	1,58,546

There may be others who have more accurate statistics. The above numbers are mainly listed to give an order of magnitude and emphasize that a damaged airplane was not an unusual occurrence but a harsh reality.

The USAAF had more casualties even in comparison with the Marines. Survival was about 50%.

While the danger from V-1, damaged planes, and German air attacks was real, fearful, and destructive, it was a danger that allowed some way of action and attempted protection.

The danger from grenades, however, was unpredictable and erratic, allowing no defensive moves. Shells came at different times, at times multiple attacks, sometimes only a sole projectile. One never knew when to go or when not to go and thus restricted any stay outside the shelter to the absolute minimum.

Uncertainty led to fear and fear led to anxiety that remained for five months.

Operation Veritable: The Western Thrust into Germany

On February 8, 1945, Operation Veritable started.

After the Market Garden debacle, the Allied had no other choice but to attack the German Siegfried Defense line directly, a reluctant task that they had tried to avoid.

Even common citizens could understand that it was a time-pressing predicament for the Allied commanders because of the Russian fast approach toward Berlin, the ultimate goal.

Initial plans to attack in December or January were delayed by the 'Battle of the Bulge' that had taken ultimate demands on troops and supplies.

When the Germans expected the attack to begin, they blew up the dikes along the Rhine River with the intent to inundate the low region from Nijmegen in the Netherlands to Cleve in Germany.

The isolated French-Canadian troops on the frontline had to retreat to a few mostly damaged higher structures, they were wet, hungry, and cold, and later rescued by amphibious equipment operations. Their rescue slowed the operation down. Allied Forces reacted by blowing up part of the dike on the west side near Nijmegen to prevent the water level from becoming too high in the inundated lowlands.

The soldiers who were still in the area had no choice but to flee to higher levels leaving everything behind. Conducting military operations in an inundated region required totally a different strategy and amphibious equipment.

All hope to end the fighting by Christmas had quickly faded.

This poor-quality photo showing Buffalo amphibious tanks gives an impression of the horrible conditions the Canadian Army had to face. Grenade impacts can be seen on the church steeple and house.

This picture shows how Canadian troops with their Bren Carrier were hiding on high locations before being rescued by amphibious vehicles. It also shows the condition of many of the civilian houses.

There are always people who can find ways to make money. In the deserted, evacuated and inundated region were many farms and houses in which everything had been left behind when the order came to evacuate. People could only take with them that they could carry.

It had been a century-old custom to build farms on man-made hillocks called *tjerpen* in the north of the Netherlands, since flooding had been a normal occurrence before dykes were built. People could not stay there because they were isolated and without the normal provisions. But the Ducks and LTVs had no trouble reaching them.

Some returning Buffalos and Ducks came back from their patrols loaded with household items for sale at very low prices. And German weapons. All bounty came from German houses we were told to justify the civilian merchandise.

Were they? How could the houses at both sides of the border be identified by the soldiers? It was tempting. Stealing from the enemy was apparently not considered stealing but considered fair bounty.

My parents and many other citizens did not buy any of the quickly dispersing items such as radios, household goods, and even furniture because of their objection to buying what belonged to others and because they had no money to spend.

Another major attack to the north must have been no longer considered because of the low terrain and rivers that limited the use of armored equipment. After achieving the initial objective of freeing occupied befriended nations, the time had come for the Allied Supreme Command to decide how to attack Germany on the enemy's own territory.

It had taken longer than planned to reach the German border.

Fighting in friendly nations had been more restricted to cause less destruction and greater consideration to the plight of the civil population. They were friends after all.

Montgomery's plan to avoid a direct attack on the formidable Siegfried Defense line by a outflank movement through the lowlands and enter Germany away from their feared defenses had been admirable but soon had proven irrational to advance over multiple rivers and canals and its surrounding dressy lands that would not support heavy mechanized equipment such as tanks and artillery.

Operation Market Garden caused an enormous loss of equipment, valuable time, and, most importantly, very high casualties. The only option left was a direct attack on Germany's strongest defense.

Not only would the fortifications be the most formidable, but the German forces were also expected to fight with the courage of desperation on their own territory.

Even to us, citizens, it was obvious that the only choice the Allied commanders had was to attack straight onto Germany's strongest defense. It was just a question of when and where.

It had been a miserable cold, and dreary winter that followed the September failed thrust north, especially for the French-Canadian forces that had to engage the enemy for months under miserable conditions.

There was no need to tell us in early February that the major military operation into Germany had started. On February 8, 1945, the frontline stalemate ended with the thundering and deafening barrages of hundreds of artillery units and tanks.

For the local citizens, it was a loud signal announcing that the long-expected assault on Germany had begun. The sound was overwhelming! It seemed that there could not have been a square yard of enemy territory that had not been hit and destroyed.

Large piles of the copper shells of the projectiles appeared that later were converted to all kinds of objects such as lamps and umbrella stands by resourceful citizens, and many were bulldozed under.

As the days progressed a large number of Churchill tanks passed through the village on their way to the frontline. It seemed to us that the slower, but more flexible tank was preferred for the assault, also because the Churchill had a greater climbing ability to cross the expected tank traps.

Ducks were used in the inundated region to carry prisoners of war back from the front, where they were taken or surrendered, knowing well that any further resistance would only cause more casualties. Because of the inundation, amphibious transportation was needed. The maximum Duck capacity was 24 people, but some had many more and were overcrowded with prisoners of war.

For a while, we stood where the Ducks entered the inundated road at the bottom of the hill and we sang '*Wenn wir fahren gegen England*' (When we sail to England), their favorite motivational war song that had for many months blared from the radio stations in occupied nations during the previous years. They were indeed going to England but as prisoners of war. But we did not sing long.

There is something sad about a defeated army and seeing tired lost people who do not know what the future will bring after giving their loyalty and effort in vain. Amazingly some German soldiers could see the irony of it all and smiled and waved at us.

Remarkable were other Ducks passing by with only one or two prisoners with two soldiers standing behind them with loaded guns. I do not know how such selections could be so quickly made under war conditions, but they were.

Sitting next to a French-Canadian driver in one of those elevated high army trucks we came by a stranded English jeep stuck on the inundated low road from our village to the main bridge in Nijmegen. I expected the truck to stop and respond to the soldiers waving for assistance.

But my driver murmured only, "Damn limeys," and continued.

Not all Allies were apparently living in harmony even though this incident may have been an exception.

There had been some signs of preparations to attack eastwards into the Siegfried Line. The inundation of the lowlands brought different equipment such as the still 'Ducks' officially the DUKW with the D for 1942 the years of manufacturing, the U for the body style and utility, the K for all-wheel drive, and the W for dual rear axis.

Another amphibious war vehicle entering was the LTV Water Buffalo, standing for Landing Vehicle Tracked, an amphibious tank powered by a Continental radial aircraft engine that made much noise, it was called the Buffalo, weight about 18,000 kg, was 10'8" wide. The maximum speed was 25 mph.

About 18,000 were made. I saw how one commander had a horrible, mutilated face, obviously from being burned. But he served nevertheless as horrible as he looked. Only much later did we understand that the Canadian forces were undermanned and that recovered wounded soldiers were re-assigned to front duty again.

The Allies also brought the Goalie collapsible boats with a wooden bottom and canvas sides that could hold 10 men, which were used during the courageous river assault that saved the vital Waal Bridge. They arrived as a flat collapsed structure.

The canvas sides could be pulled up and secured with wooden sticks. Several were left for us to fish with hand grenades. When a hand grenade is thrown into the water, some fish are stunned and can be taken from the water by hand.

When my village friend Lambert Pelen left a hand grenade with removed pin in the steel columns supporting the overhead power lines for the streetcars, it fell and exploded. He was very lucky and survived. Months later when we were swimming in Het Meertje after the threat of war had faded in the summer of 1945, Lambert was still pushing small pieces of shrapnel from his legs.

Lambert survived because of another remarkable invention that changed society, the life-saving power of penicillin. Before the 1945 liberation, it was normal for people to have infections. It was expected, it was a daily reality. The only antidote was iodine and that hurt badly when applied to a wound.

Infections were so common that it was accepted as normal. There were different stages of infections, yet soars were expected, a change that is difficult to imagine in this age of antibiotics.

Was it true that over a thousand artillery and tanks were bombarding the *Reichswald* for twenty-four hours as it was rumored? We were convinced by the thundering noise.

Ignoring our headaches civilian conclusion was that the mighty Allied Forces should be able to just walk into a destroyed area. Not a tree, house, or bush was spared it seemed when I later overlooked the area from a high point in Groesbeek.

The attack straight into the Siegfried Line was given a name; Operation Veritable.

There have been many fierce battles during WW2, but Operation Veritable into the *Reichswald*, often translated into Imperial Forest, but I suggest that Government Forest is more accurate, has not received the attention and fame of other similar battles.

This most northern defense of the famous Siegfried Line started with an inundated area between the bridgehead Dutch town of Nijmegen and the German town of Kleve.

General Eisenhower's comments after this Battle of the Reichswald. "Some of the fiercest fightings of the whole war," he wrote. "A bitter sluggish match in which the enemy had to be forced yard by yard."

Field Marshal Montgomery wrote: "The enemy parachute troops fought with fanaticism un-excelled at any time in the war. The volume of fire from enemy weapons was the heaviest which had so far been met by British troops in this campaign."

The attack was organized in three operations from north to south, Veritable, Blockbuster, and Grenade.

It was known that the German military was short of manpower and supplies. The question that can be asked as it was at that time is why the common German soldier did not surrender when the odds were zero of a positive outcome.

They as well as everyone else knew that Germany would be defeated. It was just a matter of time. Too powerful was the Allied war machine, and too desperate short was Hitler's once proud military of manpower and supplies. Too unstoppable was the Russian onslaught.

The answer must be found in the mindset of desperate and angry men who saw that their country was annihilated day and night by armadas of US and British bombers, their houses burned, their cities in flame, and their families in danger. They were now fighting in their native country, no longer on foreign territory. Political reality may not have played a role in their thinking.

Desperados, they were, fighting for a lost cause and no longer cared about survival. In their hearts, they knew that their leaders had brought this disaster to themselves and their nation through an overconfident, cruel, and fanatic regime. But it no longer was of any consequence; they defended their families and homes, a strong human instinct.

Most former German soldiers I talked to after the war were glad to be alive, accepted the past as a total misguided and irresponsible support of a brutal and fanatic regime, but still were bitter about the fate they had to endure. Not surprisingly, many still yearned for the proud times when they participated in impressive parades and demonstrations.

For them, it had been all so promising, the restoration of German pride, the booming economy, the marches, singing, and the re-emerging hope for a better future, to see it all end in catastrophes, destruction, and death.

The German High Command determined that an attack in the northern section through the *Reichswald* was too difficult to penetrate. A more southern attack was expected. But in a very un-German move against his superiors Paratrooper General Alfred Schlemm (1894–1986) who oversaw the local defense, disagreed and strengthened the defenses further north in the *Reichswald* forest and moved some of his reserves to be nearer to the northern attack. His assessment proved to be right.

While the Parachute Divisions were well-trained troops, the two German Panzer Corps were at half their intended strength. That the unit held in reserve consisted of older men mainly used for guard duties (*Sicherungs Battallion*), a weak unit consisting of men with different ailments, were clear signs of German manpower and supply shortages.

On the ultimate north side were the inundated regions of the river Rhine Plain that had to be assigned to the Canadian forces. Fighting in inundated areas is difficult, especially for the attacking forces.

German losses were estimated to be over 44000. All these round numbers hide individual tragedy, the many more wounded and maimed for life, makes one wonder about its accuracy.

The operation was assigned to Montgomery's 21st Army. He called for:

3rd Canadian Infantry Division
2nd Canadian Infantry Division
4th Canadian Armored Division
15th Scottish Infantry Division
53rd Welsh Infantry Division
51st Scottish Highlands Division

After the operation progressed, he added:

43rd Essex Infantry Division
Guards Armored Division, part of the XXX Corps
The 11th Armored Division

This is only mentioned to emphasize the Canadians' crucial (and unfair?) roles and the one Welch division to lead the attack.

Some battles become famous historical icons and the source of detailed evaluation and studies. Examples are Thermopylae, Waterloo, Midway, and the Battle of the Bulge. Other battles are mostly forgotten. One of them is Operation Veritable.

The human loss of Operation Veritable by the Canadian and British forces was very high. 15,634 men died in February 1945 (Source History Hit). To us, civilians, the Canadians were unfairly assigned to the most demanding and dangerous operations while, as stated before, it was known that they were short in manpower and supplies.

Operation Market Garden's delay allowed the Germans to set up their defenses. Was Montgomery's decision fair to send the weakened Canadian units into the most difficult assignments?

The inundation of the river Rhine flooding the plain from Nijmegen to Cleve slowed the northern flanks because the area had to be cleared with the help of amphibious vehicles. In the historic reviews, no mention was found of the contribution of the two French Canadian regiments of the 3rd Canadian Infantry division.

On March 4, 1945, the forces of Operation Veritable linked up with the US Army advancing under Operation Grenade further south.

The Western penetration of Germany had begun.

An approximation of the Operation Veritable manpower and equipment was:

	Allied Forces	German Forces
Manpower	4,00,000	90,000
Guns	2,400	1,054
Motorized vehicles	35,000	700
Casualties	15,634 (4 %?)	44,239 (49 %?)

Information from Wikipedia; Operation Veritable. I would not be surprised if these numbers are approximations only!

The combined operations succeeded with the surprising crossing by Allied Forces of the bridge across the Rhine at Remagen on March 7, 1945, which made an attack on Germany's critical industrial center the *Ruhrgebiet,* possible that caused the final collapse of the Nazi regime.

The combined efforts of Operation Veritable, the crossing of the river Rhine, and the advancing Russians toward Berlin brought Germany to its knees. Canadian forces were able to cross the river after the German resistance declined and liberated the northern Netherlands, being enthusiastically and loudly greeted by thankful citizens. The Netherlands could breathe again.

A wonderful strong united national motivation and emotion emerged because people had known the scourge of oppression and now were free to build a new and better life from ruins and four years of occupation, war and misery, a '*Herrijzend Nederland*' a 'Resurrected Netherlands'. A better, fairer and more perfect nation was ahead.

At least, for a while.

On March 3, 1945, the Picture Post wrote.

"You see, the worse of the flooding isn't the holdup it causes in our offense—we can beat that—it's the suffering it brings on the Dutch. That's bad enough now, but its effects will go on for years. Their homes, their farms, their villages, and their churches are ruined.”

“Their beasts and poultry are all drowned. The labor they’ve put into their land for generations is swept away. And all to give the Nazi’s a few more weeks or months grace before we finish them. It’s a helluva war.”

True. The price for liberty, freedom, and self-determination can be horribly high!

But it also rekindles humanity’s most precious needs for hope, faith, and dreams.

On Heroism

The word hero comes easily and frequently on the tongue in modern society, where there are now numerous 'heroes'. The word originates from the Greek *Heros*, literary a protector or defender, often related to a superhuman person or effort.

Even the word superhero emerged for those invented illustrated figures such as Superman and Superwoman.

Wikipedia describes a hero or heroine as those selfless men and women, fictional and real, who, in the face of danger through feats of ingenuity, have shown unusual courage and strength.

Webster defines a hero as a mythological or legendary figure of divine descent, endowed with great strength and ability. In years past, a hero was someone who had shown the courage to perform acts and duties far beyond established expectations.

The meaning of the word has changed. The contemporary perception of a hero is someone who performs his or her duty under difficult circumstances, such as firefighters, police officers, soldiers, and medical personnel.

There are different acts of heroism based on a hero's mental and moral state of mind and intent.

The young Hitler Youth commander who stood in the middle of the Beek village square directing the fire of three half-tracks knew that he would be shot, and so did those snipers who climbed into the Waal Bridge structure. Dying for the *Fuehrer,* and the Nazi cause, they believed, was a courageous and honorable sacrifice. Were they heroes or brainwashed human robots?

As did the Kamikaze pilots in Japan and the millions who were victimized by clever propaganda and unrelenting mental pressure. The blind following of a leader or a cause is a human instinct. When applied at the right time and under the right circumstances, it can cause a calamity, such as the over 900 who committed suicide as followers of the radical Jim Warren Jones.

"And write to my mother that he did his duty," the young Nazis sang.

To die for the Führer was an honorable act. Iron Cross decorations were assured. Even maybe the one with the oak leaves. Were they heroes? Or manipulated youth?

Acts of heroism can be based on desperation, a feeling that nothing matters anymore. So why not do something radical?

Most of the German military were tired and exhausted after four years of hardship, traveling to and from unknown nations and regions, giving it their all, only to realize that all they fought and sacrificed for was all in vain.

Even worse, their burning native cities and towns after relentless bombing raids and the desperate letters they received from home, made some give up hope and surrendered to unusual acts of bravery, because they no longer cared.

Fighting somewhere on the Russian steppe, the Balkan, and the North African sands had been different from now being faced with a fight for their nation and homes.

Aware of all the death and destruction their country had inflicted on many nations for a cause they now realized was lost and evil, they no longer cared and surrendered to a dark future without hope and thus took extreme risks that could be called heroic.

Heroism can also be instigated by fear.

The core of the Nazi regime and those who had fanatically followed it by committing cruel acts against humanity beyond any form of justice knew that they would be held accountable and the verdict for their criminal behavior would be very severe. When in 1944, the signs were clear that it would be just a matter of time before the war ended, the Nazi leaders and fanatics knew that there was no way out for them.

Just as a frightened and cornered dog act ferociously. Some tried to commit acts of mercy and care to build a defense for their day of judgment. But most used the authority they still had with renewed last-ditch energy leading to reckless behavior that would lead to acts of self-destruction for their lost cause. Heroism? Or a form of suicide?

In modern times, even sports have their heroes and heroines.

Those who excel in a sport are now also depicted as heroes and heroines, which means they were outstanding. No longer is the idea of heroism associated with danger and more with exceptional performance, thereby causing a shift in the word's meaning.

The various descriptions of heroic acts all refer to a person who was courageous behavior is admired for courage and noble behavior, at times even offering their own life to save others.

Is a firefighter who saves a child from a burning house a hero? Or is any person doing what he or she is supposed to do or has committed to do? The same is true for military acts of valor and courage. Is the policeman facing dangerous, often mentally ill criminals a hero or doing what he or she is expected and trained to do? There are many dangerous occupations.

It is often difficult to determine what is expected from those who have voluntarily committed themselves to high-risk occupations, whether an act is within the expected commitment and duty, or if it is clearly a heroic behavior beyond duty and commitment. The answers are not simple in many cases.

Is someone doing the difficult but accepted duty assigned to him or her a hero?

The truest act of heroism, in my opinion, was committed by an unknown German soldier named Ernst Grewe. Not because he did some courageous act that saved lives. He did not. Allow me to explain.

Deventer is a beautiful '*Hanzestad*', an ancient medieval free trade town on the IJssel River in the Netherlands and still a wonderfully busy and thriving modern city.

Before WW2, a College for Tropical Agriculture was established in Deventer, named the *Koloniale Landbouwschool,* educating students for plantation expertise and management, mainly for what at that time was called the Netherlands East Indies and now Indonesia. The wealth of the Netherlands had been obtained from this colony for about three hundred years.

Many students were active in the resistance during the years of German occupation; as future professionals and leaders, students often committed themselves with the idealism of youth to what they believed the future should be.

A twenty-year-old female and five male students were assigned to prevent a small bridge near Deventer from being destroyed by the retreating German army in April 1945, only a few days before the war ended. The two German soldiers who were guarding the bridge were easily taken prisoner. Most Germans soldiers knew that the war was lost and would end soon. So why resist and fight anymore?

Then the students made the fatal decision of their lives by naively taking the soldier's weapons and letting them go. The returning un-weaponed soldiers must have had no choice but to report the incident and the location of the resistance members. A strong German unit was sent to retake the bridge.

Unable to resist a superior army unit, the students surrendered. Since they were carrying weapons as civilians in a war zone deprived them of the Geneva Convention rules about 'targeted killing'. Protected are only those who are not taking part in hostilities.

Since they were carrying weapons, it could not be claimed that they did not have a hostile intent and thus also not claim that they were 'deprived of the right of a fair trial'.

The 1929, convention rules were mainly directed toward military personnel. Execution of civilians may pass legal scrutiny, but not human and moral standards. General rules can only be part of a convention. Every event has its own moral conditions. The students did not cause any harm to anyone.

The military commander nevertheless ordered the execution of the students, an extremely cruel and immoral act a few days before the war would end, a behavior of a morally disturbed man, a sick mind and typical for the fanatic desperation discussed before.

Exact details are unknown, but after the retreat of the German army, a short time thereafter, shocked neighbors found next to the executed young students including the young woman, a German soldier called Ernst Grewe. We can only guess but must conclude that he had opposed the execution or did not want to participate as a member of the execution peloton and was subsequently also killed.

What could have been another reason for the German commander to kill one of his own men?

The picture below shows the 20-year-old member of the resistance Corry Westland van Baalen-Bosch during her and her five resistance comrades' funerals attended by thousands immediately after the war ended.

On the side was the coffin of a lone German, Ernst Grewe. It is hard to imagine what trauma it must have been for him to make this life-ending decision. It did not make sense to interfere or refuse.

His refusal did not save any lives and did not do anyone any good. Others would do what he refused to do. Nobody would be saved. It was certain that the war would not last but a maximum of a few days and thereafter he could start a new life. There would be a great need in Germany for a young man like Ernst after so many of his age were killed.

For his own people, he would be considered a traitor who refused an order during frontline conditions and for the Dutch and the Allies he was just another hated German.

Nobody would ever know or probably even understand his last deed. He had everything to gain by obeying; his life and future depended on it. He was forced to follow orders for actions he was not responsible for.

Yet he did what his conscience told him was the right decision even when nobody would ever know or recognize the courage to give up his life.

He sacrificed his life for no gain to anyone nor could expect any posthumous recognition.

It is the ultimate act of courage to sacrifice even your life without saving any person or expecting honor and recognition, to simply die voluntarily for what you believed to be right.

I often wondered how the soldiers that shot him could live with the memory of murdering one of their own for what he believed. Or had it been the commander who had shot Ernst as his last desperate criminal act?

Would the soldiers in the execution peloton also remember that they assassinated a twenty-year-old woman, who did no harm to anyone, at short range? By order, yes. But they killed her nevertheless! Merciless and cowardly.

The Deventer grand medieval church was totally filled during the funeral of the young students with people standing in the aisles, emotionally shaken by the elation of the regained freedom and the sight of a young woman and five young men who paid for it with their lives.

On the side was the coffin of a lone German soldier.

Time erases memories. People can blot an uncomfortable event from their minds. As if it never happened. Most of the time. But reality and truth will prevail. In the end, reality and truth cannot be suppressed forever.

There are no monuments to recognize his deed, no silent moments to remember and honor his courage, and no flowers at his grave.

Ernst Grewe was a common man, a minor soldier—a true hero.

And so were other young people like the medical students at the University of Munich, united in non-violent opposition to the Nazi s doctrines, called the 'White Rose'.

They committed the terrible crime of throwing pamphlets from university buildings. They were caught and beheaded. As the Nazi regime beheaded some 16,000, a bloody despicable way of execution.

Among them, was a 21-year-old young woman, Sophie Scholl.

Silent heroes they are now, forgotten in the maelstrom of progressing time and fading memories.

Young people who died for what they believed in, a better world, and paid for it with their lives.

They were true heroes. And deserve to be honored and called heroes.

Chronology of Major WW2 Events

In 1944, it became evident even to civilians that Nazi Germany and its cronies had seen their final days.

It was just a question of time and the emphasis became on how to minimize casualties and destruction. German propaganda still boasted that the application of new war technology would reverse the ongoing downward trend, but not even the most committed German believed it despite all desperate fanatic efforts to boost the sagging morale.

Civilians in the occupied nations regained hope but feared acts of desperation as were experienced during WW1.

Despite the unrealistic announcements of the clever Nazi propaganda, they could no longer deny that the once boasting and victorious German military machine was now trying to defend long frontlines in the east of Russia, in the south in Italy and the Balkan, and in the west in France after D-Day.

Radio news about battles near cities and in regions that moved consistently backward clearly showed retreating frontlines despite being called controlled strategic or tactical maneuvers.

WW2 was a global and confusing war with several changing loyalties. But it ended, fortunately, like awaking from a bad dream.

The following summary is intended to provide an overview of the world-changing impact of WW2.

1919	
June 23	Peace Conference at Versailles.
1929	
October 24	Stock market crash in New York. Germany in disarray.

1933	
January 30	Hitler obtains total power in Germany

1938	
September 29	Munich Agreement between Germany, Italy, France and Great Britain about Czechoslovakian independence

1939		
March 29	Germany attacked and conquers Czechoslovakia	
March 30	France and England guaranteed Poland's independence.	
April 7	Italian troops enter Albania.	
August 29	Russian-German non-aggression pact was signed in Moscow.	
September 3	France and England declare war against Germany	
September 27	Germany attacks Poland	
September 28	Russia and Germany agree to divide Poland	
October 29	England, France and Turkey agree to protect each other	
November 30	War starts between Russia and Finland	

1940		
March 13	End of war between Russia and Finland.	
April 9	Germany attacked Denmark and Norway	
May 10	Germany attacked Belgium, France, Luxembourg and The Netherlands	
	Capitulations: Denmark	April 10
	Luxembourg	May 12
	The Netherlands	May 14
	Belgium	May 28
	Norway	June 9
	French armistice	June 22
June 4	Last British and French troops escaped from Dunkirk	
June	Italy declared war on England and France	
August 8	Begin of the 'Battle of Britain'.	
August 19	Italy attacked Somaliland	
September 2	Formation in Berlin of the Tripartite Pact between Nazi Germany, Fascist Italy and Imperial Japan to form the Axis Alliance with the purpose of conquering and controlling the world	
October 12	Germany occupied Romania	
October 28	Italy declared war on Greece	

1941	
January 16	Conflict between French Indo-China and Thailand-Japan arranges truth on Oct 31
February 17	Non-aggression pact between Turkey and Bulgaria
February 22	Special German forces under Rommel attacked North Africa
March 25	Yugoslavia becomes an Axis Alliance member
March 27	German-friendly Yugoslavian government was removed
April 5	Non-aggression pact between Russia and Yugoslavia
April 10	USA occupied Greenland
April 13	Non-aggression pact signed between Russia and Yugoslavia
April 27	German troops in Athens
May 10	Rudolf Hess flies to England
June 8-14	England occupied Syria and Lebanon
June 14	Friendship Agreement between Germany and Turkey
June 22	Germany, Romania, Hungary and Finland attack Russia
Nov. 18	England attacked Libya
December 7	Japan attacked the USA at Pearl Harbor
December 11	Germany and Italy declare war on the US.
December 19	Hitler takes control of military from Walther von Brauchitsch
1942	
January 2	Japan takes Manilla on the Philippines
January 11	Japan occupied Borneo and Celebes
March 9	Java capitulates to Japan
May 2-6	US wins the decisive Battle of Midway Island against Japan
June 12	England and Russia signed a 20-year amicable relations contract
August 7	US forces landed on Guadalcanal
August 19	English raid on Dieppe fails.
November 14	English 8th army wins the battle of Al Alamein
November 8	English and American military enter Nord-Africa
November 21	Russia begins counterattack at Stalingrad
1943	
January 4-14	Casablanca conference between Churchill and Roosevelt
February 3	German troops surrender at Stalingrad
March 30	Allies conquer the Mareth Defense Line in Tunis
April 10	Mass graves of 22,000 murdered Poles discovered at Katyn
May 10	German/Italian forces surrendered in Nord-Africa Cap Bon

July 9 and 10	Allies landed in Sicily
July 25	Italian Coup d'état. Mussolini was arrested
September 2.	Allies land in South Italy
September 8	Italy surrendered.
September 11	German paratroopers free Mussolini.
September 14	Japan leave New Guinea
October 3	Italy declares war on Germany.

1944	
March 5	Russian spring offensive started
March 21	Germany occupied Hungary
June 4	Rome liberated
June 6	D-Day, Allies landed in Normandy
July 20	Attempt to kill Hitler failed
July 21	Americans land in Guam
August 2	Turkey ceased diplomatic relations with Germany
August 22-25	Paris liberated
August 24-28	Rumania capitulated
September 2	Brussel liberated. Finland ceased war
September 4	Antwerp liberated but under heavy V-1 attack
September 17	Operation Market Garden begins in the Netherlands
September 17-27	Battle of Arnhem lost by Allies. Frontline stagnates
October 4	British troops landed in Greece and Albania
October 19	Americans landed in the Philistines
November 4	Roosevelt for the 4th time elected
December 16	The critical Battle of the Bulge started in the Ardennes.

1945	
January 12	Russian winter offensive started
January 17	Warsaw liberated
January 22	Hungary declared war on Germany
February 6-12	Yalta conference between Roosevelt, Stalin and Churchill
February 8	Operation Veritable began
February 24	Turkey declared war on Germany and Japan
March 4	Finland declared war on Germany and Japan
March 7	Americans crossed the river Rhine near Remagen
April 12	Roosevelt died
April 24	Russian and American troops meet at the river Elbe
April 25	Opening meeting of the United Nations in San Francisco

April 28	Mussolini executed and mutilated.
May 1	Hitler and Goebbels commit suicide, Dönitz German leader
May 2	Russians enter Berlin
May 5	German troops capitulated
May 7	Germany signs surrender at Reims
August 7	First A-bomb on Hiroshima
August 8.	War erupts between Russia and Japan
August 9	A-bomb on Nagasaki.
September 2	Japan signs surrender on the Battleship Missouri.

End of WW2

Germany and Japan were forced to accept the terms of their surrender which included restrictions that would prevent that the two nations would never again be able to cause the immense suffering and destruction of WW2. But the political world scene changed and with it the needs for the two industrious nations to contribute to new alliances, also military.

The German after WW2 Restrictions.

While the devastating restrictions of the WW1 Treaty of Versailles are well known for their immense consequences, German and Japanese WW2 Restrictions are much less known now that these two nations are democratic and no longer form a threat to peace.

In 1990, German WW2 Restrictions were signed 45 years after the ending of the war and after the *Wiedervereiningung*, the unification between the *Deutsche Democratische Republiek* (communist region under Russian control) and the *Bundesrepubliek Deutschland*, the free western region united again.

Military:

A maximum of 370,000 person allowed in military service. (Present numbers have been much lower and too low in the opinion of major NATO partners.)

Only conventional weapons are allowed, no nuclear, biological or chemical weapons.

No foreign non-conventional weaponry is allowed within the former DDR territory,

Territorial:

No territorial expansion is allowed of any kind including former German-speaking territories in Poland and Russia. This clause was pressed by Poland to prevent 12 million Germans expelled from regions that had been German for many generations such as East Prussia.

Japanese WW2 Restrictions.

The surrender ceremony, as it is well known, was held on September 2, 1945, on the USS Missouri in Tokyo Bay. The conditions were abbreviated:

Elimination of all who have deceived the people of Japan.

Japanese territory to be determined by the Allies.

No military forces allowed.

Economic recovery allowed.

In the surrender, the emperor is not mentioned as one who misled the Japanese people because nothing can be done in Japan without the emperor's approval. MacArthur told Hirohito that he needed him to ensure Japan's recovery, a politically very astute decision, but very different from the way German leadership was brought to justice and executed.

In a deviation caused by political reality in Asia, Japan now has a capable military again.

The 'elimination of those who deceived the people of Japan' was only tried for a short period till the 1948 general amnesty.

Section 3: Reflections and the Lasting Impact of the War

Reflections

Peace, Elation, and Retaliation

There are moments in every life that are deeply inscribed on our souls, memories, and moments that cannot be erased as long as we can live consciously.

Such a moment came for me when many sirens started to blare that horrible penetrating sound of doom with its up and down vibrations, forecasting imminent danger and destruction, hopefully later followed by the relieving steady sound telling us that for the moment, the expected and feared danger was no longer an immediate threat.

But this time the same intense noise was different, expressing a new emotion. The fear that it had instilled in us with its penetrating sound of death and suffering had made us shiver as the announcer of approaching doom as it had been for four years as our daily fate, no longer needed to be feared.

This time the sirens announced that the war had ended, and peace and liberty were regained on that day of May 5, 1945, a simple reality with a deep emotional intensity.

I stood alone and I remember exactly where it was. I let the moment enter my heart and penetrate my mind, aware of its great significance. A moment of remembrance it was, not a moment of an ecstatic celebration, but more an intense mixture of sadness for all the death and suffering that the past four years had known and gratefulness that it ended.

Thinking about tomorrow and the future had been dominated by survival, but now reached beyond tomorrow further away again toward a better world while on its horizon glimmered hope again.

No more fear, no more intense anger, no more worries about food for the next day and protection against the violence around us. No more hate? Perhaps. Time was needed to dampen emotions.

One can only truly assess the value of freedom if it has experienced what it is to no longer be free.

Hearts were filled with renewed hope. We could start to dream again! A deep-felt emotion emerged to build a better, idealistic world.

For so many, it was a time to rejoice, to finally surrender to elation as an elixir that revitalized body and mind, to let go and allow the joy of life to penetrate the soul.

But it was not so for me and many others, more a moment of contemplation it was. Of course, hope for a better future had energized the spirit, but there had been too high a price to pay for so many, too much un-erasable sorrow and pain, too much permanently disabled bodies and minds, to many families torn apart.

I remember seeing the returning victims from the concentration camps, those who had known what hell on earth is, humans with only skin pulled over skeletons still in their demeaning attire, trying in vain to emotionally sing with broken voices the national anthem when crossing the border from hated Germany into native soil.

The distant cries of wounded and dying young soldiers emerged into memories, crying for help that would not come when it was too dangerous go for anyone to go and assist him. Even to bury them.

My contemplations were rudely disturbed when I walked back home and saw a crowd of village people gather around the very simple abode on the Pompengas, the pump street, a small narrow unpaved lane across from our house.

A family lived there very quietly with three little children in a very modest house. The husband was a truck driver before the war, a tall slender man, one of those lucky people who can eat whatever they want without gaining a pound. His wife was a shy motherly woman.

Because he could drive a truck, and there were not many truck drivers at that time, he was ordered, as my father was, to join the NSKK and drive supplies to the Russian front, a probable death sentence that would leave his family without his care and protection during the approaching battles between the advancing Allies and the desperate defending Germans only a few miles from their native land.

There had been only one possibility to avoid the trauma of his feared faraway death in the ice-cold Russian steppe, which was signing up as a member of the National Socialistic Labor Union. He did, giving a higher priority to the protection of his family than to political principles. He signed and chose to stay with his family during difficult and frightening times.

Some people have the courage to uphold the principle, faith, and belief, in spite of the consequences for themselves or their family, and even sacrificed their lives in the quest for the freedom to choose, for their faith, social justice and even die for it. Such heroic courage must be highly respected and admired.

But what to do when not yourself, but your family will become victimized by your decision? This truck driver chose as his first and overriding priority the care of his family. What would one do when faced with a choice between family and principle?

History knows deeds of immense courage to hold on to faith and principle no matter the high price of even sacrificing their loved ones as Jacob was asked to offer his son. And follow through, no matter what. But not everyone is endowed with the same courage.

What would be the decision if faced with the heart-rending choice between principle and family, between acting against your most ardent beliefs and the abandonment of your loved ones?

The scene before me made me feel miserable. And deeply disappointed.

The father, who stood outside with his wife and three children, looked at the scene before him, with apathetic eyes his shoulders bent low in a surrendering gesture, while his wife sobbed silently, huddling three crying children.

They stood silently how several villagers, who had demonstrated amazing courage and commitment in assisting the Allied Forces disregarding exposing themselves to death and danger, removed the meager possession from the house and destroyed it, ransacking everything they could find. It was a futile expression of anger punishing the victims and not the culprits.

Christians pray daily, "And forgive us our sins as we forgive those who have trespassed against us."

So often empty words only!

Yes, the sorrow of friends and family lost can be deep and devastating. The need for revenge and punishment for crimes is natural. Injustice, torture, and cruelty make one cringe in blind hate.

Arrogance and abuse suffered cry out for revenge. And yet we must prevent being as cruel as those we condemn, always considering what the intent of one's behavior was.

There were also grand ceremonies with many attending when girls who had relations with German soldiers had their hair cut in shame. Some even had their heads colored with paint. The hair will grow back again. It's not so tragic. Being publicly exposed and embarrassed may hurt more.

But could Heinrich and Anneke not truly have loved each other? Cupid can shoot his arrows very unpredictably. Should love be punished? If indeed it is love. And who will be the judge if anyone's love is sincere or not?

There were exceptions.

A young village woman had a well-known romantic relationship with a German lieutenant and was shunned by the community. She only had first-aid training. When Waalheuvel became an emergency field hospital, she assisted the doctors with operations under the most primitive horrible condition possible like those recorded during the Civil War, without any or inadequate anesthesia.

Both German and Allied wounded were treated. When Waalheuvel mansion, used as a temporary frontline field hospital, came under severe German artillery fire, she asked two upper body wounded soldiers, one American and one German, to walk with her through the fighting lines to beseech the Germans to cease shelling the emergency hospital. Their own wounded were there. Destroying a hospital is a war crime.

I saw her walk away with a white flag, accompanied on each side by two courageous wounded soldiers who volunteered to go with her, one American and one German. It takes more courage than can be described to walk straight through the fighting lines where soldiers from both sides were firing from their hidden positions and past wounded and killed soldiers.

She succeeded. The shelling stopped. It was rumored that the Germans took the American prisoner of war. I do not know what happened. But I do know that the shelling stopped. After her act of courage, she was not subjected to the demeaning hair-cutting ceremonies of other girls who had dated German soldiers.

After May 5, 1945, people were living in a delirium of freedom. All the anxiety of years under occupation and war conditions culminated in moments of elation.

Above all, hope returned, as the indispensable ingredient for the pursuit of happiness.

Overall, many elated citizens were enjoying the regained freedom but did not greatly admire the temporary authorities who took over government till elections could be held. Their attitude, at least locally, was arrogant and even insulting. The ugly forces of greed and power addiction emerged.

Bitter reactions could be heard from those who did the most dangerous resistance work.

If you have the right title and name, those who had cooperated with the Nazis were soon back in their previous jobs.

Some of the people who marched in front of the parades were never in resistance. Those who did the most dangerous work were nowhere to be seen.

After liberation, some temporary authorities took the possessions of the quislings and enriched themselves as the bounty of the winners.

I, unfortunately, must agree with the criticism of the early liberation authorities from what I observed. When the German army withdrew, they left a truck in perfect condition on the Holleweg because of a lack of fuel. Trucks were in great demand to transport debris and rubbish out of the destroyed city.

My father suggested letting the truck roll into our garage so that it could be made ready and useful again when petrol would be available. But his request was haughtily refused.

Some weeks later, the temporary authoritarian people removed the tires that were most likely sold for profit, and children played with the truck and ransacked what was left till it was only good for the junkyard.

Former military commanders formed an organization named OD for 'Ordedienst', (Keep order service) intended as a temporary authority to govern the nations in the vacuum that followed the liberation. But the effort was mistrusted by many who disliked their arrogance and feared a military coup.

The mood and mindset after the war were both elations and revenge blaming all events on the defeated Germans without evidence.

As an example, a week after the war ended, a tragic explosion killed 19 people among them four children in the village of Wijhe. A German prisoner of war had committed suicide after being forced to collect landmines and bring them to ammunition storage in a factory. That was what we were told.

Years later, however, an investigation revealed totally different events. Landmines were a great threat and the resistance leadership had ordered resistance members named *Knokgroepen*, fighting groups, to identify the location of the mines but leave the de-fusing to the experts of the Canadian army.

Young, undisciplined resistance members, among them my wife's brother, wanted to do more and forced a local farmer against his will to use his horse and cart for loading and collecting the still active landmines to transport them to a storage center and out of danger.

For some unknown reason, over 60 landmines exploded. It is assumed that a landmine must have been dropped or fallen, which ignited all the collected mines.

No German prisoners of war were involved. War stories are not always accurate and biased against the enemy. Some resistance members tried to be helpful yet acted irresponsibly.

But overall, also revenge faded as time progressed, and elections were held again. The Netherlands had the good fortune of having some modest leaders who put the nation back toward justice, democracy, recovery, and prosperity, leaders like Prime Minster Willem Drees who remained living in his modest row house without protection or servants while steering the nation through the extreme difficulties of decolonization.

His strong commitment to Benelux and NATO increased international cooperation while social security took a great stride forward during his ten years of dedicated service. One of the few political leaders who did not succumb to corruption or power, a leader who never became rich, who kept the interest of the nation far above his own.

A capable modest man he was, highly respected by friends and opponents, who should be a role model for the political leaders of our present.

On Military Culture

The intent of this impression about military organizations is not to claim any professional expertise about military capability, strength, strategy, or culture, but rather what common people saw and perceived from enemy and ally. It certainly is not intended to be a scientific tactical or strategic evaluation, just a snapshot from a civilian perspective.

Military cultures reflect the character and culture of the nation served influenced by the ruling political powers at a certain time. But regardless of the political forces at a certain time, soldiers reflect the fundamental character of their native land.

Since we could observe the forces of four nations who occupied our house, I took the liberty to briefly describe the impressions these military forces made on us ordinary citizens.

The German Military

During 1940 and 1941 the German military was confident and behaved accordingly. The average soldier seemed young and healthy and between eighteen and thirty years old. Germans like to sing, and they did so very well. From their point of view and subject to clever propaganda, they believed themselves to be invincible.

The easy way multiple countries were conquered only enhanced their sense of superiority. Higher-ranked officers behaved arrogantly; common soldiers were proud to be part of a well-organized military unit equipped with superior military and well-functioning tools of war, be it air force, army, or navy.

Every soldier knew exactly what to do and what not to do and would not change even when the situation they were in demanded it.

After the German invasion of Russia, things changed. The occupying forces left in our region consisted mostly of the old and the very young and were obviously not part of the elite forces. Maintaining order in an occupied nation does not demand the same strength compared to the needed expertise to fight a strong enemy.

Older soldiers became worried and feared for their families, who were increasingly living in true hellish conditions of burning cities. Armadas of thousands of bombers flying day and night toward Germany converted the once proud convictions of victory into unexpressed doubt, concern, and fear. It could be seen in their eyes.

The failure to invade England as easily as other nations had been, especially after it had been so loudly heralded, affected confidence and, for the first time, made it clear that the tide had turned.

The Battle of Britain was more than a gallant and heroic victory; its effect induced the notion of failure and limits of the thus far belief in the unlimited strengths of the German military. But fear for the Green Police and SS kept mouths shut. At times, only cautious mentioning of the hope that the war would end soon was expressed.

The very young serving in the Hitler Youth remained as fanatic as before. Brainwashing had been very effective. To die for the Fatherland was still a great honor. They still believed in the V-weaponry promised by the Nazi regime, V for *Vergeltung*. (Retribution)

Hitler and his cronies had developed a system of decorations that would recognize valor and courage, thereby giving the decorations great value and respect other than the many decorations allotted in other nations where decorations are given for minor services such as just serving somewhere so that they barely can all find a place on uniforms and thereby lose their meaning.

German boots with their steel knobs were intended to be loud, to impress so that one could hear them coming from afar and instill fear as well as respect and gave their boots a longer lifespan. Every aspect of the German military was carefully and cleverly designed.

Germans were trained well to do exactly what they were ordered. And did not deviate from the orders they received regardless of the circumstances.

A pilot parachuting from a shot-down German fighter plane drifted close over our house. I could see every detail when he was about fifty meters above us before he landed on the ridge called the Kopsenhof. His leg seemed to be severely wounded.

Yet he had his pistol in his hand when he landed, ready to shoot even in a desperate situation and with no chance of surviving. He was lucky that he passed out, which saved his life. His action was totally hopeless and absurd for his situation, but he followed orders until the end.

Just as the soldier who swam away from the American paratroopers in a totally hopeless situation, he and the pilot did what they were told to do, even when it did not make any sense anymore.

German strength was its high technology and natural sense of order, organization, and discipline. As in some Asian countries, their parades were impressive; participation seemed to come naturally, unforced, and without opposition.

Social class differences were strictly maintained in the military and accepted as in pre-war society. A very high number of German generals were aristocrats.

WW2 remained an object of interest to many people, professionals, and amateurs. One issue studied was who the best-trained and most effective soldiers were. National pride tends to influence the evaluation. Finnish soldiers who were able to halt Russian aggression received high praise. Yet the great majority of analysts agreed that Germany had the best-trained soldiers and the best tactics and strategies.

Books from Gudrian and von Manstein became part of the instructions in several nations. The German military was stretched over thousands of miles in the East in Russia, Africa, Italy and the Balkan, and after D-Day in Western Europe, which diluted their ranks to a degree that supplies failed while facing too many enemies with unlimited resources. The leadership of the Nazi regime caused their own demise through overconfidence and arrogance.

Relations of the ordinary soldier with the citizens in occupied countries were distant but neutral. Relations with the Nazi fanatics in the Green Police, SS, or higher ranks were confrontational, feared, and angry.

Every German soldier will follow orders even when those orders no longer make sense. It seemed to be their strengths and at times their weakness. Such as the order Hitler gave that no military unit would be allowed to retreat at the Russian front, costing thousands lose their lives.

Befehl isst Befehl was their motto; an order is an order, not to be deviated from, regardless of the circumstances.

The US Military

In his most interesting book, The Eagle Squadron, author Vern Haugland quotes English Vice-Marshal Trafford Leigh-Mallory's strong opposition to forming a squadron of American pilots because his experience was that "Individually they were charming, but as a group, they were undisciplined."

The Air Marshal may have been right but not understand that, at least as we saw it, the American Armed Forces are an assembly of individualists that conform to the fundamental nature of its culture and adherence to its tradition.

Our impression, as civilians, was that Americans will follow orders, but if the situation so requires, the average American soldier will not refrain from taking individual action if deemed necessary.

Several films clearly depicted his independent spirit, such as the TV series about The Flying Tigers and later the very popular film and TV series about the MASH field hospital. Individualism was also expressed in the freedom a crew had to give their plane a chosen name and illustration that went with it.

When Hitler ordered that the German Forces fighting on the Russian front were not allowed to retreat, his orders were followed even if a situation would have saved many lives if it was against the logic of the local situation.

American soldiers would act within the intent of an order or strategy but would not refrain from deviation to save life or an advantageous maneuver. That was our impression as civilians.

War in ancient times mostly marked two opposing armies lined up against each other, followed by a ferocious clash involving thousands of soldiers.

Modern warfare, as we perceived it, and certainly the war activities after the dropping of paratroopers, led to a totally distinctive style of war where opposing parties often did not know where or how strong the enemy was. In other words, the situation was much more flexible and at times confusing.

The American individualistic style adapted more easily to this style of warfare.

Nonchalant, calm, and at times close to overconfidence was the impression they made on us. They were healthy, well-equipped, and pleasant without the rigid seriousness seen by German troops.

Our perception was of course not objective, the Allies were the liberators, the brave men that gave us our freedom back, while Germans were the despised occupants who killed and incarcerated innocent men and women, causing the ruining of our cities and the desperate decline in the basic needs to survive, who took away hope for the future.

The US Paratroopers' sense of individualism and personal freedom typified the principles of their Constitution.

The 82nd Airborne called themselves 'devils in baggy pants'. I doubt other military organizations would call themselves in such a way.

Our impression was sustained by a presentation made at Fort Benning by a former German army officer in 1965, as reported in Quora in September 2021 by C. Dodd:

"Most European armies had a standard way of doing things. We could count on British or French to recon an area and then a few days or hours later they would strike at us in the area they had done their recon work. The Americans however drove us nuts. They could recon 4, 5, or 6 different locations and then hit somewhere else where they had not done any recon at all."

"Some of the scout units, like the rangers and paratroopers, would prowl around behind your lines like they owned the place. They drove us crazy. Because you never understood what they were up to or going to do."

Especially the sentence, "They would prowl around behind our lines like they owned the place" is what we observed. Germans would operate by the book, well-planned and cunning. Americans would operate as they saw things and then decide. Both reflected their cultures.

Fighter pilot Cadweller who fought in WW2 and the Korean War, wrote in his memoirs: "Fighter pilots are smart, strong-willed and independent. Getting them going in one direction was a major feat. They had to be led, not commanded."

While TV programs seldom reflect or even can reflect reality, popular TV series such as Mash and The Flying Tigers show the individualistic mindset and behavior that typifies the US military compared to the German and Japanese strict military discipline.

A similar spirit of independence within an organized military organization could be found within Australian troops as part of cultures that evolved from the hardship of the Outback and Death Valley, where survival depended on individual courage and a strong sense of independence.

When a high-ranking general accused a bomber crew of having bombed their own troops, which was caused by a misunderstanding, he was outraged and physically tried to hit one of the crew members who said quietly, "Don't do that, general. If you touch me, I knock you down."

The general backed off, told a local officer to take care of the case, and walked away. In similar Japanese or German circumstances, the crew member would be court-martialed and even executed for insubordination.

Such an incident would never happen in a German or Japanese military would not where even fighter pilots were following orders strictly and immediately.

The Australian military approach was like the US, for instance, during the 1942 Battle of Buna-Gona in Papua New Guinea, when General MacArthur ordered a direct attack on a Japanese stronghold. The Australian officers refused considering such an attack suicidal.

Instead, they developed an outflank strategy which took two days longer but saved many lives. Such subordination would not have accepted by the

German or Japanese military. MacArthur had no choice but to reluctantly accept.

War allows some strong, egocentric, talented generals to succeed in their endeavors. Pride and competition would then become of greater importance than the goal of defeating the enemy, for instance, the contest between Montgomery and Patton during the battle of Sicily, about who would take Palermo first.

Overconfident, and, at times, even arrogant generals like Patton, Montgomery, and MacArthur would never have been found in the history books if not a global war had erupted. They knew it and did their best to ensure they would not be forgotten.

The difference in military culture is, in a way, shown by their boots. This may sound ridiculous yet is not far from reality. The German army used boots with steel knobs that made the approach of a soldier loud and obvious with the intent to impress. In parades, the sound from the stamping of multiple high-stepping soldiers was impressive.

When an impetuous German SS Commander Waeckerle committed two war crimes on May 12, 1945 by using prisoners of war as a shield and dressing his own soldiers with stolen Dutch (enemy) uniforms, the Dutch troops recognized them immediately as impostors by their famous boots. They had changed to Dutch uniforms but not their boots!

During parades, the American military walks with a normal walking routine and not with a forced gait with the intent to impress spectators, another different reflection of cultures, one to show just a willingness to defend their country when necessary, the other to glorify military commitment and superiority.

The difference between officers and the common soldier in the European military was obvious and expressed in differences in uniform and behavior. When the paratroopers came down, we could not initially recognize the difference between the ranks and only later knew that a lieutenant just had a stripe on his helmet but otherwise was dressed the same.

In concert with the American Declaration of Independence stating that "All men are created equal."

The French-Canadian Regiments

We did not know or understand at that time to the conditions Canadian soldiers were forced to live with. All Canadian soldiers were heroes in our eyes celebrated with great enthusiasm in liberated towns and regions.

But we sensed that these liberators were not showing high morale but rather many gave a subdued impression. Only long after the war did it become clear that these troops were the victims of great political tensions in Canada where intense controversies were raging about conscription versus volunteer service between English versus French-speaking Provinces.

In the English-speaking provinces, 83% of the population had voted in favor of conscription. The French-speaking Provinces preferred volunteer military service. A shortage of manpower and supplies was the result. Wounded warriors were sent back to action after recovery as I saw how the commander of an LTV tank had a horribly disfigured face.

Canada had set a rather logical priority of air force first, navy second and army third, which makes sense considering Canada's geography, but did not stimulate army morale.

Troops had been sent to England with strict orders to defend England but were not allowed to engage in war on the Continent and were given, therefore, the rather derogatory nickname of 'Zombies'. Which certainly was not boosting morale.

When this was later changed in 1944, as mentioned before, Canadian troops were sent to free the all-important deep-sea harbor of Antwerp by capturing the islands along the River Scheldt that gave access to the harbor. Greatly undermanned, the Canadians suffered terrible losses. Such as the Hamilton Light Infantry, which suffered 50 % losses.

The lack of a clear motive and the political backing caused by political stress in their native country must have affected morale. We did not know why but sensed it.

The Canadians were however greeted with gratefulness and a well-deserved image of courageous liberators in the Netherlands.

But the wet, rainy, overcast, and dark winter climate during the winter of 1944 is depressive and their assignments in the inundated region long enough to affect the most resilient spirit. Language barriers also did not allow closer interactions with the village civilians, who nevertheless profited from their generous food supplies.

Month after month dreary days of mud, chilly winds, and unpredictable dangers must have affected morale. They were not unfriendly but somewhat distant from civilians.

As mentioned before, the relations of at least some Canadians with British Forces were somewhat stressed probably based in part on at times difficult relations in Canada and their perception, or perhaps misconception, that they were doing dangerous and unpleasant assignments while the English were 'parading among the jubilant population', especially enjoying many grateful and attractive young woman.

Yet the Netherlands owes its freedom to these gallant and courageous men, over seven thousand paid for it with their lives.

The British Army

We were of course not familiar with the controversies between Generals Eisenhower and Montgomery. It must have taken all the control General Eisenhower could muster when Montgomery tore his messages apart in front of him in Belgium with Eisenhower's calm response, "Remember Monty, I am your boss."

The British soldiers we encountered were polite, correct, and quite unruffled whatever the situation and maintained dry straight-face humor only they could produce, and we often failed to understand and appreciate. The modern meaning of the word 'cool' applies.

Even during the most dangerous situations, they were factual, analytical, and calm showing no external emotions and were therefore excellent fighter pilots.

The closer relations we had with an English and Scottish soldier were most pleasant. They visited us in our shelter, were obviously good friends, and interested in our situation. When things quieted down in April 1945, they invited my sister and other local girls to a very orderly dance night where she learned the 'Hokey-Pokey'.

An English soldier approached me and asked for the 'Lavatory'. I did not know the word. My sister came by, which made his request not easier as it turned out.

I asked her, but she did not know the word either. The soldier remained very polite but must have been in great distress. But English as he was, he kept his very correct behavior.

I am sure the average US soldier would not have hesitated to show that he had to pee, but not this very correct British soldier. It finally dawned on me what he needed, and of course, I showed him the way.

A difference with the Americans was the military level of bomber crews and, particularly, the pilots. While all US Pilots and Bombardiers were officers, most European Air Forces pilots were not. An RAF Lancaster Bomber shot down near my hometown had only a non-commissioned crew, the oldest was 21, the youngest 18.

Many fighter pilots in Europe are sergeants. The social class one belonged to in civilian life was also maintained in the military.

In the US, it was not uncommon for a reserve officer to change his career as a non-commissioned officer after his reserve status ended. That would not happen in most European military. Once you belong to a class, you stay in the class. You can be dismissed but not demoted to a non-commissioned status after swearing an oath as an officer.

When the badly damaged B-17 bomber of my friend Paul Collins tried to make an emergency landing at Woodbridge, a special airfield just across the English coastline to accommodate badly damaged planes so that they would not create an obstacle when crash landing for the hundreds of planes that also needed to land.

Their hydraulic system was damaged, and thus they had no braking power. Only two of the four engines were running. To slow the B-17 down they used parachutes to bring the plane to a standstill. Just about at the same time a British Lancaster bomber made a belly landing on a cross runway.

When a truck arrived to pick up the crews of both planes, my friend sat next to the Lancaster's bomber pilot.

"You applied parachutes when you came down, didn't you?" The British pilot asked with a typical British stoic expression.

"Yes, we did," Paul said and explained why.

"Somewhat ostentatious, what?" the pilot commented straight-faced.

Such is the English character and dry un-imitable sense of humor, just a moment after making a high-risk rash landing.

The Dutch Military

And native soldiers? Relations with the local citizens were relaxed and easy. They were family, friends and neighbors.

The leadership could be divided into a small often professional group who wanted to imitate the German style of discipline and order. And, I dare to say, in vain because the great majority of the Dutch military consisted of drafted men who would agree to fight for their freedom but really did not like to be part of the military scene.

During mobilization, most soldiers did not take their assignment too seriously and also did not hesitate to express their opinion that they would rather be in their private life.

A French general is quoted to have said that the Dutch military acted as "school kids on a day out."

It may not be flattering and overstated, but there is some truth in it that the average Dutch citizen considers himself, and presently also herself, 'citizens in uniform' willing to fight for freedom and ideals, but only if it is necessary.

The few officers who tried to maintain a German-style discipline with rigor and, loud shouting, mostly from the Military Academy were treated with shoulder-heaving expressions of indifference and disgust.

True leaders, such as later my Squadron Commander Col. Benjamins, could make your blood boil, yet everyone in the squadron would have gone through fire for him.

Following a German disciplined style had its most unfortunate and sad outcome. When during the Battle of the Grebbeberg, May 11 and 12, 1940, an artillery unit under Sergeant Chris Meier withdrew when his unit came under strong German fire.

He had asked for permission, but the poor communications systems prevented contact with his superior. A hasty field Court Martial was assembled at the insistence of General Jacob Harberts, Commander of the 2nd. Corps who wanted to 'set an example'. Sergeant Meier was found guilty and executed within the frame of the four days war.

"Here, take my jacket otherwise there will be holes in it," were said to be Sergeant Meier's last words.

This episode remained very controversial after the war, probably influenced by opposition from those who were involved. Strong anti-German emotions may have influenced the hasty verdict, an explanation, but not an excuse.

Sergeant Meier was an only child. General Harberts moved to England to stay away from the emotional attacks on his cruel demand for execution during the confusion of leading an obsolete army against a superior enemy.

Exceptions establish the rule, an Old Dutch verb says.

The average Dutchman is a pioneer, trader, and adventurer but not military-inclined and prefers civilian life.

The average Dutch soldier is just a civilian in uniform.

Caucasian Soldiers

A convoy of horse-drawn typical East-European V-shaped cars entered into the village with the obvious intent to stay there. They were Caucasian; we believed them to be from Azerbaijan but may have been from the Soviet Socialistic Republic of Georgia,

Were they really a military organization, these half-military soldiers who surrendered to the German war machine, put in German uniforms, and served without carrying any weapons? To us, they seemed more like rural farmers, who obviously felt at ease with their horses, mules, and conically shaped carts.

At nights, they would dance in a row holding arms around each other's shoulders on the melody of a man playing a tiny flute.

Their officers were German, living the high life in the local mansions, riding their magnificent horses for pleasure, while their colleagues on the Russian front were frozen to death.

The German doctor was especially respected and adored. The soldiers would run to him when walking to the Waalheuvel Headquarters to carry his attaché case.

Language differences made conversations impossible. Simple words were exchanged like 'Malaka' for milk. Lost, they seemed in a totally foreign world they were forced to live in as victims of military strategy and political chess games.

They were given a choice between becoming a Russian prisoner of war or for providing simple non-military tasks. They must have known how the Nazi regime treated Russian POWs horribly. For example, *Stalag* 326, where the arriving soldiers were described in the 1941 local paper as 'Primitive and lowest white race'.

Many starved to death, initially without any sanitary facilities, some who had to dig holes in the ground covered with leaves. The death rate of POWs from US and Western European nations was 1 in 30. In the Russian POW camps 1 in 2. What choice did these men have? It is estimated that over 3 million Soviet Russians died during the four years operation of the camp.

Once forced to wear German uniforms, they were doomed, seen as traitors by the Russians and as enemies by the Allies. A return to their Caucasian homeland was made impossible, and they did not fit into the cultures where they were forced to be.

We do not know what happened to them. They may well have been part of the Georgian uprising on the Dutch island of Texel from April 5 till May 20, 1945.

Desperate people will commit desperate acts. The Netherlands was liberated on May 5, 1945. Germany capitulated on May 8, 1945. The fighting on Texel ended on May 20, 1945, 12 days after the German surrender. The local Resistance supported the Texel uprising.

812 German died, 565 Georgians, and 120 Dutch people (Wikipedia)

Simple and kind these Caucasians seemed, farmers in strange uniforms, victims of political decisions beyond their control.

There was nothing military about them.

Summary:

Cultures change with time and political reality. Once, Germans admired the military need for order and discipline. War was seen as a field for attaining honor and heroism, as it had been in Sparta long ago.

Duals were expressions of pride and honor, while the facial scars left after a dual portrayed patriotism and courage. A facial scar was a distinct sign, so much desired that some were known to have a doctor make one, certainly safer and less risky than a life-threatening dual.

After suffering the immense catastrophes of WW1 and WW2, the present German culture is close to what it is and was in the Netherlands, a necessary but no longer hailed as a glorious endeavor.

This certainly was true during the years of insufficient funding and obsolete strategy and equipment before 1940 in the Netherlands when soldiers were put into peril because politicians did not allow them to have the necessary weaponry and ammunition necessary for a fair fight.

The fundamental difference between the Axis and Allies military that was that for the nations of the Axis; Germany, Japan, and Italy, war and military were a political tool, an obsession, and a source of pride.

For most Allied combatants, war was an unwanted necessity.

Statistics

Mark Twain wrote that statistics are pliable. They are!

Yet a great number of contemporary studies are based on statistics. And even more importantly, on judicial verdicts, especially when researching the use of certain products' effects on health.

Statistics give us impressions of impact, relative importance, and value. Statistics are approximations, however, indications of trends and seldom absolute. What is included or not to make the statistic, is often debatable.

A war's deaths and wounded are accumulated in statistics, very neutral and mostly approximations in which individualism and tragedy are obliterated. Often round numbers are given as approximations and estimates in which all human factors are lost.

The statistical numbers provide us with mere impressions. War is chaos, a chaos that often prevents the facts from emerging. So many died in anonymity, never known nor counted.

The following assembled statistics I retrieved from several sources with the intent to bring forward a sense of magnitude and understanding despite its lack of accuracy.

How many people died as a result of the trauma of WW2? About 3 percent of the 1940 population died during WW2, somewhere between 70 and 85 million. Truth is that these totals are just approximations. Other approximations I found were:

WW2 Battle Death	15 million
WW2 Wounded	25 million
WW2 Civilian Death	45 million

Such approximate numbers make one cringe because of the rounded-off totals with an accuracy of plus or minus one million people. Just round numbers with possible variations of millions up or down, millions of humans who succumbed to war's violence without knowledge of where or how they may have died?

"A single death is a tragedy, a million deaths a statistic," Joseph Stalin is quoted to have said. (Goodreads)

The numbers vary depending on the sources' accuracy and who is and who is not included. For example, my friend Pietje Heinen died when his bicycle collided with a tank.

Was he a victim of the war, or was it a civil traffic accident? Statistics give an order of magnitude and allow us to have a relative impression, but the accuracy can be challenged. Statistics are indeed pliable, as Mark Twain said.

The following numbers are from the information of The National WW2 Museum in New Orleans:

	Military	Total including Civilians
Soviet Union	8.8 to 10,700,000	2,66,00,000
China	3 to 4,000,000	2,00,00,000
Germany	5 to 5,33,000	6.6 to 8,800,000
Poland	24,000	56,00,000
Japan	2 to 2,10,000	2.6 to 31,00,000
France	2,17,600	5,67,600
USA	4,16,800	4,18,500
Austria	2,61,000	3,84,700
The Netherlands	17,000	3,01,000
Belgium	12,100	86,100
Canada	45,400	45,400
Total	2,34,23,800	6,33,03,330

Even more grounds for thought are the number of war casualties as a percentage of the 1939/1940 population as published by Wikipedia; WW2 Casualties.

Nation	Percentage of citizens killed
The Soviet Union	13.7 %
Germany	8.86 %
Japan	4.43 %
The Netherlands	2.41 %
France	1.44 %

Belgium	1.05 %
United Kingdom	0.92 %
USA	0.32 %
Nation	Percentage of citizens killed

To put the horrible losses of the Russian Military in perspective; during the Battle of Stalingrad defensively from July till November 1942 and offensively from 19 November 1942 till February 1943, 418.000 men were killed, more than the total number of casualties the US suffered during WWII.

Still controversial is the 'terror bombing' of Dresden, a grand city of art and culture called 'the Florence on the Elbe River', on February 13-15, 1945, a city without industrial importance.

The official count was that between 25,000 and 30.000 civilians died, but the unofficial estimates are as high as 250,000, (Encyclopedia Britannica) because the city was crowded with refugees fleeing the advancing Russian army fearing Russian wrath for the immense suffering caused by the German attack on their nation. It is another example of a lack of factual knowledge leading to inaccuracy.

Prime Minister Winston Churchill had supported the bombing to put more pressure the Nazi leadership to surrender. It will never be known how many died in Dresden nor who they were. My aunt, Traudel, who was from Dresden, told me horrifying stories of how corpses were piled on heaps and cremated with flame throwers to avoid disease from the thousands of decaying corpses.

In February 1945, the war was in its last phase with the fighting now on the east and west fronts within German territory.

Was the bombing of Dresden an act of retaliation for the bombing of London, Coventry, Warsaw, Rotterdam, and many others European cities? If so, the Allies descended to a level so strongly condemned of their enemies. We live in a time where war crimes and acts against humanity are investigated and even punished.

While it is an almost impossible task to judge motives and circumstances of alleged criminal behavior, or to create an awareness that cruelty and a total lack of respect for human life is being investigated, it does show that even during war conditions, moral behavior is being questioned and even brought to trial.

What can be concluded from such numbers? It will not be easy to find rational and reliable answers. If the statistics are correct one of every seven Russians died in the war, which must have impacted the mindset of later Russian generations and it does explain to a degree the mindset of the Russian preset generations whose ancestors suffered immensely from West European aggression.

The break-up of the Soviet Union was nevertheless peaceful. For a common citizen, it seemed a wonder how the once global power of the Soviet Union broke up into sixteen independent nations without bloodshed. A truly magnificent achievement. Positive historical happenings unfortunately do not receive much attention in the media.

What can be concluded from these statistics is the impact the war had on nations and cultures. Even the present way nations react in contemporary times can be in part explained by the suffering their people had to endure, which, on a percentage basis means that the Russian citizens and soldiers suffered over forty times more casualties compared to US citizens.

Suffering can of course not be expressed in numbers even though the US legal system has found that suffering and pain can be expressed in money.

Traumatic memory does not end with the generations exposed to a war's horror but affects the mindset of many generations thereafter. Just as the Civil War in the US affected the mental state of many generations after, the war was long over. And still do.

Statistics are helpful and useful and provide an order of magnitude, relativeness, and size, but require awareness of inaccuracy and a good understanding of the criteria used to make the statistic.

Prosperity and Adversity

Some two thousand years ago, Roman philosopher Horace wrote:

"Adversity has the effect of eliciting talents which in prosperous circumstances would have lain dormant."(*Quintus Horatius Flaccus 65-8 BC.*)

Can anything positive come from adversity, from a war's violence and misery? Yes, it can, as much of a paradox as it may seem!

Periods of trauma and desperation may make it easier later in life for survivors to be more content and happier during better years because war experiences set the horizon of expectation at a lower level.

When someone has known hunger, adequate supplies of food are not accepted as normal, but as an enjoyable blessing. When someone knows the chilling effect of fear, times of tranquility and peace are deeply appreciated and not accepted nonchalantly as the way things are expected to be.

When someone has suffered the scourge of oppression, freedom becomes a precious gift and no longer a blasé entitlement!

Any person who has lived in a paradise of abundance and never has known adversity, prosperity becomes the expected condition and a 'deserved' right leading to over-emphasizing rights and a decline in personal responsibilities.

When there is nothing materialistically to aim for, mental illusions and extremes become attractive, often ending in addiction and demise. The emphasis on self becomes dominant while responsibilities are evaded.

When people have everything, they want, the expectation level is so high that very little is appreciated. I watched children go through the abundant packages under the Christmas tree, opening one gift after the other with an 'Oh, cool' to throw it aside, grabbing for the next present.

There seemed to be less joy in receiving and ever higher expectations, instead of receiving one orange for Christmas as a precious gift and saving slices over several days during less prosperous times.

Prosperity also diminished the care for what one owns. "If you do not take care of what you own, you are not worth having it," my generation once was taught. A contradiction in recent times of a 'throwaway culture'.

Most of all, hard times, such as wars or epidemics, strengthen the ability and resilience to deal with adversity, just as pioneers and discoverers endured pain and hunger to reach a vision of the future or fight for rights and freedom.

During times of personal trauma, life can be experienced with great intensity. Many great artistic achievements were created during times of depression and sorrow.

Prosperity, however, enhances a shallower experience of life, developing in the precepts that it is our right to have all we want and desire.

Adversity can lead to the use of unknown talents and energies while prosperity seems to lead to complacency and unrealistic expectations of a perfect, non-existing world.

Prosperous times tend to enhance unrealistic expectations and diminish the inner and mental strengths to cope with crises, setbacks, and bad luck.

The emergence of WW2's technology and its subsequent fast development will need careful human control and consideration.

Despite all death, suffering, and fear, during the years of WW2, many lived life with a deep-felt intensity, questioning life's meaning and purpose, searing for peace and contentment, and eliciting all their God-given talents.

Some researchers submit that experiencing negative emotions can ultimately lead to happiness just as failure can boost learning and experience.

To suggest that suffering and hardship can be beneficial is of course a paradox and certainly has limits when the suffering and pain experienced was so catastrophic that it irreversibly ruined life and living.

But it is true that an easy and prosperous time can lead to a more shallow and relaxed way of life while times of test and trial tend to stimulate greater intensity and the application of all given talent.

Hindsight and Enigmas

To analyze what could have been done better is a sensitive matter. Difficult decisions had to be made based on known and unknown information and, above all, the mental state of the moment.

It is always easy to evaluate decisions after all facts are known. Generals and government leaders had to make very difficult decisions that affected the lives of millions, often with inadequate or questionable information.

These decisions were made during the emotions and mental state at a specific time. It must have been a horrifying decision for President Truman to choose between hundred-thousands or millions of deaths when he considered dropping the atomic bombs.

Yet looking back as a civilian witness of the war, two events raise questions about decisions about the liberation of Europe by Allied Forces, not intended as criticism but to understand why and how two major decisions were made that jeopardized the lives of thousands of young men in battles and many innocent citizens. Decisions that must have been made on available, but often scarce and incomplete intelligence.

In his book *The Secret War*, Max Hastings wrote, "Almost everyone who participated in the secret war lied; it was their job to do so." Which must have made it very difficult to separate facts from fiction.

This author also quotes one famous Bletchley's Park expert; "Euphoria distorted the judgment of Allied commanders, blinding them to both intelligence and prudence." A harsh judgment of those who had to make extremely difficult decisions during very confusing times. Nevertheless, there is enough evidence that mistakes were made that were irrational and cost the lives of thousands.

D-Day Location

One enigma is why on D-Day the attack on the European continent was made in Normandy with its steep cliffs and difficult terrain. And far away from the ultimate goal, Germany. The decision was based at least partly on intelligence from the French resistance that the German defenses were weaker at that location. But was this so?

Later discoveries clearly showed that Germany had built amazing underground structures such as the camp near Maizy with the most modern and deadly weaponry and communication systems that caused the Allies numerous losses of life and wounded. In addition, Germany had superior tanks and weaponry that could move fast along the coast.

The resistance without a doubt did all they could to transfer the best information they could find, yet their possibilities were very limited, and thus their reports could not be totally relied upon. The information that the resistance so valiantly gathered could not have been very reliable. The Nazis were very clever in keeping large regions impossible to penetrate by civilians and were accessible only to their own military.

It is done, and it is of no use to keep questioning the past. The devastating experience during the failed invasion of the Dieppe Raid on August 19, 1942, where tanks just got bogged down in the sandy soil must have made commanders very concerned about soil that would make the effective application of armored vehicles difficult.

Nevertheless, invading the European continent further north on or near Belgian territory would have had the advantage of flat terrain, shorter distance to cover across the Canal of flights and landing forces thus less exposure to enemy fire. The point of entry would have been closer to the vital supply ports of Antwerp and Rotterdam and what ultimately was most important of all, much closer to Germany.

It took the Allies from June till February to reach the German border some 400 miles in over seven months. From the Belgian coast to Germany would have been only about 150 miles.

It has been said that General Eisenhower expressed his understandable anxiety about his decision to attack Normandy when he allegedly said, "I hope to God that I know what I am doing."

He had many reasons to be concerned. The gravel beach of Slapton in Devon had been selected for a training exercise because of its similarity with Utah Beach in Normandy. Exercise Tiger from December 1943 to April 1944 was an unmitigated disaster that cost some 750 young men their lives by friendly fire and German E-boat attacks (small and fast torpedo boats in Germany called *Schnell Boots* or S-boats).

The D-Day rehearsal had been a failure. No wonder that General Eisenhower had grave concerns about his most difficult and aggravating decision that would cost so many soldiers their lives while the outcome was far from certain.

Operation Market Garden

After France was liberated with the joining of the D-Day and Southern Armies, the Allies were ready to focus on their ultimate target: Germany.

Civilians were unaware of the actual strategies developed by the Allies but it did not take a military expert to know that:

The Battle of the Bulge proved that Germany still was a military power. Desperate people are dangerous. The Siegfried Defense was known to be a formidable defensive structure. The Russians were advancing toward Berlin forcing the Allies to do all that they could to prevent Russia, an ally in the quest to conquer the Axes, yet still a mistrusted Communist country, would take all of Western Europe despite the Yalta agreement.

Any attempt to outflank the Siegfried Defense was initially considered impossible because of the low terrain and the many rivers and canals that needed to be crossed. General Eisenhower apparently preferred a broad front strategy that would cause force the desperate German defenses to spread their forces thinly that also had to face the fierce Russian attack from the east.

Germany was short of supplies as a result of the daily bombing and a lack of basic resources such as fuel. The very wide frontline would have been impossible to provide adequate manpower and supplies. Somewhere a weakness had to be expected and could be taken advantage of, especially with the fast-motorized divisions under the already legendary General Patton.

Field Marshal Montgomery nevertheless proposed a strategic plan to go around the Siegfried Line Defenses via the Low Countries to attack the all-important industrial area of the *Ruhrgebiet* on the north side of the river Rhine that had for centuries and since the Roman Era a cultural divide.

His plan was to end the war by Christmas 1944 based on the knowledge that the *Ruhrgebiet* was essential to supply the German military with the needed supplies.

Both Generals had a lot of experience and knowledge about military operations and had the advantage of intelligence information. It was not an easy task for General Eisenhower, however, to keep unity and cooperation between the Allied Forces.

The distribution of supplies remained a very sensitive subject. But General Eisenhower gave in to Montgomery's plan, probably only reluctantly to keep peace and cooperation with a known arrogant Field Marshal whose plan had the approval of the very influential Prime Minister Winston Churchill.

Author Max Hastings wrote in his book *The Secret War*:

"The little Field-Marshal's neglect of crystal-clear intelligence became a major cause of the Western Allied failure to break into the heart of Germany in 1944."

It seemed so obvious that it would be very hard to drive The British Relief Force eighty miles up a single Dutch road when the surrounding areas were impassible terrain for mechanized weaponry.

The question can and should be raised even by non-military trained civilians, whether it had been a reasonable assumption for the paratroopers of Operation Market Garden to take eight passable undamaged bridges of which it was known that they all were wired with explosives that could easily be activated on a simple command of the retreating Germans?

Or to fight in a region where all heavy military equipment such as tanks and artillery could only advance over one main road since the lowlands were too difficult for tanks and other heavy equipment?

It is sad that the English army such as the XXX Corps blamed the failure on the American paratroopers while the highly respected American journalist Walter Cronkite who landed with a glider of the 101st Airborne stated firmly that "They (the paratroopers) kept the road open for the second British army and it was their failure that they were delayed."

The fact is that neither the American and British Airborne nor the British Second Army should be blamed for the debacle. The fundamental mistake was made by the planner of the largest airborne operation of WW2 who assigned gallant and courageous troops to an impossible mission.

***

Why question what happened so long ago? Because too many young men died needlessly. It should be questioned not with the intent to criticize but to prevent such fundamental and wrong decisions will never be made a gain. It happened in WW1 as so excellently reported in Van Praag's 1939 book Days of Our Years that generals made knowingly or unknowingly fundamental mistakes that cost thousands of young soldiers their lives. And twice as many civilians.

Every person should be held responsible for his or her decisions. Even generals are servants of the people of their nations and should be accountable for what they did or failed to do.

Questions should not be asked to condemn but to learn from failure.

Justice, Injustice, Revenge and Reparations

A German Proverb: *Recht has nicht der, der Recht hat, sondern der, der Recht bekommt.* Justice is not achieved by those who have rights, but by those who receive it.

Fanatic national and intolerant political systems by the leadership of three Axis nations, Germany, Japan, and Italy caused immense suffering during WW2. Geneva Conventions rules were violated, war crimes were committed, and moral and basic human dignity standards were ignored.

What happened to bring their main responsible leaders to justice?

A legal judiciary prosecuted German war crimes.

Japan's war crimes were mainly judged by one man, General MacArthur.

German war crime prosecution continued till at least 2022.

Japan's war crimes prosecution ended in 1949.

Italian leader

Benito Mussolini was executed, and a lynch mob mutilated his body.

Germany's leader Adolf Hitler committed suicide.

Japan's leader Emperor Hirohito remained a highly respected ruler in his palace surrounded by wealth and service.

Should circumstances of political reality compromise justice? General MacArthur's decision to 'use' the emperor's influence to bring Japan back to recovery from a devastated nation was certainly effective and probably considered reasonable. But at the cost of justice.

The 1925, Geneva Protocol banned biological and chemical warfare. The Japanese representative signed the contract. But the agreement was never ratified by the Japanese parliament, the Imperial Diet, and thus was not legally binding. It was a clever way to show a friendly face to the world while allowing them to do what they wanted.

One example was among others the Japanese creation of Unit 713 in Manchuria to research biological warfare under the flowery name of 'Cherry Blossoms in the Night', located in a former lumber mill.

The name the organization was given was also very misleading: 'The epidemic prevention and water purification department' it was officially called.

In this horrible place over three thousand humans, including children and pregnant women, were subjected to incredible torture and death, sarcastically referred to as 'logs' because it took place in a sawmill.

Besides many others, the experiments included.

- Injecting potent bacteria and viruses
- Exposure to infested mice and fleas
- Syphilis experiments after pregnancy by rape
- Frostbite experiments till limbs were frozen
- Pressure experiments till death
- Centrifugal experiments till death
- Vivisection

While German concentration camp criminals were searched worldwide, prosecuted, and punished, Japanese researchers, criminals under the leadership of Shiro Ishii, who with his Unit 713 committed the most horrible and most terrible human experiments on thousands of prisoners, male and female alike. Yet he died peacefully in 1959 and was never prosecuted in exchange for handing the data accumulated from his horrific experiments over to the US Government.

A somewhat confusing issue is the way Western civilization and Japanese culture evaluate responsibility. In Western civilization, the emphasis is on the individual who committed or instigated criminal acts. Japanese society has a broader approach of *'rental'*, solidarity, which in essence holds the organization or group responsible.

If a player in a sports team for instance commits an offense, the entire team is held responsible according to Japanese judgment. Should Japanese war criminals be prosecuted therefore by the laws of Japan or Western civilization?

Fair and legal justice is not always simple. Should justice be based on the principle of 'an eye for an eye and a tooth for a tooth' as propagated in major cultures and religions or should forgiveness be considered for repenting sinners as it is part of Christian theology: "Forgive us our sins as we forgive those who sin against us." which recognizes that evil exists and that nobody is perfect.

A general amnesty was declared in Japan in 1949, four years after the war ended.

The principle that justice should be blind was replaced in Japan's case with an open-eyed priority on economic revival and practical reality.

Atrocities, torture, cruelty, suppression, and death cry out for justice and revenge. Callous disrespect for humanity, evil pleasure in suffering, and fanatic blindness that justified genocide cannot and must not escape objective justice. Political maneuvering should never suppress justice.

Former researchers of the infamous Unit 713 later obtained high positions in Japanese post-war society, such as the Governor of Tokyo, and head of the Japanese Olympic Committee, a clear and obvious indication that, in contrast with the German general attitude, Japanese society never accepted remorse for past criminal activities.

Justice should not be influenced by revenge as a retaliatory action against injustice with the intent to harm the wrongdoer. Retaliation is a violent response to injustice. Retribution seeks a moral response to injustice.

The Nuremberg Trial of German war criminals was revengeful and retaliative. MacArthur's decisions regarding Japan were practical, political, and economical, allowing Japan to become a respected and prosperous nation quickly, but justice was ignored.

A comparison.

The German Nazi government committed hideous crimes by murdering millions in concentration camps.

Japan committed hideous crimes, especially in China, Korea, and many other Asian concentration camps. Prisoners of war were tortured and cruelly executed. MacArthur decided that the emperor should remain outside the criminal court although there was clear evidence that nothing happened in Japan without the emperor's consent.

Japanese trials were limited to what MacArthur decreed to allow Japan to recover sooner. The recovery needed the emperor's support as the absolute authority of the Japanese culture and nation.

Germany admitted their wrongdoing and erected monuments in remembrance of the victims of past atrocities.

Japan denied the atrocities committed during the war and instead built monuments in remembrance of the 'victims' of the A-bomb.

Prince Azaka, who condoned the massacre, torture and theft of 300.000 people in Nanjing was never prosecuted because he was a member of the royal family.

German Arthur Seyss-Inquart, who saved thousands of lives by allowing Operation Manna and prevented the military scorched earth tactics, was hanged.

To investigate and prosecute the war crimes Japan committed during WW2, the International Military Tribunal for the Far East (IMTFE) was established consisting of representatives from eleven countries, Australia, Canada, China, France, India, the Netherlands, New Zealand, and the Philippines, the Soviet Union, the United Kingdom and the United States.

With such a variety of experiences and a mixture of legal experts from various legal systems, major disagreements could not be avoided about whom to try or how to try them. The first IMTFE convened in April 1946 and lasted two and a half years. One major issue was whether Emperor Hirohito was responsible or not.

Since the well-intended multiple-nation tribunal could not reach a unified way of prosecution, the Supreme Commander of the Allied Powers, General MacArthur, acted and arrested 39 suspects, most of whom were members of General Hideki Tojo's war cabinet. Six defendants were sentenced to death and 16 to life imprisonment but received clemency soon thereafter.

The IMTFE did what was possible with such a variety of nations and different legal practices and laws. But in the end, whatever happened was the decision of one man, MacArthur.

Mac Arthur's statement that occupations can become more of a problem for the occupational forces than for those occupied was practical and allowed a fast recovery. Nevertheless, justice was ignored for practical political reasons.

It has been claimed that the emperor was only a puppet in the hands of his military commanders, which may well be true. Nothing happened, however, without the consent of the god-like monarch. The facts are that the atrocities committed by the Japanese equaled the Holocaust.

Japanese cruelty knew no limits. There are many examples and incidents. In Janjing, two officers—Yoshiko Mukai and Tsuyoshi Noda—had a friendly contest in 1939 about who could kill the first one hundred Chinese including women and children with their swords. Even more chilling were the mass rapes of women and young girls often ending by the soldiers by thrusting their bayonets into their victim's vaginas.

While attempts to do justice in Europe were in general fairer, exceptions were still made if it serviced the Allies such as Wernher von Braun, an SS *Obersturmfuerer*, (Major) who developed the V-2 that cost thousands their lives or life-long mutilation yet became with some 127 other Nazi engineers and scientists respected US citizens.

Von Braun was sitting between President Kennedy and Vice-President Johnson during presentations.

An overview of how justice was executed for the Axis nations:

	Japan	Germany
Were human rights violated	Yes	Yes
Were inhuman experiments committed?	Yes	Yes
Were all those who committed the atrocities prosecuted?	No	Yes
Did the nations admit guilt and accept responsibility?	No	Yes
Were victim memorials erected and maintained	No	Yes
Were reparations paid to victims?	No	Yes

To maintain fair and neutral justice during and after a war is probably an illusion. Did the Allies also commit war crimes by bombing cities like Dresden or Tokyo where only defenseless citizens were the victims? War is violent and cruel which leads to humanity's most base instincts.

In Europe, German prosecution continued of everyone involved directly or indirectly for decades and even more than seventy years after the war.

In Japan, all prosecutions ended as early as October 1948.

In Europe, enemy leadership was held accountable wherever they could be found. A hundred-year-old guard of a German concentration camp was put to trial in 2021, as was a 96-year-old secretary, 76 years after the war and 73 years after the Japanese amnesty!

After WW2, there were immediate executions in several occupied nations, for instance, the leader of the Dutch Nazis, Anton Mussert as there were for the leaders and guards of the concentration camps, who were immediately executed both men and women, some after a trial, some without a trial.

For justice to be fair, it must be swift as required in the Constitution Amendment VI "the accused shall enjoy the right to a speedy and public trial," a requirement we seem to forget when a person can be twenty years on death row and thereafter executed. Yet if justice lacks objectivity in an atmosphere of emotional revenge, verdicts may prevent fair and objective justice.

German Nazi leader Arthur Seyss-Inquart was hanged in 1946. Yet by allowing foreign and enemy bombers to drop food during intense fighting conditions, which he did even when he easily could have refused because it was an enemy operation, he saved thousands of lives. Should not that also have played a role in the verdict? Or that he limited the scorched soil demand from withdrawing military leaders?

Should Rudolf Hess, after his aborted attempt to negotiate peace deserve a lifetime of solitary incarceration?

Most early verdicts of Nazi war criminals were reduced significantly in the 1950s only some five years after the war, an indication that the many verdicts had been made when the emotional cry for revenge was high.

"The passion and glamour of the time" Supreme Court Justice William O. Douglass called it in his critical commentary of the Nuremberg trial.

Most disturbing was the final phase of the Nuremberg trial, the execution. How could the US military select Master Sergeant John C. Woods as executioner? Woods was previously discharged for being psychopathic in 1930. Execution by hanging was selected to emphasize the severity of the crime. Execution before a firing squad was considered too honorable.

Woods had been the main executioner of the hanging of 34 US soldiers. He had lied about his previous hanging experience. Woods and his assistant military policemen Joseph Malta may have intentionally calculated the length of the ropes too short so that the accused would not die from a broken neck but from a slow suffocation.

Was the opening also made purposely too small so that the convict had bleeding head wounds during the fall? On October 16, 1946, ten men died in the gymnasium of the courthouse in an apparently botched hanging that strangled several instead of a quick death. It took Joachim von Ribbentrop and Fritz Sauckel 14 minutes to die and Wilhelm Keitel 28 minutes.

Who declared the prisoners dead? Was a report written? Who recorded their last words? Whatever may have exactly happened, there is no doubt that it was a shameful ending to the much-hallowed Nuremberg trials, an ending that was a violation of the very principles of the USA.

It takes great minds to judge fairly and avoid emotional revenge toward peace and prosperity as for instance, the Marshall Plan to recover the German economy which also greatly helped the US economy of that time.

It will always be difficult, however necessary, to find a balance between speedy and fair justice and justice free from understandable yet often questionable emotions for revenge shortly after the commitment of a crime.

In an interesting series of discussions and interviews on French TV24, the plight of the estimated over 100,000 French men and women were studied born of French women and German soldiers during the occupation. 'Horizontal Collaboration' it was called.

While initially condemned as shameful, soon, these mothers and children integrated into a normal status in society in which the past wrongs faded away in the realization that no one is perfect.

In conclusion, justice was differently applied toward Germany as it was toward Japan. For political, economic, and financial reasons!

Hasty and emotional trials shortly after a war ended and feelings and emotions are still understandably high, can affect justice.

Justice between the two major enemies, Germany and Japan was executed differently in duration and effort for political reasons.

At the cost of fair and open justice.

***

To the victors go the spoils. The conquerors gain benefits and knowledge beyond the usual spoils such as surrendered weapons and equipment.

But should it also include data and information assembled from inhuman experiments that would never be morally and legally permitted in the victorious nations? Is such information justified even when it could be beneficial for the people in the victorious nations?

An example is the horrible test made by the Japanese Unit 713 did regarding syphilis, a disease that threatened every military organization and civilian. The immorally gathered information was submitted to the US on condition that the criminals who committed horrible and inhumane tests on thousands of innocent people, would not be prosecuted.

Between 1945 and 1959 a secret intelligence operation was established in the USA, named Operation Paperclip, that brought some 1600 German scientists and engineers to the USA with their families because of their advanced knowledge and experiments, in aeronautics and rocket science, architecture, electronics (guiding systems, radar, satellite) material science, medicine, physics, chemistry and chemical engineering.

When it was revealed in the media that it included Walter Schiele, who assisted the human experiments at Ravensbrueck Concentration Camp, he immigrated to Argentine with the help of the US Military.

"Suffice to say that German developments at the end of the war helped submarine development worldwide and contributed to the design and success of the US submarine program," Jay Bazzinotti in Quora April 2017.

At the same time, the Russians brought 2200 German specialists to their country in Operation Osoaviakhim, a total of over 6000 with their families, all assembled during one night on October 23, 1946, despite the immense suffering of the Russian people during the German aggression.

***

In August 1945, a Potsdam Agreement demanded that Germany should pay a reparation of 23 billion dollars but mainly in machinery and manufacturing equipment, technology and forced labor (reparation labor). Is forced labor the same as slave labor? Was not forced labor by the Nazis condemned?

As a result, delegates from former occupied nations were send to Germany plundering whatever they could find in the remnants of the destroyed German industry.

And what was found and returned was not much after the very destructive Allied bombing of the German manufacturing industry. As an engineering student I was assigned to the rescue of an at least fifty-year-old lathe with a cracked base. It was, as most of what I saw returning from Germany, just a piece of junk ready for the scrapyard.

When I gained permission to visit my grandparents by bicycling over 150 miles in a day on a one gear old bicycle, I saw the devastation in Bremen where for miles one could not see what it once had been houses or streets. But in the rubble three walls were erected, a tarpaulin spread over it while in a brand-new stamping machine was working at maximum capacity. The crates outside were marked 'For Mutual Defense'. A present from the Marshall Plan.

While the outdated and defect machinery was returned to the nations from where it was stolen, Germany started with new modern machinery. Who became the winner?

Observing the devastation in Bremen I thought that it would take decades to recover from destruction. When I came back five years later, one could see hardly any traces that there ever had been a war.

About fairness in reparations, it is estimated that 11 million people died in Nazi concentration camps among them about 6 million Jews. Israel was paid over $800000 for rehabilitation of survivors. French and Dutch Railroad paid reparations for the transportation of Jews. Most Jewish survivors and families were paid reparations. The remaining five million were not.

War is evil. Evil exists. Human justice is imperfect. These are simple truths!

This reality must be accepted, especially for those who combated the existence of evil, sacrificing their lives, or must cope with a life-long physical or mental disability.

And those who survived unscathed, at least physically, with however memories of fear filled moments, anger, anxiety, frustration and nightmares.

More than a war WW2 was, more than the Von Clausewitz definition that war is but the continuation of diplomatic relations other than with peaceful means.

Italy paid 125 million dollars reparations to Yugoslavia, $105K to Greece, $100K to Russia, $25K to Ethiopia and $5K to Albania.

There are many confusing figures and statistics about reparations paid by the Axis nations but also about the US. Reparations were made in different ways.

The US also paid reparations to some 49 nations according to a 1952 treaty. The payments ended in 1977.

Japan seems to get off easy because China and Russia did not demand reparations. A payment of some 6.67 million dollars to the International Red Cross for the horrible suffering of their POW and citizens seems insulting.

"Massive reparations have been paid to the state of Israel in the name of the Jewish people at large," (Encyclopedia Britannica) Over 14 billion dollars?

Two similar responsible nations, Germany and Japan were again treated differently! And responded differently.

The issue of reparations is complex and will never be satisfactory and is even still ongoing in disputes regarding reparations between Germany and Poland. The fairness of reparations will always be questionable. Estimates can only be very rough calculations during chaotic circumstances and questionable estimates. Relative values of the destroyed property will always be seen differently by the receiving and the paying party.

The fact remains however that Japan's reparations were minimal compared to what Germany paid and was forced to pay.

Acts of Desperation

It is not popular to say anything positive about the cruel and brutal regime of the Axis nations. But it is important to strive for objectivity and avoid being blinded by emotion or hate.

The facts are that Hitler, and his cronies must have known that the war they had started was lost after the last desperate attempt to turn the tide during the Battle of the Bulge had failed and after all desperate efforts to halt the Russian onslaught had turned into chaos during their retreat. They also must have realized that they would be held accountable for the crimes committed and that any defense of their actions would be futile.

The Axis did not instigate biological or chemical weapons. They could have during their last desperate hours. The impact could have been a calamity for soldiers and civilians never known before. But it did not happen.

It has been suggested that Hitler's reluctance to use biological and/or chemical weapons may be attributed to his own experience when he was gassed in Belgium during WW1.

Germany had a stockpile of some 12000 tons of sarin gas so named after the four inventers working for the chemical giant I. G. Farben who mixed phosphorus with cyanide into a horrific lethal chemical substance.

The Allies considered the use of non-lethal gases. After WW1, Winston Churchill as Secretary of War favored the use of gas to shorten conflicts. The application of non-lethal gases that would disable the enemy temporarily but not fatally, was considered a humane use of a weapon.

Desperate people are prone to turn to desperate irrational acts in a mindset of: "I am going down but I will take you with me." In their last evil acts, Nazi leaders could have released their huge stockpiles of chemical and biological arsenal. They did not. But they could have, as they had during WW1 with the use of chlorine.

We cannot even imagine the consequences of these horrible weapons being activated for the military and probably even more for common citizens. If attacked with lethal gases or biological weapons, the Allied Forces would have retaliated in similar and probably even greater consequences.

Japan was ready to apply biological warfare under direction of microbiologist/monster Shiri Ili under the romantic name of 'Cherry Blossoms in the night'. He had it all worked out as planned, the North American West Coast would have seen swarms of infected insects. The A bomb prevented putting their plans into action which may be seen as another justification for this ultra-destructive weapon.

Should we recognize that the potential catastrophe was avoided? I believe we must for the sake of truth and objectivity. The Nazis refrained from the chemical warfare Germany had applied in WWI. The dropping of the atomic bombs prevented Japan's plans.

Some opinions claimed that the Nazis did not have the ability to apply their chemical and biological weapons because they did not have control of the air. But this argument is not realistic. It does not take a huge armada of bombers to cause a calamity of chemical and biological destruction.

They certainly had enough Kamikaze pilots, who under the right weather conditions, could have caused another hell on earth. The war that exposed humanity's most evil nature could have been even worse!

The US used the ultimate destructive weapon, the atomic bomb, to end a war that could have otherwise would have cost millions of lives.

The Nazi leadership could also have used an ultimately destructive evil weapon in their desperate situation. The truth is that they did not.

The Power of Hope

Hope is the waking of dreams.

Aristotle

It is a simple truth: hope motivates and energizes, regardless of condition or situation.

Hope is the inevitable ingredient for survival that enables tenacity and courage even beyond reality. What gave prisoners in concentration camps the inner strength to deal with the hideous environment of starvation and brutal torture?

Would it not have been preferable to surrender lives that knew only suffering without decency, affection, or mercy and end all suffering after endless years of confinement? But they did not. Because they still saw a glimmer of hope!

When I had the privilege to teach a decade at a prominent US university after retirement, I asked seniors before graduation who had a better student life; contemporary students who had excellent facilities, laboratories, libraries, and electronic devices, sports and athletic availabilities, parties, and entertainment, or my post-war generation who studied in unheated rooms, had no cars, miserable living conditions and had to work at the top of their capacity to stay above the level of elimination because of the limited positions available, without adequate facilities, and classes in makeshift accommodations in the still damaged buildings.

The answers were mostly hesitant, but most students believed that contemporary young people had the obvious advantage and the better deal.

I submitted that this may be questioned because the post-war generation's precious gift was the conviction that the future would be bright, a strong expectation and hope that we would build a better and more just society, and sang, "Never shall there be a war again."

There was a sincere conviction that every morning would be better than the day before, a common unity, a perhaps unrealistic but wonderful conviction that there would never be war again, and a deep-felt motivation to charge ahead toward a better world. It was naïve and somewhat over-idealistic but sincere. Hope was alive and motivating!

Do most contemporary students believe that the future is bright? Answers came hesitantly and far from convincing. Global perspectives have opened new concerns about the environment, overpopulation, and artificial intelligence.

A more densely populated world allows closer interactions through amazing technologies that create better knowledge and understanding but also cause tensions between cultures and nations that were formerly more separated and distant. Immigration and its diversity demand also led to stress and demands for adjustments.

Do the present young people believe that their future is bright? Do they look to the future with dreams and hope?

Dante Alighieri put his now famous phrase "at the gate of hell."

"Abandon hope all ye who enter here."

Hell, according to Dante, is where there is nothing any longer to aspect, reach, live for, and motivate. Hell is where there is no longer a future light when living in darkness. Hopelessness saps the will to continue. Also when living during times of prosperity.

It was hope that gave the concentration survivors the courage to go on and not surrender to the temptation of ending living in a human-made hell.

When prosperity has reached its pinnacle and all possible desires are satisfied, where to go from there? Drugs and a world of non-reality? Dr. Calhoun stated that some problems, even some unhappiness, are necessary to maintain mental health.

Hope can be alive or absent regardless of society's level of prosperity, during times of affluence and poverty, peace and suffering.

For the pursuit of happiness, hope is essential.

Lasting Impacts

Rights and Responsibilities

A healthy balance between rights and responsibilities is imperative for any free and democratic nation to prosper.

Before WW2, responsibility dominated over rights, personally and collectively.

After WW2, rights dominated over responsibility.

Pre-WW society demands for a focus on responsibility was evident in societal behavior and discipline in education.

A focus on rights became obvious in the post-WW2 era. The United Nations concentrates on human rights and rights are at the forefront of the judiciary and in society at large. While human dignity and rights emphasis are positive trends, a less laudable aspect is the blame culture that emerged from the emphasis on rights enhanced by a legal system that invented the rather absurd notion that suffering and pain can be compensated with money.

Which culminated in outrageous verdicts benefiting mostly lawyers who can become instant millionaires from catastrophe and calamity, thereby earning the international nickname of 'vultures' which impacts the USA's global reputation.

The remarkable shift in rights versus responsibility can be attributed to a renewed awareness during and after WW2 of decolonization, self-determination and democracy.

A fair balance between personal and collective rights and responsibility is imperative for free nations to flourish.

One way to achieve a better balance would be by a Bill of Responsibilities added to the Bill of Rights demanding that every right is irreversibly bound to a responsibility to ensure care for the life one initiated, for family and relatives, for civil behavior and restricted use of insult and vulgarity.

In the US and other free and democratic nations, freedom is seen as the main principle of society, freedom to move, freedom of speech, and freedom of political choice.

Personal freedom, however, should be accepted against the backdrop of social responsibility. Everyone is part of a society that demands that individual freedom is restricted by considerations of how our personal choices and behavior affect our neighbors.

One can choose for instance to have the freedom to prefer loud sounds, which however may irritate or affect the people who exist around us in a fast-increasing population density. We don't live alone. We are responsible for our behavior and how our freedom can and will affect those around us.

A fair balance between rights and responsibilities was indirectly emphasized by the famous speech of President John Kennedy in his inaugural speech in 1961 when he said;

"Ask not what your country can do for you; ask what you can do for your country."

Individualism is highly regarded in relatively new cultures such as the USA and Australia; in older cultures, such as Japan, societal responsibility is prioritized.

Rights should dominate, but only with the acceptance of societal and personal responsibility to achieve higher level of mental health and human interaction.

Toward a more perfect society.

Gender Equality

Rightful attempts for women's rights started with the 20th Century suffragists. Yet before WW2, the possibility for a woman to enter multiple professions and crafts was still extremely limited. Only very few women succeeded in penetrating male territories, such as Marie Curie.

Society, at that time, had, by law and tradition, separated the male and female expected tasks and territory. Men had to be the providers, and women had to care for the household and children.

Christianity's influence ensured that women were expected to be a helper to their husbands and act subservient. In the Dutch language, the term for women was *'het zwakke geslacht'* the weak gender, a very demeaning but very expressive terminology.

Men were seen as strong, physically and mentally, and women were judged as sensitive, elegant, and gentle.

The global war demanded that men were needed in the military often in places they had never known before. Women took their usual assignments, especially when the need for manufacturing war equipment was high. Rosy the Riveter showed that women could do everything males had performed and did well.

Women also were flying planes and performing other potentially dangerous occupations. The outcome was predictable. Once women had opened the gate to all occupations traditionally held by men, there was no return to pre-war restrictions possible anymore.

A post-war development connected to gender relations was the introduction of birth-control medication which reduced the fear and the consequences of sexual intercourse.

Unrestricted sexual relations changed the relations between the genders by lowering the fear of pregnancy, but also diminishing the romance and chivalry that once kept the interaction between men and women at a more limited, but possibly higher level. Sexual intercourse became less restrictive and frequent at the cost of romantic ideals.

Every progress also kindles some counter-movements. More women have now penetrated what once was a strict male territory than men working in traditionally women's territory because the male working territory was much larger.

Consequently, tensions between the genders evolved when both women and men aimed for the same opportunities. Women consider it their right while men feel threatened.

Inevitable was a subsequent more assertive behavior of women in the traditionally male territory to ascertain equality in the gender competition at the cost of the traditional and past demure and elegant manners expected from women.

As a result, women became military combatants.

"War does not have a woman's face," a Russian proverb says.

Yet Russia had women pilots aged between 18 and 24 years in 1942. There still is a reluctance to deploy women in positions of peril but the US now has women as fighter pilots, a very demanding as well as dangerous assignment.

Gender equality in the military has been given increased attention progressing toward the level presently common in Israel.

Gender equality that emerged during WW2 will probably continue and reach a level of total equality, but also prompt gender competition that pulls men and women alike from the instinctive human divisions, tasks, and traditions maintained ever since our species emerged.

The experiment of Dr. Calhoun in the 1960s at the National Institute of Mental Health with mice where population density and the lack of male mice to control their territory caused a separation of the genders ultimately resulting in the cessation of reproduction.

All mice died after a total gender separation set in when both genders were prevented to live in accordance with their basic instincts because of overpopulation. When there were only a few mice left, the decline did not reverse itself.

Humanity should not be compared to mice because of the gifts of moral consciousness and reason. A potentially fatal gender separation can be avoided by an awareness that with unlimited career opportunities for both genders, competitive tensions can affect gender relations.

From Dr. Calhoun's experiment, humanity can learn that both genders have fundamental instincts that must be recognized to maintain a healthy mental society.

Political and social movements, such as equal rights for women, tend not to cease when the objective has been obtained because the movement's energy and inertia will often lead to more extreme visions and expanded goals and expectations. Will total gender equality result in harmony or demise?

Contemporary thoughts and concepts are radical compared to historical perceptions and standards regarding homosexuality, transgenderism, and behavior that were seen as unnatural or immoral in most historical cultures and religions.

WW2 became again the catalyst that caused revolutionary changes in mindset and behavior, also regarding the fundamental and all-important relations between men and women.

Space Visions

With the development of the German V-2 rocket, the space era began.

For centuries, humanity explored the celestial skies in amazement and wonder without thoughts of reaching beyond the limits of our planet.

The subsequent space race between Russia and the US for space hegemony started the human interest in searching and entering the universe beyond planet Earth. Yuri Gagarin circled around the earth, and Neil Armstrong made his first step on the moon.

What changed human behavior, however, were the communication satellites that make it possible to obtain instant information and can tell us exactly where to go via GPS. Visiting libraries is no longer needed, nor asking questions to knowledgeable people. Google knows and has the answers, thanks to satellite communications. It is no longer necessary to stop and ask where someone lives or where to go.

Human brains no longer need to store information because all the information is externally available with a touch of the fingers if electricity and the internet are available.

Hubble gave us a view of a universe with its endless dimensions and time beyond our grasp to comprehend and by ending all previous illusions that our planet and world were at the center of a starry realm and humanity's assumed significance.

Fits aced with a glimpse of, by our perceptions, weird macro, and micro realms and its incomprehensible behavior ended centuries of doctrines and dogmas people lived by and reduced our planet's importance to nil.

Space research and increased knowledge had a broadening effect on the human perspective of the past and future. Discovery and understanding of the universe reached far beyond the endless search of astronomers by changing the perspective of the minor role humanity plays in the mind-boggling dimensions of time and space of an incredible universe.

Where once humanity's understanding of humanity's past was some three to four thousand years, now, scientific evidence points to four of five billion years since the Big Bang exploded.

The exponential knowledge that had its origin during the WW2 war affected religious and spiritual perceptions of the role humanity plays in a fast universe where its impact and perception demanded a total change in understanding of our planet and its inhabitants.

And so did inevitable impressions of the greatness of a creating force of a universe beyond human understanding. Space research and discovery demanded a re-conception of the condition of our planet and species in an endlessly expanding universe.

Space research and knowledge greatly enhanced scientific understanding, changed our perspective of who we are as humans, and challenged traditional perceptions of religion and faith.

Visionaries predict travel and immigration to other planets.

A totally new awareness emerged of time and distance with a renewed understanding of how the physical world around us develops and operates.

And with little understanding of why the micro and macro realms exist.

Humanity is on the threshold of new perceptions and understanding.

Also of our vulnerability, of powers can threaten our very existence.

It all began with the V2 rocket technology of WW2.

Globalization

The initial application of several types of jet engines was, as can be expected from totally new technology, difficult and complicated. Yet an era of smooth and safe high-altitude travel became possible and affordable, opening up global experiences by millions traveling every to the most remote corners of the earth.

History taught us about huge migrations that took place in ancient times over hundreds of years. The same number of travelers now migrate during summer vacations.

Communications also progressed to immediate and again affordable global contacts via satellites.

From post-WW2 technology emerged a new human experience called globalization which broadened understanding and awareness.

Transatlantic crossings may be a good comparison.

When the founder of the Du Pont Company arrived in the US on January 1, 1800, it had taken three months to overcome storms, inclement weather, food, and water shortages. Passengers certainly got to know each other very well when imprisoned in small uncomfortable accommodations and poor food.

A new way of crossing the Atlantic became possible with the development of the steam engine in luxurious ocean liners such as the Normandy, the Queen Mary, and the United States It still took about two weeks till about 1950 with greater comfort and luxury and enough time to interact and develop temporary or permanent relations.

In modern times, a great number of flights offer many Atlantic crossings between six and nine hours. There is no need to interact anymore during travel. Thousands of safe and reliable airplanes offer flights with a forecasted accuracy within minutes about the arrival time and the duration of the flight. Computers steer the planes safely and accurately.

Passengers no longer interact because there is no need for the short duration. During the flight the interaction is mainly with TV or other electronic devices available at most passenger seats. The connection changed to technology again instead with each other.

Nations and cultures interact more than ever before. Vacationers, professionals and businesspeople can be found in previously isolated most remote corners of the planet.

Global minded people became less bound to their culture to celebrate diversity.

Major airports such as Atlanta, Beijing, London and Tokyo process between fifty to over hundred million travelers every year. Distances are no longer measured in length dimensions but in hours of flight.

Modern media also provide detailed information about the most remote corners of the planet. More people migrate to different nations and cultures which improves understanding, but also can cause a decline of traditions and cultural identity. A new humanity of the global citizen is emerging.

Globalization leads to diversity and greater appreciation and understanding of unknown countries and cultures, but also, to tensions that were not evident when living conditions were experienced more separately.

Diversity is like minestrone soup that tastes delicious if well prepared. But the individual tastes of the ingredients, such as onions, squash, tomato, celery, and many more lose their specific taste or at least minimize it.

In those countries and unions impacted by globalization, cultures fade away. Traditions and beliefs can only be maintained privately to gradually diminish by the interacting and inter-maraging generations, are lost in the diversity of many old cultures in language, art, dance, expression, wisdom, dialect, and traditions developed over centuries.

Diversity and globalization bring people closer. But there is a price to pay by diminishing cultural richness and a closer sense of belonging.

Its development is, however, irreversible in a globally exponentially increasing population with its new worldwide vision.

Environmental Concerns

Before WW2, humanity paid little attention to global warming and environmental concerns, the main focus was on economic survival, political tensions, and the threat of war. Unaware of the possible consequences, health-threatening pesticides and fertilizers were applied, mechanics cleaned their hands in tetraethyl lead-containing gasoline, asbestos was used in industry and households, all paints were oil-based, and so on.

After WW2, a new awareness and knowledge emerged triggered by global warming concerns, the exponentially increasing population, and environmental concerns. Humanity become increasingly aware of its responsibility to care for our amazingly beautiful planet for present and future generations.

Ovid, however, warned that the source of the problem is often ignored when all emphasis is on the effects, not the cause. He wrote: "The cause is often hidden, but the effects are visible to all."

Reducing carbon and other damaging emissions is indeed necessary as is ending deforestation and other damaging and destructive human activities. Much has already been achieved. The air we breathe is much cleaner than it was a century ago.

The source of environmental problems is regrettably not, or seldom addressed, during environmental conferences and UN emphasis and information, which is the exponential increase of the global population, from 2 to over 8 billion during my generation. Humans pollute and need shelter and food thereby destroying nature to provide space, ingredients, and materials.

The climate on planet Earth has been changing for some four billion years from the impact of immense universal energies and powers. Since the exponential population increase of our species, questions have emerged about whether humanity can influence the climate.

Many scientists confirm that that is indeed happening while others remain skeptical. Whether climate change is caused by external universal forces or internal human activity remains a difficult problem to solve.

But in either case, humanity has a responsibility to preserve and protect the beauty and natural development of planet Earth by eliminating, or at least reduce, all harmful influences on life and natural evolution of our beautiful but vulnerable planet.

For whatever the cause may be, human caused or not, drastic and global information, awareness and action must be taken to reverse the present self-destructive path of air and water pollution and the out-of-control accumulation of trash and waste.

Lest we self-destructs and irreversibly destroy our beautiful planet.

The Post-WW2 Age of Technology

The key players in the drama called WW2 are well known and will be remembered, national leaders such as Eisenhower, Churchill, and Stalin and generals, among them. Zhukov, Montgomery, Patton, Yamamoto, and Rommel. Their decisions and activities influenced the outcome.

Other people who had a decisive impact are less known. Will Marian Rejewski and the Polish Cyber Bureau, the Frenchman Gustave Bertrand, and most of all, Alan Turing be remembered?

They and their teams deciphered the German Enigma code and build the Bombe and Colossus Machines at Bletchley in England that even broke the more sophisticated Lorenz Code. They saved lives by the information they were able to distract and contributed to the intelligence on which the military strategists depended and that led to victory.

Their amazing intellect opened a totally new era of science and technology that rapidly and exponentially developed into what is leading toward artificial intelligence, intelligence from machines instead of the human brain, systems that may have already achieved a certain self-awareness.

How sad that the genius of Alan Turing was driven to suicide at the early age of 41 by highly questionable moral judgment without receiving recognition for the immense contribution he made.

Advanced WW2 technology has improved life on our planet allowing people to live more comfortably and with less suffering and pain compared to the pre-WW2 era.

It is easy to quickly adjust to better circumstances that soon become the norm. Or as it is often heard from advertising, everyone now 'deserves' the comfortable life gained by advanced technology. Expectations advance quickly during prosperous times.

The shadow side of the age of technology is technology dependence.

During ages past, education systems focused on filling the brain data banks of pupils with information through learning 'by heart'. What was not known had to be learned from reading, listening and investigating. And remembered. Searching through encyclopedias or in a library stimulated curiosity.

In modern times, there is no longer a need to store information in our brains because it is available immediately and completely from amazing information sources such as Google, Bing, Wikipedia and others.

Will this lead in the future to brain reduction and capability when information storage and knowledge is no longer needed because it is instantly and unlimited available externally through technology?

Is there a danger that humanity becomes totally dependent on external information and problem solving, so that the individual ability to form opinions no longer exists and humanity gradually becomes technology-dependent robots?

WW2 taught us the danger of a 'herd instinct' in which people become victimized by a demagogue or political ideology, but can technology dependence also victimize people when the individual loses his or her rational self?

Medical technology allows longer lives! Wonderful healthcare, diet research, and medical technology made it possible for mankind to live longer. The National Geographic Society predicted that the children now born can expect to become 120 years old, which causes a dilemma for the balance between working and retirement years while putting more pressure on a declining labor market.

During the past generation global population increased from 2 to over 8 billion who will need employment in an era where technological developments increasingly requires less human effort. Human ingenuity will be able to provide food, vertical cities can be built to provide shelter, and energy sources will be discovered and developed, but employment cannot be created where there is no demand.

Very clever and impressive advances in technology may also have a confusing side-effect by a fading recognition between what is real and what is artificial, an open and dangerous possibility to make people believe in what is supposed to be real but is fake.

What to accept as real and what as fiction remains then an enigma that can be used in everyone's best interest by eliciting joy and imagination but is a frightening tool in the hands of ruthless and power-addicted politicians.

Technology is rationally indifferent and can serve humanity well. But has neither soul nor consciousness, no knowledge of good and evil.

Humans are instigating and applying artificial intelligence. It will be able to bring sheer unlimited progress. But humanity's brain capability can no longer follow or control its lightning speed.

Many leading scientists and visionaries warn that AI's capability can become beyond human control and even lead to humanity's demise! Caution is imperative. But will it be impossible to stop progress? The age of technology's impact has begun.

The catalyst that initiated the age of technology was World War 2.

Before WW2, most technologies were fundamental and understandable for the common citizen; the needed energy came from fossil fuel, coal, and a steam based medium. Structural connections were riveted. Internal combustion engines could be understood and repaired by self-educated mechanics.

Slide rules were popular instead of computers. Typewriters were mechanical. Telephones were at the edge of progress and cable connected. Craftsmen used their physical energy instead of powered tools.

A transatlantic letter took five weeks. Most writings were readable and formal. To find out where one wanted to go needed knowledge of geography and the ability to read maps. Knowledge came from printed books and was acquired by going to libraries to study the subject with encyclopedias and the help of some card system, a time-consuming effort in quiet surroundings.

Most libraries were very attractive places. During the search for a subject many interesting pages had to be crossed which led to being easily distracted by another subject encountered on the way to the subject searched for. Notes were taken by handwriting.

People count without the help of calculators and developed a feeling for numbers and approximate outcome.

Telephone calls were kept short because using the telephone, certainly in public phone booths, was expensive. And annoying when someone inside the booth would take his or her time while ignoring the impatient line waiting outside.

After WW2, answers to questions are provided by electronic external sources, immediately and effectively to whatever question comes to mind. Any person can be reached globally with just a few touches and yes, you can see any person also wherever he or she is on the planet.

Very clever technologists have performed miracles far beyond even the most daring pre-WW2 visions.

What more can be asked for? Contemporary communication has already reached a level of perfection people in pre-WW2 times could not even dream about.

Comparing pre-WW2 and post-WW2 communication and information availability, it is easy to admire and enjoy modern global miracles.

But only if the needed energy is available and as well as connections to the internet.

When an electrical network failure occurs which is not an unrealistic assumption during ever higher electrical demands, and when satellite connections can be interrupted and disturbed by universal influences such as solar storms, will future generations be able to find their way, know to get information, and how to get in contact with others without technology?

Will they still be able to understand where to go and how to get there? The Pre-WW2 generation could. Will future generations also?

Most of all something precious will be lost expressed with the simple word awe, a feeling of mystery and wonder. When everything can be seen, an overabundance of possibilities suppresses experiences and dreams.

The handwriting was once an expression of self. Now all written communication uses the same very effective but sterile systems often using abbreviated words and expressions that no longer implement the art of expressing a situation or feelings with articulate well-chosen words.

Dr. Calhoun's experiments indicated that some unhappiness may be needed to fully enjoy happiness.

Technology may be able to satisfy our needs to know and discover. But humans are burdened and blessed with instinct and feeling that technology cannot provide. We are after all a spiritual entity.

Pre-WW2 people were unaware of cholesterol, vitamins, or even blood pressure. One died of 'old age'. Care for the many war wounded created a surge in medical knowledge and development.

We do not believe in pain I heard doctors say. This immense contribution to our generation is now accepted without much thought. In years past, many young women died horrible death giving birth, half of the children never reached the age of ten and so many cried for weeks on end in hellish pains!

As for instance, the skeleton of a man called 'the Archer' found in a grave near Stonehenge in the United Kingdom, probably an important man, whose cheekbone was half eaten away by an infection.

What hellish pain he must have suffered as so many had for thousands of years? Before WW2 the most used pain drugs were opioids with the inevitable effect of being addicted in addition to the misery of their affliction. How blessed the present generations are.

A medical procedure that once required several weeks in a hospital is now performed as an out-patient. Organ and bone replacements progressed, and many illness are cured with antibiotics.

Humanity changed from a pre-WW2 communal interactive society to a technology-instigated individualistic lifestyle where no longer knowledge is accumulated in people's minds but obtained from external technological sources, as long as they are available.

Despite the wealth and abundance of the present era, the future will be shaped by those who still have faith and ideals, who learned to cope with adversity and thrust forward no matter the obstacles that may be encountered.

Hope for a better tomorrow emerged from unrealistic but wonderful expectations rising from the ruins of World War 2.

World War 2 caused an eruption of technology that was initially triggered by German war technology and forced an even greater response from the United Allies.

Most technology is serving mankind well, especially in the medical wonder of modern times and for instance in the smooth ever increasing travel possibilities. Atomic energy's horrific possibilities keep nations in a frightening balance in the knowledge that its consequences could equally endanger both opponents.

Thus, a war, WW2, irreversibly changed humanity from the communal interaction practiced since its onset to a technology-dependent and addicted species that may surrender their individuality and communality to a soul-less, sterile, lightning-fast, superior technology that can operate beyond humanity's intelligence and consciousness.

Section 4: Summary and Conclusion

Summary

Technology spiraled upwards before and during WW2 driven by German and Japanese fanatic illusions to conquer and control the world.

Allied nations united to destroy the evil aggression and, with the intensity and motivation only a war can elicit, countered with even greater technological development.

The subsequent impact changed the way humanity interacts.

The war acted as a catalyst for rapid change.

Would these changes also have been actuated without the urgent motivation to stay ahead of the opponent's developments?

It is a fair question to ask. There are of course no clear answers to this question. Without the strong military and survival motivation a global war of great magnitude required, it must be assumed that the pace of change would probably have been much slower in a peaceful civic world.

What would have initiated the development, such as the V-2 space technology? Would the enormous financial investments have been allocated during an era of tranquility? Would the resources have been available? Probably not, when other social needs would have received greater priority.

WWII was more than a gigantic global military battle.

The war ended. Its influence remains.

War technology changed the way societies interact.

Before WW2, people interacted within their community.

After the war, technology's amazing momentum was perfected, and jet engines became effective and reliable allowing smooth travel at high altitudes. Rocket technology put a man on the moon and allowed satellites to circle the planet. Computers rapidly changed human capability and behavior resulting in a more individualistic connection to technology instead of each other.

Over seventy years have passed since the Second World War. Local wars occurred in Korea, Vietnam, and the Middle East. But another global war was prevented.

Modern destructive weaponry could cause the demise of the defending nations as well as any attacker. Immensely destructive remote-operated weaponry could even threaten the existence of our species resulting in more international and regional negotiations.

Other urgent issues such as environmental concerns now receive global attention. Sanctions are applied, with limited success that are nevertheless a much better means to discourage violent confrontations.

Advanced technology has made the perception of our world smaller. Global awareness and knowledge advanced.

Which hopefully will avoid the vagaries, suffering, and fear of another global war that could erase the great progress made in humanity's improved standard of living and prosperity.

WW2 triggered fundamental, irreversible changes in human behavior, interaction, and expectations.

1. Communal activities and interactions declined. So many live closely compacted in massive structures in overpopulated towns, yet human interaction declined by turning to technology instead of traditional communal lifestyles. Available technology fosters individual connection via technology that started with television and was further enhanced by many other technological capabilities such as Smart Phones, Facebook, and computer games.

2. Jet propulsion enabled smooth and affordable travel, allowing millions to see many regions of the planet at a reasonable cost leading to greater global knowledge and understanding of different nations and cultures and a wider perspective compared to pre-WW2 standards.

3. Immediate information and knowledge can be easily accessed if electricity and the internet are available. The limitless information sources of Google, Bing, and Wikipedia replace communal interaction, the art of debate, and discussion. Personal, brain-stored data attained from learning by heart are no longer necessary thereby surrendering to technological dependency. External information sources reduced the need for personal knowledge, and the need to

supply the brain's data bank with thoughts, knowledge, and memory, suppressing human talents of imagination, visions and dreams. External technology sources may ultimately lead to a reduction of human brain capacity into a robotic state and external resource dependency.

4. Women successfully contributed during the war in diverse occupations traditionally done by men which changed the age-old role of women in society toward gender equality. Professional opportunities for women advanced but also led to increased gender competition and tension that evolved into higher divorce rates, single parenting, and the demise of the family as the fundamental structure of society.

5. Post-war prosperity fostered expectations of higher levels of social affluence and rights, which led to a decreasing sense of personal responsibility and the blaming of external sources or persons for all misfortune, and an imbalance of rights over responsibilities.

6. Medical technology greatly advanced health and longevity and reduced suffering by enhanced pain management.

7. Military weaponry development during WW2 after the dropping of the atomic bomb and its frightening consequences forced powerful nations to avoid world-scale conflicts and maintain an uneasy cautious approach.

8. The space program started its development with the German V-2 rocket, which, besides giving an insight into the mysterious realms of the universe, changed the perception how insignificant our species is in the endless dimensions of space and time.

Conclusion

The technology initiated and developed during WW2 gave rise to a technological era that changed the way humanity interacts, processes information, and collects knowledge. Stunning new technologies enhanced prosperity and knowledge beyond the expectations and visions of years past.

But technology can only be to humanity's benefit when it can still be managed and controlled by humans. Artificial intelligence, however, can be difficult if not impossible, to subject to human will because of its dazzling speed beyond human ability to follow and grasp.

Contemporary humanity has become individualized by technology's impact. Information can now easily be manipulated and influenced by political propaganda, companies, or individuals. Democracy, the chosen way of living in harmony, is now threatened by unlimited barrages of information that make decision-making ever more complex for common citizens, especially when clear perceptions of what is real or fake have become more difficult to determine and questionable.

Future generations must decide to live as technology-depended robots or maintain humanity's amazing brain's capacity to collect information and process facts from fiction in parallel processing separate from the technology deluge. To remain human, it will be necessary to enhance and preserve humanity's talents of imagination and spiritual and moral instincts that are absent in indifferent technologies. Technology must serve humanity, not control it.

Science and technology advanced human understanding of brain-challenging discoveries in micro and macro worlds beyond comprehension. The more we have come to know, the more we must realize that we know very little. Most of what scientists discovered and applied are *how* the macro and micro realms exist and progress, but not *why*.

WW2 was the catalyst for an exponential advance in science and technology. Humanity benefited greatly from advanced knowledge and its technical application, especially in health care.

Epic technological advances encompass the dangers of self-destruction and that humanity may become controlled by and dependent on indifferent lightning-fast artificial intelligence that threatens self-determination, basic instincts, and moral consciousness of good and evil, WW2 changed the way humanity lives and interacts.

May it be toward a renewed pursuit of happiness and peace and may what is good and noble always triumph over ever-present evil.

And may the lasting impact of the technology that originated and emerged from WW2 benefit humanity's peace and prosperity.

References

Bos, Jan, *The Battle of Nijmegen*: Taking the Bridges over the Waal, WW2 History Magazine.

Ryan, Cornelius, *A Bridge Too Far*, Simon and Schuster New York.

Devlin, Gerard, *Silent Wings*: *The American Glider Pilots of WW11.*

Hastings, Max, *Bomber Command, Churchill's epic campaign*, Touchstone, 1979.

Hastings, Max, *The Secret War*, Harper Collins Publishing, 2016.

Hoagland, Vern: *The Eagle Squadrons.*

NPS: *De Oorlog, Mobilization, Nederland's Leger, Declarative van 28 Augustus,* 1939 (The War: Mobilization, The Netherlands Army, The Declaration of 28 August 1939).

Axis History Forum, Moylan Interview, Judgment at Nuremberg, a 1961 Film directed by Stanley Kramer.

Stichting De Greb, *De Slag om de Grebbeberg, Leger en Mobilisatie* (The battle around the Grebbeberg, Army and Mobilization).

WW2 Peoples War: The last Flight of Lancaster, 189 by David Kirk.

HARK (Hulp Actie Roode Kruis): *De Gemeente Ubbergen in de Frontlinie.* (The County of Ubbergen in the war zone).

ARKO Boeken: Deventer 1940-1945.

L de Jong: The Kingdom of the Netherlands in World War Two.

The National Interest Magazine: The Focke-Wulf 190.

M.J Adriani Engels and G.H.Wagenaar: *Nacht over Nederland* (Night over the Netherlands).

General Sir John Hackett: I was a Stranger. Chatto & Windus, London 1978.

Verzetmuseum (Resistance Museum*) Eten in oorlogstijd.* (Eating during the war)

Wikipedia; *Regeringsbrood* (government's bread).

Pierre van Paassen: Days of our Years, Hillman-Curl, New York 1939.

Delaware's World War II Fallen: 2nd Lieutenant John M. Butler (1918-1944).

'Op Maat' Levensverhaal (Dutch translation company).

The warfare History Network.

Bakels, Floris B, "Dertien dagen in Mei" (Thirteen days in May) Kok Kampeen, 1990.